Managing Projects

Pearson
Education

Managing Projects
Building and Leading the Team

DAVID BODDY
University of Glasgow

An imprint of Pearson Education
Harlow, England · London · New York · Reading, Massachusetts · San Francisco · Toronto · Don Mills, Ontario · Sydney
Tokyo · Singapore · Hong Kong · Seoul · Taipei · Cape Town · Madrid · Mexico City · Amsterdam · Munich · Paris · Milan

For Cynthia

Pearson Education Limited

Edinburgh Gate
Harlow
Essex CM20 2JE

and Associated Companies throughout the world

Visit us on the World Wide Web at:
www.pearsoneduc.com

First published in Great Britain 1992

ISBN 0273-65128-5

British Library Cataloguing-in-Publication Data
A catalogue record for this book is available from the British Library

Library of Congress Cataloging-in-Publication Data
Boddy, David.
Managing projects : building and leading the team / David Boddy.
p. cm.
Includes bibliographical references and index.
ISBN 0-273-65128-5 (pbk.)
1. Teams in the workplace. 2. Project management. I. Title.

HD66 .B62 2001
658.4'04—dc21 2001036567

10 9 8 7 6 5 4 3 2 1
05 04 03 02

Typeset in 9.5/12.5pt stone serif by 35
Printed by Ashford Colour Press Ltd., Gosport

Contents

Preface

To survive in the current business environment management is under constant pressure to change what they do and how they do it. Someone has to be responsible for putting these changes into effect, for managing the practical detail, for making the change happen. They usually work with the support of some form of project team, which may or may not help their enterprise.

This book is for such people, who wish to understand more fully what the job of managing such project teams involves. They may be studying project or change management as part of a qualification, or they may have some direct project responsibilities. They may, for example, be managers whose staff are affected by change or who are themselves responsible for implementing a project. Whatever their role, they can benefit from having a fuller and more accurate perception of the project process. The aim of this book is to help those studying, or responsible for managing, a change project to be more confident and skilful in understanding the human aspects of change, especially the project team.

The book is a direct successor to an earlier text (*Take the Lead: Interpersonal Skills for Project Managers*, Prentice Hall, 1992), but most of the material in the present work is new. Like the earlier book, it is based on the author's research with many project managers, responsible for delivering real projects in organisations of all kinds.

Some of the research was conducted specifically for this book. For the earlier work we worked with a group of eight managers over a period of about six months, using a variety of methods to secure and validate their first-hand accounts of managing projects. Many of the insights and evidence gained in that research is still relevant, and reappears at points throughout this work. Since 1992 the author has continued his research into information systems projects, and other kinds of organisational change, especially supply chain partnering. This work too has provided insights into project management, which appear in this book.

Finally, a further group of nine active project managers took part in a research project specifically designed to provide new empirical material for this book. They work on a wide range of organisational change projects, and provided written analyses of their recent activities, in accordance with a prepared brief. They were each interviewed about their experiences, and attended two group meetings at which the emerging themes were discussed. This direct empirical material has of course been presented within the context of other empirical and theoretical work on project management, organisational behaviour and managing change.

The structure of the book, and the relationship of the chapters to each other, is set out at the end of Chapter 1. Each chapter follows a common format, with a short introductory section leading to learning objectives. After the main text of each chapter (containing boxes with short practical illustrations) there is a case study with questions. This is followed by a summary, chapter questions, suggested further reading and references. Each chapter also contains a 'notepad' feature that encourages readers to relate the topic of a section to their experience, or that of their organisation.

Acknowledgements

This book has been made possible by the work of many managers who have attended my Executive MBA courses or who have taken part in the research I have conducted in their organisations. Their willingness to discuss their experiences and exchange ideas with people from other backgrounds has ensured that the book is firmly grounded in management practice. Without their contribution, the book would not exist.

I also acknowledge the contribution of the reviewer of successive stages of the book, whose comments and suggestions were of great value in shaping the final version. My thanks also to Geraldine Lyons at Pearson Education who has worked with the book from commissioning to final delivery.

David Boddy
April 2001

We are grateful to the following for permission to reproduce copyright material:

Table 2.1 and Figure 2.1 from Mapping the dimensions of project success in *Project Management Journal* Vol. 28, No. 2, pp. 5–13, published by Project Management Institute (Shenhar, A.J., Levy, O. and Dvir, D. 1997); Figure 3.2 from *Becoming a Master Manager*, published by J. Wiley, New York (Quinn, R.E., Faerman, S.R., Thompson, M.P. and McGrath, M.R. 1996); Figure 4.1 from *Project Management*, published by Gower Publishing, Aldershot (Lock, D. 1996); Figure 4.2 from *Business Information Systems* (Chaffey, D. 1999); Figure 4.3 from *The Rise and Fall of Strategic Planning* (Mintzberg, H.); Figure 4.4 from *The Ethics Method*, published by Associated Business Press, London (Mumford, E. and Weir, M. 1981); Figure 5.3 from Elements in the control cycle; Figure 6.1 from Benefits of a stakeholder analysis; Figure 6.5 from *Exploring Corporate Strategy* (Johnson, G. and Scholes, K. 1999); Figure 6.6 from Managing in four directions; Figure 7.1 from A typical project board structure for a small project in *Making Project Management Work for You*, published by Library Association Publishing, London (MacLachlan, L. 1996); Table 7.1 from Individual self-management: analysis of professionals' self-managing activities in functional and cross-functional teams, in *Academy of Management Journal*, Vol. 41, pp. 340–50 (Uhl-Bien, M. and Graen, G.B. 1998); Figure 7.2 from *Thinking Beyond Lean*, pp. 29–34 (Cusumano, M.A. and Nobeoka, K. 1998); Table 7.3 from *Learning from Cross-functional Teamwork* pp. 12–13, published by Institute for Employment Studies, Brighton (Kettley, P. and Hirsh, W. 2000); Figure 7.3 and Table 7.4 from *The Wisdom of Teams*, published by Harvard Business School Press, Boston, USA (Katzenbach, J.R. and Smith, D.K. 1993); Table 8.2 from *Groups that Work (and Those That Don't)*, published by Jossey-Bass, California

(Hackman, J.R. 1990); Figure 8.2 from *Influencing Within Organizations* (Huczynski, A.A. 1996); Figure 8.3 from *Organizational Behaviour: An Introductory Text* (Hackman, J.R. and Oldham, G.R. 1980); Table 8.5 from *Management Teams: Why They Succeed Or Fail* by Butterworth Heinemann, Oxford (1981), source www.belbin.com; Figure 9.1 from Idealised stages of group development; Figure 9.2 from *Group and Organizational Studies*, Vol. 2 (Tuckman, B. and Jensen, N. 1977); Figure 9.4 from Steps in setting objectives; Figure 9.5 from *Take the Lead: Interpersonal Skills for Project Managers* (Boddy, D. and Buchanan, D.A. 1992); Figure 9.6 from *Organisational Behaviour: An Introductory Text* (Huczynski, A.A. and Buchanan, D.A. 2001); Table 10.1 from Influence tactics in upward, downward and lateral influence attempts in *Journal of Applied Psychology*, published by American Psychological Association, Washington (Yukl, G. and Falbe, C.M. 1990); Tables 10.3 and 11.3 from *Organizational Dynamics*, Winter, pp. 4–17, published by Elsevier Science, Oxford; Table 11.2 adapted from A theory of human motivation from *Psychological Review*, 50, pp. 370–96, published by Thompson International (Maslow, A.H. 1943); Table 12.1 from Managing your boss in *Harvard Business Review*, published by HBSP (Gabarro, J.J. and Kotter, J.P. 1980); Figure 12.2 from Example Weekly Progress Report; Figure 12.3 from *Managing Information Systems: An Organisational Perspective*, published by Pearson Education, Harlow (Boddy, D., Boonstra, A. and Kennedy, G. 2001).

Belbin Associates for information from *Management Teams: Why They Succeed or Fail* by Meredith Belbin (*see* www.belbin.com); John Wiley & Sons Limited for an extract from *Managers Divided: Organisation Politics and Information Technology Management* by D. Knights and F. Murray, © John Wiley & Sons Limited 1994; and Walter de Gruyter GmbH & Co KG for an extract from 'Managing product development projects: on the significance of fountains and deadlines' by Lindkvist, Soderlaund and Tell published in *Organization Studies* Vol. 19.

Whilst every effort has been made to trace the owners of copyright material, in a few cases this has proved impossible and we take this opportunity to offer our apologies to any copyright holders whose rights we may have unwittingly infringed.

Part 1

Projects and organisations

1 An introduction to managing projects

Introduction

People managing large projects depend on other people. Some will be immediate colleagues or members of the project team. Others will hold more senior positions, or belong to other departments or organisations. The project manager needs to influence them to do something new or different, in a changing and uncertain context. This is risky, and requires well-developed skills for dealing with other people. Mastering such skills can be highly rewarding – not least because people can use them in other high-profile management roles. This book should help them develop and use such skills more successfully, more often.

This chapter sets the scene, outlining the range of projects to which the book is relevant. It shows that while each project is unique, they also have something in common. This is the need to achieve an acceptable level of performance, through managing people in a volatile context. The chapter compares the job of managing projects with the demands of managing a routine activity. It concludes that people can use the skills required to manage projects in many other management roles, especially in volatile areas of business.

Objectives

After reading this chapter you should be able to:

- summarise the features that are common to major organisational projects;
- compare the task of managing a routine activity with that of managing a project;
- anticipate how this book could help someone responsible for managing a project;
- understand the distinctive perspective of this book.

Projects and project management

Senior managers constantly propose new ways of doing business. Someone has to turn the bright idea into working reality, usually through managing it as a project. A project describes a set of activities to change something, or create something new. It is a job that is done once, and is distinct from continuing, routine activities. This covers a great deal of human activity. The focus here is on relatively large organisational projects, and on the work of those responsible for implementing them.

Their job titles vary. Sometimes the line manager does the work, alongside his or her normal duties. In other cases, people from a support function such as engineering, management services, information technology, or human resources take a leading role. They may be called project manager, project planner, internal consultant, business analyst and so on. They may be the formal manager of the project, or someone involved as a member of the project team. For convenience the book uses the term project manager, but the reader need not interpret this term too narrowly. The titles do not matter: what does matter is that the meaning of the activity is clear to all those with whom the project manager comes into contact. Whatever the title, senior management needs formally to designate the person responsible as the project manager. They also need to publicise that fact, to ensure that others recognise their role and their relationship with the project. Senior managers need to make it clear that they have launched the project and that they expect the (named) project manager to deliver the project within some specified time and budget limits.

To do this the project manager will need to work with other people, and influence them to work in a particular way. People may need to meet deadlines, show unusual commitment, change established practices, commit resources – and make many other adjustments. Some will be simple and unproblematic. Other changes will be awkward or controversial, perhaps going against deeply held beliefs. To make progress the manager cannot just draw up a schedule, or set out a critical path. He or she needs to understand (amongst other matters) human motivation, team development, and how to influence people.

These people will take different roles in the project. Some will be members of the project team – which itself takes many forms. Others will be senior members of the organisation, or from other organisations. Some may be full-time, others will work on the project only occasionally. The project manager needs to be able to influence them all.

The book uses published research and original empirical research into contemporary projects in most sectors of the economy. This empirical work has led to the distinct perspective of the book towards projects and their management. The volatile and competitive business environment means that many projects are highly uncertain activities. Structured methods of project management are of limited value in uncertain and ambiguous conditions. Those responsible for the project need to influence a wide range of interested parties, using both personal skills and institutional support. They need to deal with the processes and politics of projects.

These skills are not new or unusual. People can develop them by applying principles about the nature of projects, the processes they involve, and ways of influencing people and teams. Principles cannot prescribe how to deal with each unique situation. But the project manager familiar with the principles developed through the book should be able to apply them to their project problems. By building this part of their repertoire, they will make incremental yet sustainable improvements in the way they do the job.

Unique projects, common features

Projects are a step into the unknown. They are an attempt to combine ideas and activities into something new, often being the building blocks of wider strategic changes. Managers create projects to deal with an infinite variety of organisational changes. The ideas and examples presented in this book have come from work with project managers responsible for major changes which have included:

- a new information system in a local authority service;
- a new facility in an oil refining company;
- a European-wide order processing system in a computer company;
- implementing an Enterprise Resource Planning system in a chemical company;
- organisational restructuring in a public agency;
- reorganising manufacturing in a semiconductor company;
- a new 'care pathway' through a hospital for patients with dementia;
- creating a new joint venture to process transactions for an oil company.

In one sense each of these is unique – they happen once, in a particular business, at a particular time, with a unique set of players. A method that suits one business may fail in another. Anyone managing a project needs to craft an approach which works in that situation.

However, in other senses projects have features in common. First, they involve meeting performance expectations. People expect projects to produce something new or different – even if what they expect is ambiguous and changeable. These expectations also compete with criteria of time and cost. People have different expectations, and their priorities shift. Figure 1.1 illustrates this dilemma. Meeting one criterion is usually at the expense of the others.

Second, projects depend on people, not techniques. Clearly techniques like work breakdown structures, process mapping, planning, scheduling and estimating are valuable. But the work that these techniques plan and record is done by people. Without their work there is nothing to plan or monitor. So project managers need to influence other people. They are typically from different levels and functions,, and will be pursuing personal as well as organisational goals. They will weigh the criteria of cost, time and performance differently. Projects that involve organisational, human and political issues will raise particularly sensitive issues. How people deal with these issues will affect the outcomes.

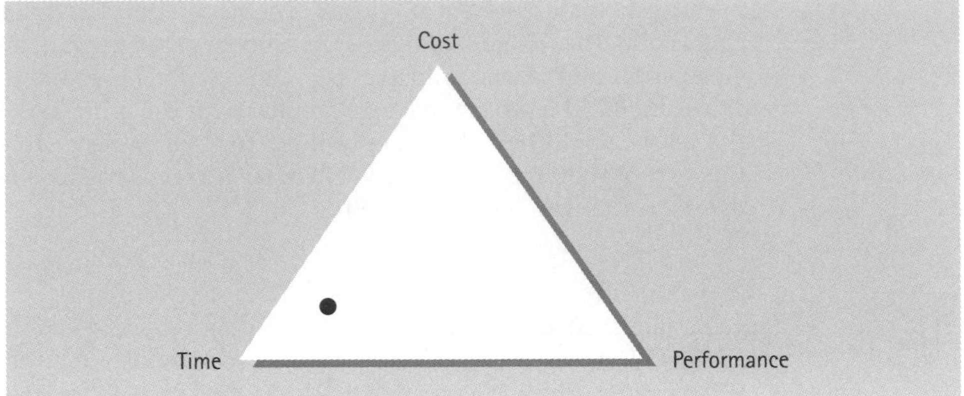

Figure 1.1 Conflicting project criteria

Third, projects take place within a context. People create a project because they want to change something – to change some part of the context in which people work. That project itself takes place within the existing context – which the promoters intend it to change. The project manager attempting to influence people does so within that context, and this will help or hinder the project. Finally, the elements of that context (which Chapter 2 deals with fully) also affect each other – changes set off ripples that lead to further change.

The common features of apparently unique projects provide opportunities for learning. Project managers may not learn much of value to their situation from the substantive topics of other projects. They can learn from others' experience in dealing with the common themes of influencing people to meet fluid performance criteria in a volatile context.

NOTEPAD 1.1

Your project

You will gain more from your work on this book if you are able to relate the ideas presented to a project (recent or current) with which you are familiar. Make some notes in response to the questions below. Later notepads will invite you to connect your project to other ideas.

- Write a brief account of a project with which you are familiar.
- Who initiated it, and why? What are the intended outcomes?
- What is your role in the project?
- What do people expect of your project, in terms of Figure 1.1? What conflicts are you experiencing between the criteria?
- Who are the main parties that you need to influence?

How distinct is project management?

Is managing a project different from other kinds of management job? In some respects there are clear differences between managing a project to create innovation and managing an established system to maintain stability. However, broader changes in the business environment appear to encourage less stability, and more innovation.

Examples of stable systems include a payroll team in a finance department; delivering a regular service, such as a library or non-urgent clinic; or running a well-established and repetitive manufacturing operation. Their managers focus on stability. The role involves getting things done within relatively stable working relationships, using information from reasonably regular and constant sources. From time to time, of course, a change occurs, as managers introduce a new product or a new working arrangement. After that temporary disturbance the system returns to its normal, relatively predictable routines.

Projects are different, as they represent a departure from current activities. People establish them to create a new facility, to change the way people receive information, to create a new business unit, to change customer service – and for an infinite number of other reasons. They mean managing one-off change, requiring separate systems and unusual management structures. These are somewhat apart from the regular operation.

Table 1.1 compares the roles of those managing a system with those managing a project.

These differences are becoming less clear-cut as organisations of all kinds become more responsive to changing conditions. They adopt more flexible forms of organisation, such as those outlined by Charles Handy (1990) or Rosabeth Moss Kanter (1990). As product life cycles shorten, and as technology provides new ways of producing goods and services, exceptional disturbances are no longer one-off events. They are the normal way of working in many businesses.

Managers make changes to the working system which have deadlines, requirements, budgets and ambiguity. These changes depend on coordinating how individuals and resources adapt the operation to the new circumstances. Managers

Table 1.1 Managing systems and managing projects

	Managing a system	*Managing a project*
Task	Familiar	Unfamiliar
Staff	Full-time, permanent	Part-time, temporary
Roles and duties	Established patterns	Uncertain, variable
Culture	Role or power	Task
Working relationships	Established cooperation	Negotiable
Authority	Clear, reflects position	Ambiguous, little direct
Coordination	Hierarchical	Network/matrix
Information sources	Established, routine	New, uncertain
Momentum	Maintained by system	Threatened by system

change their organisation's structure and expect staff to be more flexible and creative. Fewer people are likely to be managing stable systems, and more are likely to be in roles that resemble project management. The line manager's job may be to manage a series of projects. The box gives an example of this approach.

Oticon – managing the business by projects

This Danish company is one of the world's five largest producers of hearing aids, with about 1200 staff. It has its own basic research and production facilities and stresses the high engineering and design quality of its products. To counter intense competition it made radical organisational changes. People do their work in projects. Management appoints the project leaders, who then have to recruit their team. Employees choose whether to join – and can only do so if their current project leader agrees. Previously most people had a single skill; now all have several. Chip designers have skills in customer support, for example. Employees can work on several projects at once. These arrangements allow the company to respond quickly to unexpected events and to use skills fully. Different backgrounds mean more insights.

They have no departments and no formal structure, just teams. The Chief Executive, Lars Kolind referred to this as 'managed chaos'. The company tries to overcome the dangers by developing a very strong and clear purpose and mission. It expresses this as being 'to help people with X problem to live better with X'; and a common set of written values. There are no titles – people do whatever they think is right at the time. The company counters the potential chaos of this by building underneath the flexible organisation a set of clearly defined business processes. The absence of departments avoids people protecting local interests and makes it easier to cope with fluctuations in workload. Changes to the physical environment and communication systems encourage direct person-to-person communication, and hence the project team arrangement.

Source: Based on Bjorn-Andersen and Turner (1994) and other material

This uncertainty or lack of structure is not in itself a sign of management failure. Rather it is inherent in the nature of current business life in an uncertain environment. This makes it much less likely that structured methods can handle all the problems. It becomes more likely that the emphasis needs to move towards the human, organisational and political aspects of management.

If that is the case, then the approach outlined in this book will apply to a much wider range of roles than those formally designated as project managers. If work involves dealing with ambiguity and uncertainty, and with how people respond to that, then the approach in this book will be relevant.

The perspective of this book

There are many good books about managing projects (such as Lock, 1996; Mayler, 1999; Woodward, 1997), dealing with the structured aspects of the task. They show the value in the right conditions of using well-established techniques of analysis, planning and control. They typically focus on construction projects in which external factors affect the project in relatively predictable ways. They concentrate on projects that are 'free-standing' creations, rather than changes that are embedded in the operations of the enterprise.

This book is different. It deals with major organisational and other changes that are novel, and where there are usually different interests. Not only is the outside world likely to change during these projects; so too will the actions of the interested parties. This implies that political and interpersonal aspects of projects will matter. The book gives most attention to these.

Managing a project is essentially a practical task, yet project managers need an accurate mental picture of what it involves. They need a theory of project management to guide their actions. Chapter 4 provides the theoretical bases of the book, but a short preview may help. This includes the ambiguity of performance measures in novel projects, the emphasis on influencing people rather than using techniques, and on managing the context.

Projects aim to create something, and project managers expect to be measured on how well they meet expectations. The difficulty is that expectations are likely to change in the course of the project, so that the manager is aiming for a moving target. In a rapidly changing business world plans are frequently overtaken by events and changing circumstances. Projects evolve during implementation, as key players adjust to external changes. People often only discover the full potential in an emergent, step-by-step process of discovery.

Second, project managers work by influencing other people who have different interests and values. In part they do this by using their individual personal skills. These are often not sufficient in themselves, but need the support of good structures and institutions, including a project team. These can be a powerful device, but only if the project manager is able to develop them effectively.

Third, projects do not take place in isolation. As the project manager seeks to influence people affected by the project, this process will be affected by past events (the historical context), and by the contemporary context. The interaction between the project and the context has major implications for the way project managers do their job. It is a constant theme throughout this book.

Figure 1.2 illustrates how these themes relate, and how the four Parts of this book deal with them. Part 1 sets the scene, considering the nature of projects and the context in which they occur. Part 2 concentrates on the work of those managing a project. Part 3 focuses on managing the team, while Part 4 deals with managing those beyond the team.

Real projects are usually messy, complicated affairs. The manager grappling with that awkward reality is right to be sceptical of neatly packaged solutions. The book recognises the reality of managing difficult and often controversial projects. It does not present an idealised view of the process. It identifies the obstacles that get in the way of applying good practice, and helps the manager to discover ways of overcoming these. And if the preferred methods do not work, what other lines of action might be available? There is often a difference between the way managers dealing with change would like to act, and the way others oblige them to act.

The book is intended for people who are both busy with a change project, and who may be studying the topic at the same time. It aims to provide a road

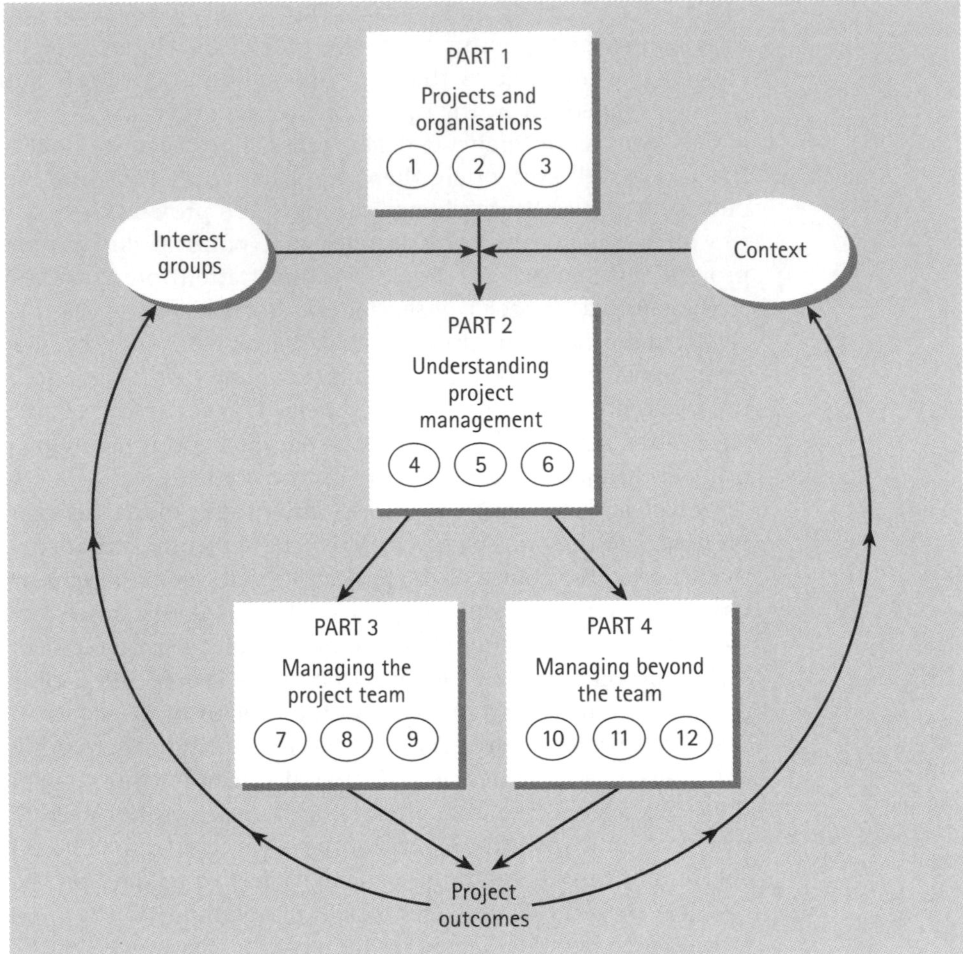

Figure 1.2 Plan of the book

map for those managing projects, thus helping to avoid some of the hazards and pitfalls. Although for ease of explanation the book has the four Parts shown in Figure 1.2, reality is not that tidy. Something always goes wrong in major changes, and no book will change that.

CASE STUDY

The maintenance scheduling project

The manager was an experienced project engineer with a national energy business. His boss put him in charge of a project to develop an enhanced computer system to support maintenance scheduling in an engineering department. The system would work from existing maintenance records to issue automatically the instructions for engineering staff on which jobs they should deal with on particular days. It would also record when they had finished the job. Head Office had initiated the project, not the local department in which it would operate.

The Director promoting the idea was keen to use a system already being used in another part of the company. The project manager continues the story:

'He has clearly defined the system requirements on the basis of how he sees the problem. Now that I have started work I am getting into the politics of the situation. The information the system collects will show senior managers how their operational managers are performing. So I decided it was important to communicate with area managers, talk about the system, talk about what the objectives are. Not really to get them on my side but to impart a fuller understanding that the system is not really intended to spy on them. It should help them improve their performance and the department's performance.'

So I have spent a great deal of time over recent months with the area management. I would like to think I have been successful in showing them the way we are heading. Though at this stage they seem to be a bit uncertain and to be honest a little bit dubious.

In the midst of that the proposed system has been reviewed technically, including how the data will be transferred from the existing system. I have been meeting with the computer professionals and am reasonably confident that will work. A new development is that the Director has discovered that the other part of the company will charge us heavily if we use their system. So I now have to do a cost justification of that and other systems to get a clearer picture of the options. The managers in the areas became interested in that as well, wondering if they were committing themselves to productivity gains in the future. You have to be careful about the politics.

Having done an appraisal on seven options it was clear that the best was one using PCs with the possibility of linking them into local networks. I have now become the promoter of this option and interestingly enough the people who were least in favour of it were the computer people. They perhaps saw a weakening of their power base. They have a vested interest in mainframes, and do not want the company to adopt a PC option.

Eventually it's up to the Director to decide which way he wants to go. I like to think that by managing this project the way I have done the area managers are more aware of what is going on and that they have a point of view. Previously they would have just had a mainframe thrust on them from Head Office without discussion.

Case study questions

1 How would you describe the context in which this project manager is working?

2 Use the suggestions in Table 1.1 to indicate how his role will differ from that of someone working on a routine task.

3 Who will the project manager need to influence?

4 Are there any similarities or differences between this project and the one you described in Notepad 1.1?

Summary

This chapter has introduced the topics of projects and project management. These are an increasingly important aspect of managing, and how well a manager deals with them will have an impact on their career. The nature of projects is changing, away from relatively discrete, physical, construction-type projects, to those that are deeply embedded in the way organisations work. This has implications for the skills required to manage them.

The key points from this chapter are:

- Managers create projects as a way of responding to changing business needs, so they are central to organisational performance.
- All managers are likely to have some responsibility for managing a project, or be part of a project team, irrespective of their primary role.
- While the substantive topic of each project is unique, they all have some common features.
- These common features are the need to balance conflicting performance criteria, to manage the context, and to influence other people.
- While project management is different from the management role which emphasises stability, it is increasingly close to the modern role which emphasises flexibility.
- The main theoretical perspectives which the book develops are the influence of context, the emergent nature of projects, and the need to influence others.
- The ideas in the book draw on recent empirical work on a range of current projects.

Chapter questions

1 Why are projects becoming a more common aspect of management work?
2 What are the conflicting performance criteria that project managers face?
3 What features are common to all projects?
4 In what ways does Oticon 'manage the business by projects'?
5 List four ways in which project management may differ from managing a routine system.

Further reading

After an introductory chapter, the most useful further reading is probably that which examines specific projects in depth. Suggestions are:

Clark, J. (1995) *Managing Innovation and Change*. London: Sage Publications. A long-term study of major production and organisational change in Pirelli, the Italian tyre and cable company.

Drummond, H. (1996) *Escalation in Decision-Making: The Tragedy of Taurus*. Oxford: Oxford University Press. An absorbing account of a high-profile project failure at the London Stock Exchange.

References

Bjorn-Andersen, N. and Turner, J.A. (1994) 'Creating the twenty-first century organization: the metamorphosis of Oticon', in Baskerville, R. *et al.* (eds) *Transforming Organizations with Information Technology*. North-Holland: Elsevier Science BV.

Handy, C. (1990) *The Age of Unreason*. Boston, MA: Harvard Business School Press.

Kanter, R.M. (1990) *When Giants Learn to Dance*. London: Unwin.

Lock, D. (1996) *Project Management*, 6th edn. Aldershot: Gower.

Mayler, H. (1999) *Project Management*, 2nd edn. London: FT Publishing.

Woodward, J. (1997) *Construction Project Management*. London: Telford Publications.

2 Each project has unique features

Introduction

Each project evolves in a unique situation. Project managers try to achieve the project objectives by influencing other people in a particular setting, at a particular time. Nobody has made that change, in that organisation, in those circumstances. Nevertheless research into many projects indicates several common dimensions. Project managers can use these to diagnose which aspects of the project may need special attention.

This chapter begins by considering the dimensions of project success. The second section shows how to assess the forces driving and restraining a project. It then identifies eight features which project managers have found to be significant in their projects. If such features make projects unique, they also place different demands on the people managing them. The project manager who is aware of the landscape being crossed knows what to expect, and what that means for the job.

Objectives

After reading this chapter you should be able to:

- **express clearly which dimensions of effectiveness matter most in a particular project;**
- **outline and illustrate the idea of the forces driving and restraining a project;**
- **list eight features that make projects unique;**
- **analyse a project using the diagnostic tool presented.**

Measures of project success

Interest groups use different criteria to assess the effectiveness of a project. As Pinto and Slevin (1988) pointed out, 'Projects are often rated successful because they have come in on or near budget, and achieved an acceptable level of performance. These characteristics may be used because they are the easiest to measure and they remain within the realm of the project organisation' (p.67). These, however, are essentially internal and short-term measures of project efficiency. They ignore the possibility that a project may run efficiently in its terms, but fail to meet customer expectations, or the longer-term needs of the business.

Was the Millennium Dome a success?

The Millennium Dome cost an estimated £854m, and attracted 6.5 million visitors – far more than any other attraction in the country. Many commentators criticised the quality of the exhibits. Here is an extract from an interview with the Chief Executive Pierre-Yves Gerbeau:

Q: *Has the Dome been a success?*

A: The difference between success and failure lies between two figures: The 12 million visitors that were originally forecast, and the one year we had to make it a success. Twelve million visitors was never a realistic forecast but it was the measure by which we were judged. One year was never long enough to make an attraction like the Dome financially viable . . . Personally I think we have been successful. We have made 6.5 million people very happy. Our satisfaction rate is 88 per cent – 90 per cent if you ask how happy people were with the staff. We have been slaughtered by the media, but we have turned the Dome around and made it one of the premier attractions in the world . . .

Q: *The latest estimate of the cost of the Dome is £854m. Can you justify that?*

A: Yes, I think so. If you look at how the East End of London was compared with now, I think there has been a great improvement. It was a wasteland, and now the transport is better. Businesses have moved in . . . and 1,400 new homes. It's much more alive now . . . And 6.5 million people have come and had a wonderful experience.

Source: *The Independent*, 30 December 2000, p. 4

The limitation of internal measures has encouraged people to devise those which take account of other dimensions. Shenhar *et al.* (1997) proposed (from surveys returned by 127 managers of new product development projects) four dimensions of project success, summarised in Table 2.1.

Table 2.1 Dimensions of project success

Dimension	*Description*
Project efficiency	Was the project completed on time and within budget? A useful measure in itself, as efficiency adds to competitiveness, but not sufficient
Impact on the customer	Does the project meet performance or functional specifications? Is the customer satisfied with what has been delivered, using it fully, interested in further work, etc.?
Business and direct success	Is the project providing the sales, income, profits or other benefits that were expected? Market share? New processes or other direct effects on the organisation?
Preparing for the future	Has the project helped to prepare the organisational and technological infrastructure for the future? Is the firm more prepared for future opportunities? Building new skills?

Source: Based on Shenhar *et al.* (1997)

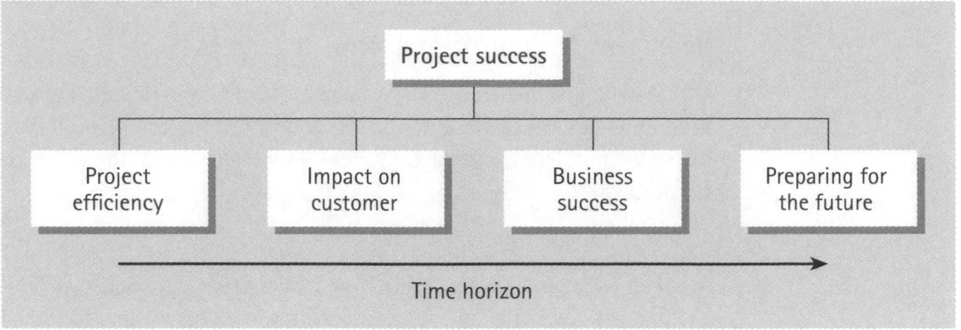

Figure 2.1 The four dimensions of project success
Source: Shenhar *et al.* (1997)

They also suggest that the significance of these measures will vary between projects, and will change over time, as shown in Figure 2.1.

During the project, and in its immediate aftermath, the efficiency criterion will be dominant. As time passes, it becomes easier to assess the contribution of the project to the other dimensions. They suggest that management should 'look at the short-term and long-term benefits of the project and judge its performance on the outcomes of all dimensions' (p. 11).

Driving and restraining forces

In considering how to move a project forward from the present position, managers need to take account of the circumstances surrounding the project, 'including the total social field: the groups and sub-groups involved, their relations, and their value systems' (Lewin, 1947, p. 14). Lewin pointed out that any social system is in a state of temporary equilibrium. Driving forces are trying to change the situation in directions which they favour. Restraining forces push the other way to prevent change, or to move it in another direction (see Figure 2.2). The project manager faces this equilibrium, 'which can be changed either by adding forces in the desired direction, or by diminishing the opposing forces' (p. 26).

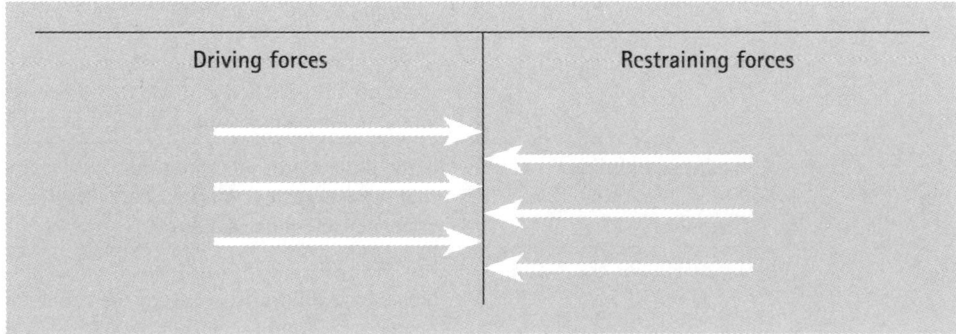

Figure 2.2 Force field analysis

Driving forces encourage change from the present position. They encourage people and groups to give up past practice, and to act in ways that support the change. Driving forces can take many forms – such as a newly available technology, an inadequate business process, or the support of a powerful player. Conversely factors such as the already installed technology, shortage of finance, the opposition of powerful players or the company culture can be restraining forces. They encourage opposition, inertia and the maintenance of existing practice.

Project managers can 'add forces in the desired direction' by, for example, stressing the advantages of the change, emphasising the threat from competitors, or making the benefits seem more attractive. Alternatively they can seek to 'diminish the opposing forces' by showing that the problems will not be as great as people fear, or pointing out that difficulties will be temporary.

Lewin observed that while increasing the driving forces could produce change in the desired direction, it could also increase tension amongst those 'forced' to change. The change may then be short-lived, or offset by the negative effects of the tension. Because these secondary effects may go against the interests of those promoting change, he suggested that, as a rule, trying to reduce the forces restraining change is the wiser route.

External events can trigger and drive change: new competition, a change in legislation, the activities of a pressure group, a chance conversation. Information from any of these sources can trigger change. People with sufficient power can use these and countless other external signs to justify a proposal.

An external driving force re-establishes a project

One of the projects studied for this book was a plan to upgrade the Social Work Information System (SWIS) used by staff in a local authority. A manager initially proposed the system in 1996, and she made some progress. A reorganisation, budget cuts and limited enthusiasm for the project by the Head of Social Work meant that enthusiasm waned, and the project was deferred. In 1999 the need for the system became more urgent. Legislative change required the authority to provide much more detailed information on clients, staff workloads and overall performance before they could receive extra funds. The old information system was unable to provide the management information to meet these requirements. This external change acted as a trigger to re-establish the project, and the authority provided funds to establish a new SWIS – with the support of the Head of Social Work.

Source: Personal communication

They can also use internal triggers to promote change: new management priorities, problems with technology or facilities, the emergence of organisational or staff problems. People use these events to build a case that becomes a driving force for change.

External and internal forces only trigger and drive change if someone sees them, recognises they are important, is willing to act and is able to make something happen. Perceptions matter, because what may be a clear signal to one person is no more than a faint possibility to another. Information that seems authoritative to one may seem biased and superficial to another.

The project manager can use Notepad 2.1 to analyse the implications of these ideas for their project.

NOTEPAD 2.1

Driving and restraining forces

Make a list of the forces that are driving and restraining your project, laying it out as shown in Figure 2.2.

- How might you try to reduce the restraining forces?
- How have these forces affected the shape and priorities of the project?
- How can you use external pressures, trends and events to support proposals for change, in a way that is more convincing than internal pressures?

Understanding the driving forces can help project managers realise why a project has come to life at this time. They can use them to communicate the urgency of the case to those they are trying to influence. On occasions it may also give a warning signal – such as when the driving force appears to come from one fragile source, rather than a broadly accepted view. This will affect whether signals trigger and continue to drive the change in a powerful way, or whether they fade and disappear.

They can also assess the forces restraining a project. These include limited energy and time. There may be so many signals that people have difficulty keeping track. Even if they see important data, they may be so busy with current work that they cannot act on it. There may not be enough resources, there may be uncertainty or scepticism about the benefits, or opposition from groups who see their privileges threatened.

Conducting a force field analysis is a useful diagnostic device, to help the manager identify the forces bearing on the project, and in planning the best approach to moving forward from the inherited position.

Diagnosing the change

Not all projects are difficult. Even within one that is generally challenging, some aspect will be easier to handle than others. Research with many project managers (see Preface) has identified eight features which distinguish one project from another. The project manager can use these to diagnose where the main challenges are likely to arise. They are:

- core/margin;
- novel/familiar;
- rapid/gradual;

- controversial/uncontroversial;
- changing goals;
- outside links;
- senior stance;
- other changes.

Core/margin

How close is the project to the core operating activities of the organisation? At one extreme, projects aim to change an activity which is marginal to the business, or which is in a background, supporting role. Examples could be a project to computerise the payment of pensions to ex-employees, or one to relocate some administrative functions. These may be useful changes, but not ones that enhance or threaten the survival of the business.

At the other extreme are projects whose success or failure is critical to the business. They are the means of implementing the broader strategy, such as a new on-line service for a bank, or creating a web site for an established retailer. They affect core operating processes, basic technologies or visible aspects of the business and its reputation. Published examples include:

- a new branch accounting system in a travel agent with many retail outlets (Boddy and Gunson, 1996);
- the Taurus and Crest systems to automate the settlement process at the London Stock Exchange (Currie, 1997);
- major cultural and management changes in a local authority (Keen and Scase, 1998).

The closer the project is to the core of the business, the greater the risks and potential rewards for the project manager. They are likely to face particular pressure to meet (possibly conflicting) performance criteria, and to do so quickly.

Novel/familiar

Does the project involve introducing novel, untried solutions, or established, familiar ones? Some projects centre on systems that others have used in similar situations. People understand the setting and the likely solution at the start of the project. Apart from the minor operating problems to be expected in any organisational activity, people can reasonably expect that the project will go according to plan. Examples include a plant engineering company building a standard refinery; a chain store opening an additional retail outlet; or a company introducing an established training regime to a new part of the organisation. Such projects are relatively structured and programmed.

Others depend on much learning and discovery during the project itself. The ideas floated are novel and contain a high degree of uncertainty. Someone

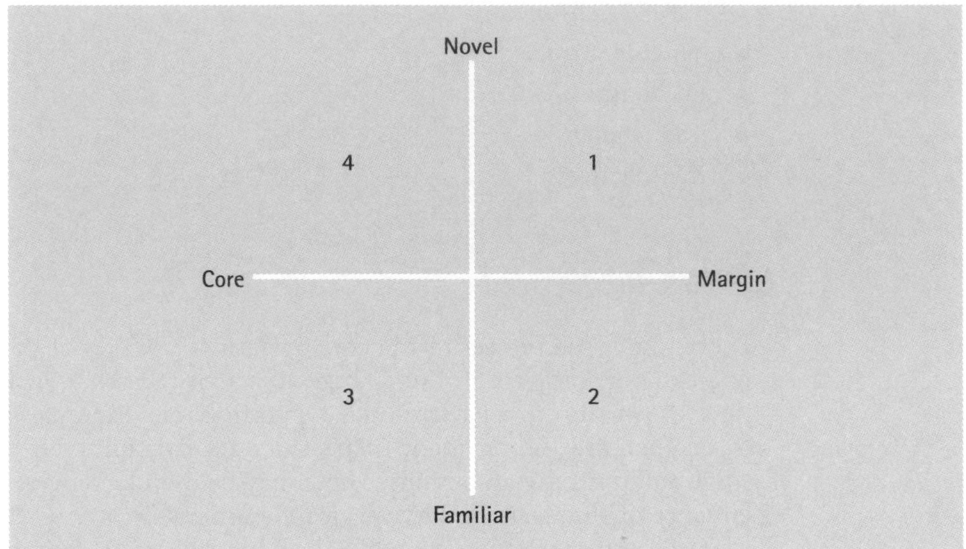

Figure 2.3 The four quadrant model of projects

has to develop the system or procedure, and they do not know at the outset how they will achieve the specification. Clark's study of a huge manufacturing reorganisation by Pirelli (Clark, 1995) is one example. Another is the business process re-engineering project (named the Columbus project because it was practically a journey into the unknown) undertaken by The Royal Bank of Scotland (Currie and Willcocks, 1996). People know the general intentions of such projects but not how they will get there, or what the specifics of the finished activity will be like. The activity will necessarily be relatively unstructured, unprogrammed, open.

The degree of novelty affects the project manager's task of influencing others. The more novel the project, the greater the uncertainty and provisional nature of successive steps. There will be changes of plan on the way, and uncertainty about the finished state.

Figure 2.3 shows these two critical dimensions of projects. This book is likely to be of most help to those who are managing projects in Quadrant 4. These are projects that are core to the business, and at the same time involve designing novel solutions. That will make it a difficult project to achieve on time and within budget.

NOTEPAD 2.2

Projects in Quadrant 4

- What examples of projects can you identify that would fall into Quadrant 4?
- What demands would they place on the project manager?
- How would they differ from the demands of a project in Quadrant 2?

Rapid/gradual

What is the pace of change? Senior managers usually expect rapid change, and urge the project manager to achieve this. They expect quick results and become impatient with requests for more time for design, testing, training or consultation.

Successful speed . . .

This project was to install a customer accounting system in a chain of retail outlets. The project manager and the equipment supplier estimated that installation could start in 12 months. The managing director supported the project enthusiastically, as he saw that it would be very beneficial to the business. He insisted that the first systems be installed within six months – which turned out to be feasible and brought great advantages quickly.

Source: Boddy and Gunson (1996)

Excessive haste leads to important issues being neglected. Staff feel under extreme pressure to cope with fast implementation, while continuing to work on the existing methods. Other projects go at a more gradual pace, perhaps with a sequence of carefully defined phases. They could involve the careful evaluation of pilot projects before extending the change to a new site. Managers see planning and preparation as a necessary part of the process and do not press the project manager to cut corners or to produce quick results.

Successful deliberation. . . .

An ambulance service was implementing a computer-aided command and control system into its control rooms. The change would represent a radical departure from previous methods, and failure would expose the service to severe public criticism. Senior managers insisted that the software designers worked closely with operational staff to design a system that met their needs. They also allocated time and money for training, and assured staff that the new system would only 'go live' when staff were confident that they could use the system. They also implemented the system gradually, using lessons from earlier sites in later ones. The system worked well, and was readily accepted by staff.

Source: Boddy and Gunson (1996)

Pressure to implement a project rapidly inevitably leads to a search for short-cuts. These can work, but bring substantial risks. The project manager should carefully assess those risks, and decide if they are acceptable. If not, they need to consider how best to influence senior managers to set a less demanding timetable.

Controversial/uncontroversial

Will there be a fight? Some projects arouse strong disagreements. Major production or administrative reorganisations, rationalisation projects or major changes in a service are not neutral, technical matters. They threaten established interests, who may disagree fundamentally about the direction of the change, or indeed about whether it should happen. An example is the study by Knights and Murray (1994) of major change in an insurance business. Others arouse no such controversy, as everyone concerned accepts the desirability of the change. If disagreements arise, they are about means, not ends. Effort goes into the solution, not into managing deeply held disagreements.

The implication for the project manager is that controversial projects will be more difficult and demanding to complete satisfactorily.

What do these features mean for the project manager? While each contains threats and hazards, they also offer opportunities for career visibility and promotion. Table 2.2 summarises these for the features so far.

Points to remember:

- Different people will see the same project differently. What seems a familiar problem to one is novel to another. Such differences may reflect background and experience, or that one has considered aspects of the project the other has overlooked.
- Views will change as the project moves forward and people gain experience, or as unexpected difficulties arise. A project that starts controversially may become less problematic as people work on it.

Table 2.2 Threats and opportunities in project types

Feature	*Threats*	*Opportunities*
Core	Senior management pressure Penalty of failure severe Heavy responsibility	Career visibility Rewards of success Resources OK
Novel	Failure to find solution Cost and time over-run Someone else gets there first Resources underestimated	Boost to career Track record Loose budget Result hard to compare
Rapid	Pressure for quick results and corner-cutting Indirect aspects ill-considered	Loose budget New job soon
Controversial	Differences harder to manage Information distorted Significant resistance	More credit for success Backing from winning side

Other challenges for the project manager

Figure 2.4 illustrates four other challenges that project managers have to deal with to varying degrees.

Sometimes the factors in Figure 2.4 work in the project manager's favour, and help them to progress the project. For others they become major obstacles, and require sustained attention. They are only partly under the manager's control, often reflecting how other players interpret and react to events.

Changing goals

The goals of a project evolve in a dialogue between senior management and project management. In small, structured projects goals are not likely to change once the project is under way. Those managing novel projects find the goals change. Even if sponsors set clear goals at the outset, changing circumstances make it necessary to change them. This is a feature of the world that business operates in, and which shapes the job of the project manager. Boddy and Buchanan (1992) reported several examples, shown in Table 2.3.

Goals sometimes change because of 'scope creep', which occurs when people add new features to the original specifications. The case study of Chapter 1 also provides a final illustration of how goals remain fluid as a project gets under way. A few months into the project the manager commented:

> *'Now . . . the director has decided that he is looking for a cost justification for having the system at all – especially now he has discovered an extra cost he had not anticipated. For the first time, the "do nothing" option is arising.'*

To some extent changing goals are inevitable in novel projects – this reflects the inherently emergent nature of both strategy and the projects which implement it. The implication for the project manager is perhaps to manage expectations, so that people expect to experience some shifting of goals, and understand why

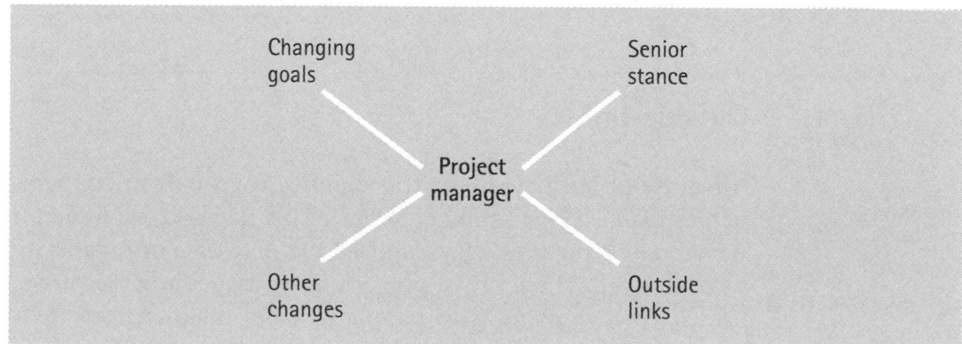

Figure 2.4 Other challenges for the project manager

Table 2.3 Sources of changing goals

Source	*Example*
Market changes	'This project is only half-way through implementation – but already we're introducing significant changes to cope with new areas of business which the sales and marketing people have succeeded in obtaining'
Senior management priorities	'We've only done about 30 per cent of the scheduling devolution programme, when all of a sudden up pops this new thing, which is going to take over all my time. It's always a balance between the priorities of getting something done that is secure and can last, and doing something that is obviously coming under pressure from a very severe business need'
Lack of clear strategy	'The specification of what the refinery was to produce was difficult to prepare, as it proved impossible to get the marketing director to be quantitative about the products he wanted to make and sell . . . It was also clear there was no plan to process the by-products which would arise. All of these factors made project management very difficult, as there was a basic lack of clarity about the product range, the expected sales, or what technology would be used'

Source: Boddy and Buchanan (1992)

this occurs. Equally they need to be ready to manage the implications of such flexibility for other aspects of the project.

NOTEPAD 2.3

Changing goals?

- Have the goals of your project changed during the work?
- What led to this change?
- What effects has it had on the project?
- How can you deal with it?

Outside links

A feature of business life is the significant growth in cooperation between companies (Sako, 1992; Faulkner, 1995). This has also happened in the public sector where new structures, characterised by 'networks of organisations' (Walsh, 1995) have evolved. These broad policy trends shape tangible projects, many of which now involve working with people in other organisations. Many IT projects now cross organisational boundaries. As such they are likely to require changes in more than one organisation, which are not directly within the authority of the project manager.

Projects usually require technical expertise or resources from people in other departments or organisations. While this has many advantages, it also brings risks – others are not necessarily as committed to the project as those who are managing it.

Neglecting to manage suppliers . . .

A small oil refining company embarked on a project to build a new plant. They lacked the experience to design the process, or the engineering of the plant, so decided to work with an engineering contractor. This link worked well, but severe difficulties arose later when the work being done by a piping sub-contractor was unsatisfactory, causing a critical delay. The same company suffered dramatically when it received an unexpected announcement that there would be a three-month interruption in its supply of crude oil. Alternatives were not as suitable, and caused technical and marketing difficulties: 'We were negligent in our approach to our suppliers, in that we did not adequately sustain a relationship with them, and they did not advise us of their impending refinery closure.'

Source: Boddy and Buchanan (1992)

A project based in one department may need others to agree to changes in their ways of working. Separate functions acquire different cultures and ways of working which may be difficult to reconcile with the project requirements. Some may be receptive to change, and keen to move ahead quickly; others need longer to adjust. They have different priorities, reflecting their part of the business, and other demands on them. The project manager is competing for their time and commitment against other priorities.

Senior stance

The attitude of top management towards the project is critical. They cannot give detailed guidelines, and may not even set out a clear blueprint for change. But their actions and words affect the ability of the project manager to influence other people. They shape part of the context in which the project manager works.

Are they visibly behind the idea of change, willing to give it the resources it needs, and with reasonable expectations of what the project can achieve? How demanding are they, how tolerant of risk and delay? Will there be pressure for short-cuts, or do they see the value of getting the change right, even if it takes longer?

The project manager needs to know who is behind the change, as a powerful sponsor or champion will see the project through the difficult times. The champion for change – the person who will push the changes through, cajoling the doubters and supporting the project in time of difficulty – is usually a senior manager. The project manager should also know how powerful the person promoting the project is, and whether their support is reliable. This project manager felt exposed:

> *'The newly appointed Warehousing Director initially demonstrated a high degree of ownership and support for the proposal. Although this arrangement worked well in the early stages, the Director lost interest in giving the scheme his personal attention. He preferred to concentrate on matters of "strategy", and allowed "urgent matters" to take precedence.'*

It is also prudent to assess if any members of senior management oppose the project, and how sustained that is likely to be. A project may run counter to the basic values and beliefs of some senior managers, or threaten powerful interests. If significant groups or individuals are intent on undermining or disrupting the change, the management problems will be markedly different from those experienced in less controversial changes.

Building and sustaining ownership is more difficult if goals are changing and there are many outside links. Wide links or dependencies mean genuine commitment has to come from a correspondingly wide range of functions and levels. Shifting goals can lead to the erosion of commitments already established.

Other changes

Volatile environments mean that change is more frequent, and so comes in clusters. Almost all the projects included in the research for this book took place at the same time as other major changes. Sometimes these were other aspects of the same broad project, and therefore were to be expected. More often the turbulent environment of the organisation was prompting several simultaneous responses (see also Clark, 1995). Multi-project situations bring more uncertainty. There will be more competition for resources, and more scepticism as staff observe yet another change being launched. Table 2.4 summarises the threats and opportunities of these features.

Table 2.4 More threats and opportunities in project types

Feature	*Threats*	*Opportunities*
Outside links	More uncertainty Harder to predict effects Slower to secure agreement	Career visibility Rewards of success
Changing goals	Loss of credibility with others Cost and time over-run	Can use to justify delay Claim extra budget Result hard to compare
Supportive senior stance	High expectations	Career visibility Access to resources
Other changes	Competition for resources Initiative fatigue	Climate receptive to change

Spotting the pitfalls

Project managers can assess where trouble is most likely to arise, and what that means for how they need to manage the change, by using the checklist shown in Table 2.5. It brings together the features of change projects discussed above. Projects can be reviewed against these features, by placing a tick at the point on each of the scales which most accurately describes the project. High scores indicate where trouble is most likely to arise. Later chapters of this book should enable managers to handle many of these features more confidently and effectively.

A low total score suggests a problem with relatively clear boundaries, a relatively clear set of agreed objectives, and where the steps to achieve the result are fairly predictable. A change of this sort is 'hard', 'structured' or 'bounded'. It may be a challenging and demanding result to achieve; but it deals with well-known issues.

A high total score suggests a more ambiguously defined activity, with disagreement over objectives, and little certainty about how to achieve them. The change is relatively 'soft', 'unstructured', 'unbounded'. It will raise different problems from those experienced in managing a more structured project. There will be more uncertainty, more changes to plan, more political activity, more compromise. The route to be followed will not be clear.

Do people share the same view of the task on which they are working? The project manager will be vulnerable if others see the change in structured terms, when the manager sees it as ambiguous and political. They may then use the wrong approach, expect a fairly straightforward activity, and become impatient with delay while people resolve their differences.

Change management is about introducing some structure into an unbounded, unstructured problem. It is about turning an apparently insoluble mess into a soluble difficulty, by reducing the uncertainties to manageable proportions. This can be done by gathering information that will help reduce or eliminate successive areas of uncertainty. By assessing the level of uncertainty in respective areas of the project, it may be possible to see those which can be dealt with now, and those which need still to remain ambiguous.

Others connected with the project can share this understanding. Once the project manager is clear about the nature of the task, it becomes easier to pass that to others, to develop a common picture.

Table 2.5 Project profile tool

Significance:	Margin	1	2	3	4	5	Core
Solution:	Familiar	1	2	3	4	5	Novel
Pace:	Gradual	1	2	3	4	5	Rapid
Intentions:	Uncontroversial	1	2	3	4	5	Controversial
Changing goals:	Rare/minor	1	2	3	4	5	Often/major
Outside links:	Few	1	2	3	4	5	Many
Senior stance:	Supportive	1	2	3	4	5	Unsupportive
Other changes	Few	1	2	3	4	5	Many

CASE STUDY

Digital Europe, Part A

Until its merger with Compaq, Digital Europe was the European manufacturing and distribution operation of the Digital Equipment Corporation, one of the leading players in the world electronics industry. At the time of this case study the European Division had seven plants making different products within the Digital range. The plants had a high degree of autonomy and often competed with each other for the 'charter' to make new products. At the same time they had to cooperate because systems sold to customers were usually built with parts made by several of the European plants. So there was also competitive pressure to improve Europe-wide systems. A senior manager from one of the European plants recalls his experience of managing one such attempt:

'I was asked to attend a meeting with a group of people who were interested in "order fulfilment". They showed me some data about how long it took our competitors to process customer orders and how reliable their delivery promises were. It became very clear to me that this was a major area of opportunity for our company. Our products were good – we would do very well competitively if we could put in systems and administrative processes that were equally sharp. It was a yawning gap and something had to be done.

'I volunteered to pull together a group of people from our other facilities and put our thoughts together. We gathered people from each location who understood order scheduling and who also had a vision of what it could be like. Between August and September we had two five-day meetings and came up with some ideas which I then drafted into a formal document. This stated the problem and gave some indication of a solution. The next problem was how to enable that plan.

'I then began a round of presentations to plant staffs around Europe and to our European management team, describing to them the problem and suggesting to them a way forward. People received the paper well. However, it was also very clear that people were beginning to be wary of what it was going to take to correct our internal processes and systems. The company had attempted major pan-European redesign work before and had failed miserably because the divisions would not accept the solutions. European-wide programmes, therefore, had a bad name.

'Over the last year my part-time team has done much work with each of their plant staffs to convince them of the need for the order fulfilment project. My European functional boss had also been working with the European management team to convince them of the need for major investment. We agreed to do a presentation that looked at all our processes and systems in order fulfilment. The aim was to get the commitment and investment that we require from the managements of the separate European plants.

'My functional boss and I therefore spent many long hours doing this. It was the culmination of about 15 months of part-time work, with the best brains we have available to try and get our corporation to move forward. We were now at the point where we needed some more legitimacy. We managed to gather our European staff team in Ireland for about six hours and we did our presentation. We clearly captured the interest, imagination and energy of the group, and very clearly they were going to

find a way even though we have no formal budget. It was an excellent culmination of 15 months' work, though in many ways it was just the beginning.'

Source: Information provided by the manager

Case study questions

1 Is this project being driven by external or internal forces?

2 Where would you place it on Figure 2.3? Would people in different plants in Europe put it in the same place?

3 Why are outside links so important to the project?

4 How has the project manager sought to influence the stance of senior managers towards the project?

5 Use Table 2.5 to identify where the pitfalls may be in this project.

Summary

This chapter has shown how the elements in the context combine in unique ways to shape the task facing the manager of a particular project. It has described these, and shown how managers can use them to diagnose the nature of their project.

The key points from this chapter are:

- It is possible to identify forces that are driving and restraining a project.
- The project will move forward if the driving forces are greater than the restraining forces.
- The elements of the context combine to produce projects that vary in their significance, novelty, speed and controversy.
- These have critical implications for the task of the project manager.
- Other challenges arise from the phenomena of changing goals, outside links, senior stance and other changes.
- Assessing these factors with the aid of Table 2.5 will help the project manager to decide where to focus effort.

Chapter questions

1 Are external driving forces likely to be stronger than internal ones?

2 Do you agree or disagree that reducing restraining forces is more likely to produce results than increasing driving forces? Give examples to support your view.

3 A manager uses Figure 2.3 and concludes the project is in Quadrant 4. The Board thinks the project is in Quadrant 3. Why might this difference have arisen, and what are the implications for the project manager?

4 Review the threats and opportunities which different kinds of projects represent (Tables 2.2 and 2.4). Do you agree with the lists, or are there items you would add?

5 What specific difficulties do you think that 'changing goals' will cause for relations between a project manager and their team?

Further reading

Kharbanda, O.P. and Pinto, J.K. (1996) *What Made Gertie Gallop? Lessons from Project Failures*. New York: Van Nostrand Rheinhold. A highly readable (and sometimes contentious) account of a wide variety of classic project failures from around the world, leading to some valuable lessons.

Pettigrew, A.M. (1985) *The Awakening Giant, Change and Continuity in ICI*. Oxford: Blackwell. The classic account of ICI's long-term programme of radical transformation. Provided the empirical source for Andrew Pettigrew's theories on the context of organisational change. A long book, but worth the effort.

References

Boddy, D. and Buchanan D.A. (1992) *Take the Lead: Interpersonal Skills for Project Managers*. Hemel Hempstead: Prentice Hall.

Boddy, D. and Gunson, N. (1996) *Organizations in the Network Age*. London: Routledge.

Clark, J. (1995) *Managing Innovation and Change*. London: Sage Publications.

Currie, W. (1997) 'Computerising the stock exchange: a comparison of two information systems', *New Technology Work and Employment*, 12, 75–83.

Currie, W. and Willcocks, L. (1996) 'The New Branch Columbus project at Royal Bank of Scotland', *Journal of Strategic Information Systems*, 5, 213–36.

Faulkner, D. (1995) *International Strategic Alliances: Co-operating to Compete*. Maidenhead: McGraw-Hill.

Keen, L. and Scase, R. (1998) *Local Government Management: Rhetoric and Reality of Change*. Buckingham: Open University Press.

Knights, D. and Murray, F. (1994) *Managers Divided: Organisation Politics and Information Technology Management*. Chichester: John Wiley.

Lewin, K. (1947) 'Field theory in social science', *Human Relations*, 1, 5–41.

Pinto, J.K. and Slevin, D.P. (1988) 'Project success: definition and measurement techniques', *Project Management Journal*, 19, 67–73.

Sako, M. (1992) *Prices, Quality and Trust: Inter-firm Relations in Britain and Japan*. Cambridge: Cambridge University Press.

Shenhar, A.J., Levy, O. and Dvir, D. (1997) 'Mapping the dimensions of project success', *Project Management Journal*, 28, 5–13.

Walsh, K. (1995) *Public Services and Market Mechanisms: Competition, Contracting and the New Public Management*. Basingstoke: Macmillan.

3 Projects interact with their context

Introduction

The task of managing a project is deeply influenced by the context in which it takes place. The context includes history, because what people remember of earlier events affects how they respond to current proposals. It also includes the contemporary setting, both within and beyond the organisation. Managers create projects to change some aspect of the organisation. At the same time the existing (inherited) organisation helps or hinders project performance.

This chapter outlines the significance of the context to project managers. It then identifies the main elements of that context, as these represent areas of management action. People are likely to observe several elements of the context, and to respond to them in the light of their interests. If that is the case, can the project manager create a context that gives coherent, consistent signals to those affected? Creating an adequate process for managing the links between project and context will help.

Objectives

After reading this chapter you should be able to:

- outline a theory of the interaction between people, the project and their context;
- identify the elements in that context;
- show why the context also includes the processes of project management;
- use the approach in a project with which you are familiar.

An interaction approach

Why do people act the way they do? One view is that a person's interests and inclinations shape their behaviour. People understand what they are doing, have information about the consequences, and make conscious decisions to satisfy their interests. Those who take this view emphasise individual free will, and the scope that people have to choose what they do. An alternative position is that social institutions condition human behaviour. People occupy roles in society and organisations. These roles, made up of the expectations of others, determine what people do.

A model that most accurately represents the situation facing a project manager combines both approaches. An interaction approach, building on the work of Orlikowski (1992), expresses the widely applicable idea that people act within their context. The rules and norms of behaviour in that context encourage them to act in a particular way. How people in practice respond to those rules produces a 'revised' context which is what now shapes behaviour. The relation between people and context works both ways.

In organisational life, managers construct a context which they believe will achieve their objectives. Other people socially construct the context when they decide how to react to the formal position – which features to reject, ignore, use or adapt to suit their ways of working. With repetition these practices become accepted as the way to do the job. They create the working context for that situation, which is now part of the context shaping human action. People shape institutions, and institutions then shape people.

In the same way, project managers work within the existing organisational context, but reshape some aspects to encourage behaviour that supports project objectives. They try to create rules to encourage new behaviour. Other players interpret those rules in their interests, and these now form their context.

Applying the interaction model to information systems

The interaction model implies that, to a degree, people modify any system throughout the phases of design and use. As they use the system they adapt it to suit the particular circumstances. They experiment and improve. Some systems offer little scope for this – designers have ensured that users must use the system in a set way. Others have more scope for local interpretation. Intranets are a good example, as their content depends on human action. People have to enter and maintain information that makes the site worth using. If the site (part of the new context) contains little of value, staff will not bother to use it. The more flexibility that is possible, the less useful it is to consider technology as an objective, fixed entity with predictable effects: 'Technology does not impact on a social context, or vice versa but, over time, each shapes the other' (Kimble and McLoughlin, 1995).

This idea of continuing interaction between people and their context gives insight into projects of all kinds. For example, Boddy *et al.* (2000) used it in their work on supply chain partnering. This is an approach to inter-firm business relationships in which companies develop practices that encourage collaborative rather than adversarial behaviour. A move towards partnering depends on the players working in an (unfamiliar) collaborative way. The separate contexts of the two companies initially caused difficulty. They had varied histories and cultures, so the staff approached common problems in different ways.

> *'One of the biggest problems we had was that . . . they are a very old-established engineering company, and they think that way . . . It was attitudes, the way they want to do business . . . Flexibility didn't seem important. Whereas to us it was critical. Compared to us turnround is slow. We work in minutes and seconds – they work in weeks and months!'*

To preserve the relationship, those running the project gradually created a new context to encourage cooperative behaviour. They made significant changes in order processing and manufacturing facilities, created new staff roles and created new structures to solve problems. These changes in context encouraged people to act more cooperatively together, ensuring the success of the project.

So the notion of understanding and managing the context is fundamental to the approach of this book. What are the elements that make up that context?

Identify the elements in the context

A familiar place to start is with Leavitt's (1965) model, in which he proposed that organisations consist of four interacting elements – task (or objectives), technology, people and structure. Later work has identified the influence of power (Buchanan and Badham, 1999; Markus, 1983; Pfeffer, 1992) on behaviour. Power models emphasise, for example, that change affects the interests of people unevenly. Others emphasise the role of culture, because these may encourage or discourage innovation and commitment to change (Lorsch, 1986; Martin, 1992). More recently attention has turned to the transformation processes used to deliver outputs and services (Peppard, 1995). Boddy and Macbeth (2000) found that the provision of adequate resources had a statistically significant effect on the outcome of projects. Combining these sources gives seven empirically grounded elements (Figure 3.1) that make up the context of a project:

- **business processes** – the way the companies have designed the processes for moving materials and information;
- **technology** – the type and location of physical facilities, machinery, and information systems;
- **resources** – mainly the financial resources available to the organisation;
- **structure** – the way tasks required to deliver goods and services are divided and coordinated;
- **people** – their knowledge, skills, attitudes and goals;
- **culture** – the prevailing norms, beliefs and underlying values that characterise the organisation;
- **power** – the amount and distribution of identifiable sources of power.

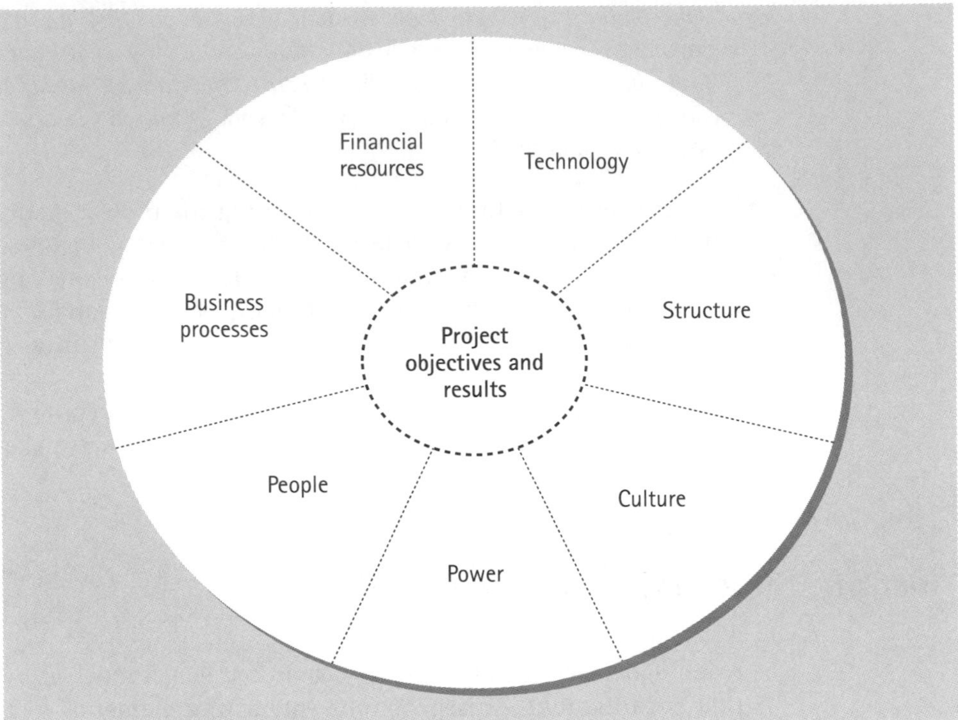

Figure 3.1 The context of a project

NOTEPAD 3.1

Your project

- Use the headings in Figure 3.1 to analyse the main features in the context of your project.
- Which are having the greatest effects?
- Are they helping or hindering the project?

The project is intended to change the context

Projects aim to change one or more elements of the organisational context – in the expectation that this will encourage people to work in ways that support the project objectives. Project managers (such as those implementing the supply chain partnering project described earlier) start within the existing context. They reshape some aspects of the context (putting in a new business process, or changing a structure) to encourage behaviour that supports the new system. They create 'rules' (Walsham, 1993) that they hope will guide the behaviour of other staff involved in the activity. The latter socially construct the context as they begin to work within these new rules. This happens as people begin to use the new system, and decide which aspects to ignore, use or adapt. The interaction between people and context continues as the system evolves.

Changing the context in a supply chain project

Boddy and Macbeth (2000) studied two companies as they tried to move towards a more cooperative supply chain relationship. Managers in both companies introduced changes to the context of work – technology, processes and work-roles. All of these were designed to create a context which encouraged more cooperation, and closer interpersonal links. For example the supplier's sales coordinator:

> *'There is a close relationship with my opposite number in Sun. We speak several times a day, and he tries to give me as much information as he possibly can.'*

Sun staff echoed this:

> *'What makes (them) different is that you're talking to them daily . . . The relationships are a bit different – it is a bit closer than an ordinary supplier where you don't have that bond. Dealings are more direct. People are becoming more open with each other.'*

Both groups came to appreciate the others' requirements and tried to make things easier for them. Sun staff learned about the supplier, and vice versa. Both spoke of 'harmonising expectations'.

Source: Boddy *et al.* (2000)

As people become used to working with the new system, their behaviours become routine and taken for granted. They become part of the context which staff have created informally, rather than those formally responsible for designing the change. These informally created aspects of the context may or may not support the intentions of those who initiated the project and designed the new system.

The context affects the project

Contemporary context

While the project aims to change the context, the contemporary context itself will help or hinder that attempt. All of the elements of Figure 3.1 will be present as the project begins, and individually will have some influence on how people react to the proposal. To take just one example in some detail, the prevailing culture – the shared values, ideals and beliefs that hold an organisation together – affects how people view a change. Cultures develop as members work together to deal with problems, and in so doing develop shared assumptions about the external world and their internal processes. As firms grow, sub-cultures develop within them. Members are likely to welcome a project that they believe fits the culture or sub-culture. They are likely to resist one that conflicts with or challenges the culture.

A significant element in organisational culture is the set of values which guide members' actions. Quinn *et al.* (1996) proposed that these values represent the perspective that members typically take towards two inherent tensions which occur in any organisation. These are between flexibility and control, and between maintaining the internal system and adapting to the external environment. The resulting four cultural types (shown in Figure 3.2) summarise the competing values within an organisation on how to manage it.

The cultural types are:

1 **Open systems** (external, flexibility). People have an open view and see the external environment as a vital source of ideas, energy and resources. Examples: start-up firms, new business units – organic, flexible operations.

2 **Rational goal** (external, control). People see the organisation as a rational, efficiency-seeking unit. They define effectiveness in terms of production or economic goals. Examples: established firms, sales management units – mechanistic.

3 **Internal process** (internal, control). People largely ignore the environment, tending to look inward. Their goal is to make the unit internally efficient, stable, controlled. Examples: utilities, public authorities, back-office operations.

4 **Human relations** (internal, flexibility). An emphasis on the human relations view of organisation, with a focus on informal, interpersonal relations rather than formal structures. Examples: professional service firms such as legal practices, small consultancies.

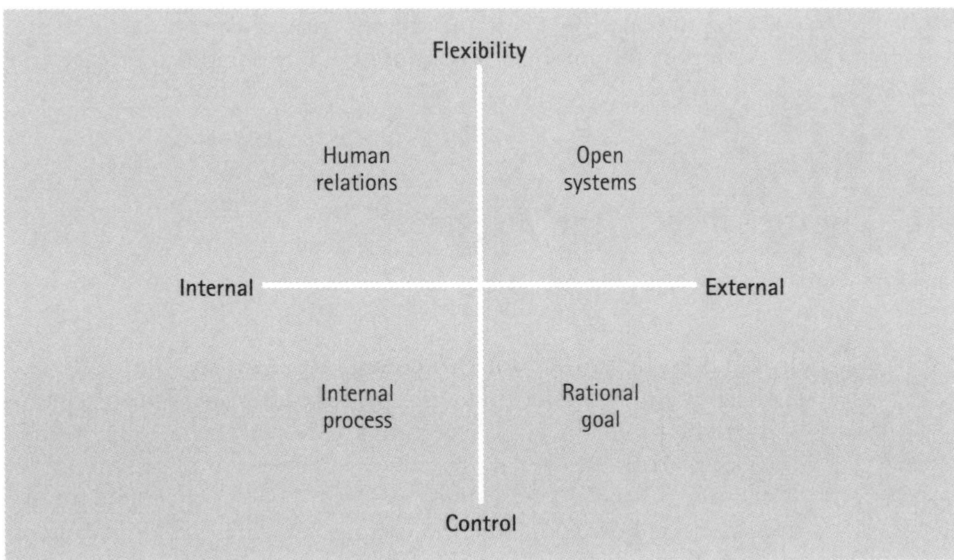

Figure 3.2 Types of organisational culture

Source: Based on Quinn *et al.* (1996)

NOTEPAD 3.2

Culture, organisation and your project

- Decide which of these cultural types best describes your department or function.
- Has that affected the way people have reacted to change projects?
- Try to do the same analysis for departments affected by a project on which you are working.
- What do your results imply for managing projects, and for this theory?

Intuitively, we can sense that people holding the values of these four cultures will react differently to many things. For example, they are likely to have different views towards a project to implement a new IT system. We would expect people in a mechanistic, relatively stable organisation to welcome systems that give more control over what is happening, or that promote order and predictability. They may not welcome those which increase access to information or which expose people to more external ideas. They threaten established methods.

This idea received some informal empirical support in discussions with staff in a major European financial services company. The group were able to identify several areas of the company which matched the cultural types, and to describe their different views towards various Internet proposals. For example, those in an 'internal process' culture (typically performing routine back-office data processing functions) were hostile to Internet ventures. They appeared to others to be 'stuck with their own systems', which were so large and interlinked that any change was threatening. Staff in new business areas of the company ('open systems') were much more positive, seeing the Internet as a way towards new business opportunities.

If the prevailing culture supports the application envisaged, then people are more likely to accept it with enthusiasm and commitment. If there is a mismatch between the culture and the Internet proposal, the promoters will experience resistance or lack of commitment.

The same is true of other elements of the context, implying that the project manager needs to be aware of which aspects of the context will be supportive, and which represent potential obstacles.

How culture impeded an Intranet project

Newell (1999) reported how a bank attempted to create a Knowledge Management system based on Intranets. The aim was to enable staff across the global organisation to share information (irrespective of which division they worked in) to support service to global customers. The project ran into difficulties because the bank had a tradition of autonomous business units. Given this culture, they responded to the Intranet initiative by creating their own, unconnected Intranets. The project had served to strengthen the barriers within the company rather than dissolve them.

Historical context

While the contemporary context is evidently the product of history, it is important to emphasise this historical dimension. Change, and any project, is an evolutionary process, which takes place within the historical and contemporary context of the organisation. As Pettigrew *et al.* (1992, p. 269) observed: 'The importance of temporal interconnectedness – the need to locate change in past, present and future time – should be stressed.'

Management seeks to implement change against a background of previous events. Past decisions shaped the organisation context as it is today. They affect its receptivity to change and its ability to change. As the Sun case showed, the past affects how people react to current requirements. The project manager in the Chapter 1 case study also experienced this, as he sought to find the views of the area managers. He recalled:

> *'There are so many changes taking place, they are more or less numb, and this is simply another change which they are just going to have to take on board. The result is that they are somewhat passive and neutral, and when I ask what their requirements might be, the response is usually "you tell me".'*

The promoter of a major project in a multinational also experienced the effects of history, as he tried to raise enthusiasm amongst his colleagues:

> *'They were a little sceptical and wary of whether it was actually going to enhance our processes. Major pan-European redesign work had been attempted in the past and had failed miserably. The solutions had not been appropriate and had not been accepted by the divisions. Europe-wide programmes therefore had a bad name.'*

Beliefs about future history also affect how people react to a current proposal. Those who are optimistic about the future of the business and of their place within it tend to be more receptive and open to change than those who feel threatened and vulnerable.

Other levels

The context represented by this model occurs at several levels – such as operating, divisional and corporate. People at any of these levels will be acting to make changes in their context – which may help or hinder the manager of a particular project. For example, a project at one level will often depend on decisions at other levels about the resources available.

The manager leading a refinery team experienced this problem:

> *'One of the main drawbacks was that commissioning staff could have been supplemented by skilled professionals from within the company, but this was denied to me as project manager. This threw a heavy strain and responsibility on myself and my assistant. It put me in a position of high stress, as I knew that the future of the company rested upon the successful outcome of this project. One disappointment (and, I believe, a significant factor in the project) was that just before commissioning, the manager of the pilot plant development team was transferred to another job.*

He had been promised to me at the project inception, and I had designed him into the working operation.'

Another manager summed up the ever-present threat:

'I've got to check every day that they're still working on my project.'

Acting to change an element at one level will have (hard to predict?) effects at this and other levels. Any elements of the context, such as business processes, technology or the rest may change, for reasons quite unconnected with a given project. The effects may be unintended, but may nevertheless have significant implications for the immediate project. There is thus no certainty that people see themselves within a coherent context that encourages them to work towards the success of the project. It is part of the manager's job to create that context. Even then, events beyond management's control will affect results.

NOTEPAD 3.3

The context of your project

- What aspects of the contemporary context, shown in Figure 3.1, have had most effect on a project you are familiar with?
- How have historical factors affected people's reactions?
- Were the effects positive or negative for the project?
- Did those managing the project take sufficient account of these contextual factors?

The process of projects – managing the interaction

The final point to make in this chapter is that the context of a project also includes the processes through which it is managed. Chapters 4 and 5 deal fully with this topic. So far this chapter has dealt with the substantive aspects of the context. Equally important are the processes available to (or created by) the project manager with which to manage the project.

Sometimes there will be established processes and systems, and some form of methodology with which to manage projects (such as the widely used PRINCE method, described in Chapter 4). More often project managers themselves will need to create appropriate ways of doing the job. At the very least this is likely to mean assembling a project team, and ensuring team members work together satisfactorily towards the project objectives.

The purpose of such mechanisms is to ensure that the project activities have adequate links to the wider context. They provide a channel of communication between the project and wider events. They enable people to know what is going on, what they need to do, or where to focus their effort. If they work well they can be more than the sum of their individual members, as people not only contribute their ideas, but exchange them with others to produce creative solutions to project problems.

CASE STUDY

Kwik-Fit

Until Ford acquired the business in 1998, Kwik-Fit was Europe's largest independent tyre and exhaust retailer. Tom Farmer had created the business in 1971. The core business was still the drive-in, 'while you wait' fitting of replacement tyres, exhausts, batteries, brakes and shock absorbers. The company also offered engine oil and filter change services and supplied and fitted child safety seats. In 1995 it began to sell motor insurance.

To build a dominant national position, the company had to provide a standard of service that would, in the words of the Kwik-Fit slogan, achieve '100% delighted customers'. Factors which customers valued included location, cleanliness, speed, quality, price and having parts in stock.

A small central management team worked in Edinburgh, led by Tom Farmer. The main operating company, Kwik-Fit (GB), had five geographical divisions. Day-to-day management was in the hands of a management board between the main board and the divisional management. Management throughout the company was in direct contact with market conditions facing the depot managers and staff. Their job was to support the depots, not to dominate them:

> *'We're not a big organisation – we're a collection of small businesses... in our company culture, Head Office is seen as a support operation. Our structure is very flat, inasmuch as if we wanted to change something tomorrow we could do it – we haven't got a hierarchy that has to be gone through.'*

Farmer believed firmly in keeping the number of administrative staff as low as possible. Every transaction inevitably generates administration – notably to account for the day's revenue, and to replenish stocks. In the early years, the company used a manual administrative system. Records of transactions, receipts and stocks were kept on paper in boxes and files. As the company grew (both organically and by acquisition) the administrative system began to fail. Farmer initiated a project to computerise the administrative processes.

The first computer system consisted of Electronic Point Of Sale (EPOS) terminals in each depot, linked to a mainframe computer at Head Office. This would allow all details of the day's transactions in each depot to move to Head Office overnight for immediate processing.

Source: Boddy and Gunson, 1996

Case study questions

1 How did the context shape Tom Farmer's approach to the IT project?

2 Which cultural type does the company correspond to?

3 How has the project changed the context (use Figure 3.1)?

4 How would you expect different players in the company to react to the new context?

5 What processes of change is the company likely to use, given what you know of its context?

Summary

This chapter has introduced the major theoretical perspective of the book, which is that people need to manage projects within their context. It has also indicated the empirically grounded elements that make up that context, and which represent areas for management attention.

The key points from this chapter are as follows:

- What people do depends on their context, which is itself the result of human action.
- This context consists of a limited number of elements.
- These elements are technology, business processes, resources, structures, power, people and culture.
- A project is an attempt to change one or more of these elements to change organisational performance.
- At the same time, the inherited context will itself affect the ability of people to change the context.
- The contextual elements are present in both a historical and contemporary sense, and at different levels of the organisation.
- The context also embodies the processes through which people manage projects.

Chapter questions

1 What is meant by the interaction approach? Use an example to illustrate your answer.
2 How does it differ from other perspectives on human behaviour mentioned in this chapter?
3 What are the elements which make up the context of a project?
4 Why is a project 'intended to change the context'?
5 What is the basis for distinguishing between the different cultural types identified?
6 Why will cultural type affect reactions to a project?

Further reading

Buchanan, D. and Badham, R. (1999) *Power, Politics and Organisational Change*. London: Sage Publications. A detailed and empirically based analysis of the politics of change, which implies that the project manager who lacks political skill will fail.

Dawson, P. (1994) *Organisational Change: A Processual Approach*. London: Paul Chapman. A fuller discussion of the process perspective on change projects.

Keen, L. and Scase, R. (1998) *Local Government Management: Rhetoric and Reality of Change*. Buckingham: Open University Press. A thorough analysis of a long-term study of a large local authority. It traces how the authority embarked on a programme of radical organisational and managerial reform. In doing so it illustrates many of the issues discussed in this chapter.

References

Boddy, D. and Gunson, N. (1996) *Organizations in the Network Age*. London: Routledge.

Boddy, D. and Macbeth, D.K. (2000) 'Prescriptions for managing change: a survey of their effects in projects to implement collaborative working between organisations', *International Journal of Project Management*, 18, 297–306.

Boddy, D., Macbeth, D.K. and Wagner, B. (2000) 'Implementing collaboration between organisations: an empirical study of supply chain partnering', *Journal of Management Studies*, 37, 1003–17.

Buchanan, D. and Badham, R. (1999) *Power, Politics and Organisational Change*. London: Sage Publications.

Kimble, C. and McLoughlin, K. (1995) 'Computer based information systems and managers' work', *New Technology, Work and Employment*, 10, 56–67.

Leavitt, H.J. (1965) 'Applied organizational change in industry: structural, technological and humanistic approaches', in March, J.G. (ed.) *Handbook of Organizations*. Chicago: Rand McNally.

Lorsch, J. (1986) 'Managing culture: the invisible barrier to strategic change', *California Management Review*, 28, 95–109.

Markus, M.L. (1983) 'Power, Politics and MIS implementation', *Communications of the ACM*, 26, 430–44.

Martin, J. (1992) *Cultures in Organizations: Three Perspectives*. Oxford: Oxford University Press.

Newell, S. (1999) 'Ebank: A failed knowledge management initiative', in Scarbrough, H. and Swan, J. (eds) *Case Studies in Knowledge Management*. London: IPD.

Orlikowski, W.J. (1992) 'The duality of technology: Rethinking the concept of technology in organisations', *Organisation Science*, 3, 398–427.

Peppard, J. (1995) *The Essence of Business Process Reengineering*. New York: Prentice Hall.

Pettigrew, A.M., Ferlie, E. and McKee, L. (1992) *Shaping Strategic Change*. London: Sage Publications.

Pfeffer, J. (1992) *Managing with Power*. Boston, MA: Harvard Business School Press.

Quinn, R.E., Faerman, S.R., Thompson, M.P. and McGrath, M.R. (1996) *Becoming a Master Manager*, 2nd edn. New York: Wiley.

Walsham, G. (1993) *Interpreting Information Systems in Organisations*. Chichester: Wiley.

Part 2

Understanding project management

4 Theories of change

Introduction

Project managers act in accordance with their personal theory of the task. This guides how they try to influence others in the volatile context of the project. Other players, including those on the project team, will have their own theories. They may have thought consciously about these, observing and interpreting previous projects. Alternatively, they may have based them on habit and established practice, with no consideration of other approaches. It may help project managers to compare their current theory of projects with some alternatives.

This chapter outlines four contrasting perspectives – project life cycle, emergent, participative and political. These alternatives are not necessarily in conflict. Each may work in the right conditions, which the project manager needs to assess.

Objectives

After reading this chapter you should be able to:

- **distinguish between four alternative perspectives on project management;**
- **decide which is most appropriate in the circumstances of a particular project;**
- **appreciate how the choice of model affects the skills that project managers need.**

Project life cycle approaches

Much of the advice given to those responsible for managing projects uses the idea of the project life cycle. Projects go through successive stages, and results depend on conducting the project through these stages in an orderly and controlled way. The labels vary, but major themes are:

- define objectives clearly;
- allocate responsibilities;
- fix deadlines;
- set budgets.

People often refer to these approaches as 'rational-linear' models of change. They reflect the assumption that planned change in organisations unfolds in a logical sequence, that people work to the plan, and that they notice and correct deviations from the plan. For some projects, and for some parts of other projects, these assumptions are reasonable. In those cases, rational-linear models give valuable guidance to those introducing change. If the assumptions are not correct, the manager who relies on this approach will not succeed.

In this model successfully managing a project depends on specifying these elements at the start and then monitoring them tightly to ensure the project stays on target. Ineffective implementation is due to managers failing to do this. For example Lock (1996), in his authoritative and highly regarded text on project management, identifies the 'key stages' of a manufacturing project, shown in Figure 4.1. He advises project managers to ensure that the stages are passed through in turn, 'until the project arrives back to the customer as a completed work package'. He also points out that: 'Clockwise rotation around the cycle only reveals the main stream. Within this flow many small tributaries, cross-currents and even whirlpools are generated before the project is finished' (p. 16).

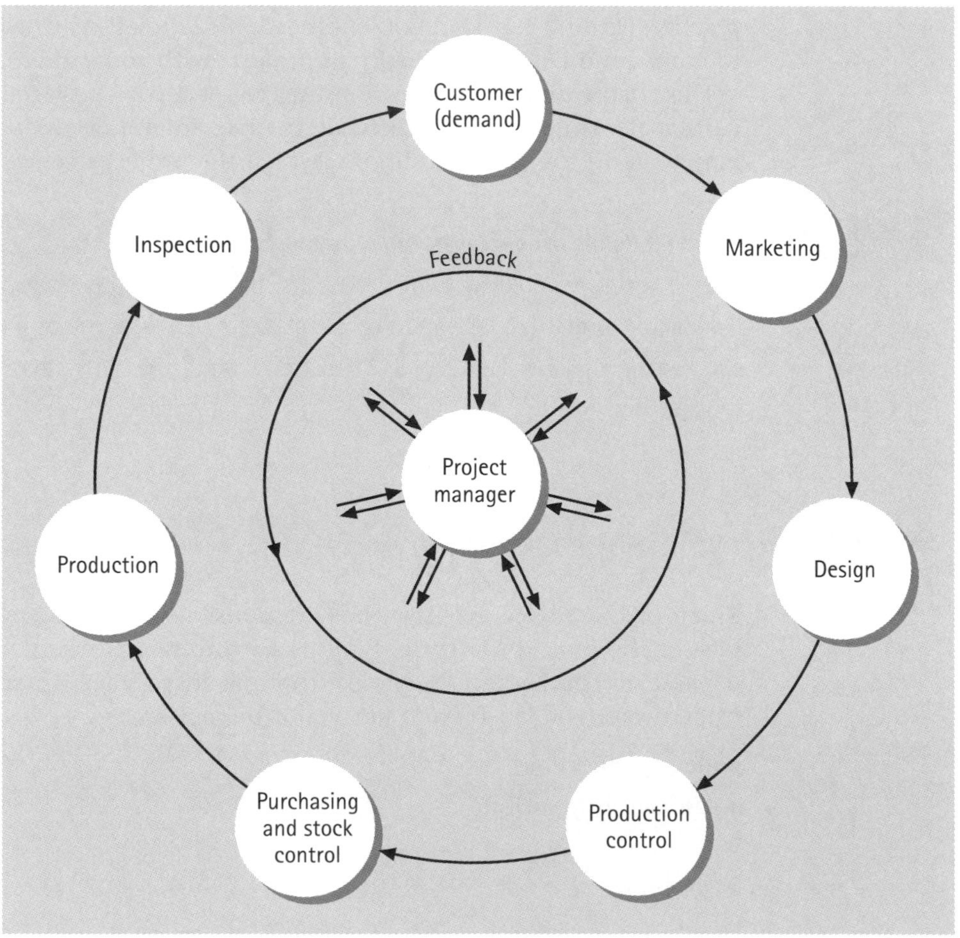

Figure 4.1 A manufacturing project cycle

Many books on project management (such as Lock, 1996; Woodward, 1997) present advice on tools and techniques for each stage of the life cycle. The project manager relying on this approach is expected to be skilled on two primary dimensions. First, with respect to the substance or content of changes introduced (whether this is a computerised management information system, a new factory building or a revised payment system). Second, with respect to planning and project control. They have to define outcomes and the necessary activities to reach them. They must monitor progress, and take remedial action to minimise deviations from the plan. Skills in dealing with 'human factors' or 'behavioural issues' are seen as important, but tend to be another item on the list (often the last item). They appear to be subordinate to the issues concerned with project planning and control.

Those advising on IT projects often take a similar approach, recommending a variety of 'system development life cycle' approaches. The development life cycle is an iterative process through several phases. Figure 4.2 (based on Chaffee, 1999) illustrates these.

The Systems Development Life Cycle model was developed to bring some order to the task of developing computer-based information systems. It consists of the steps of:

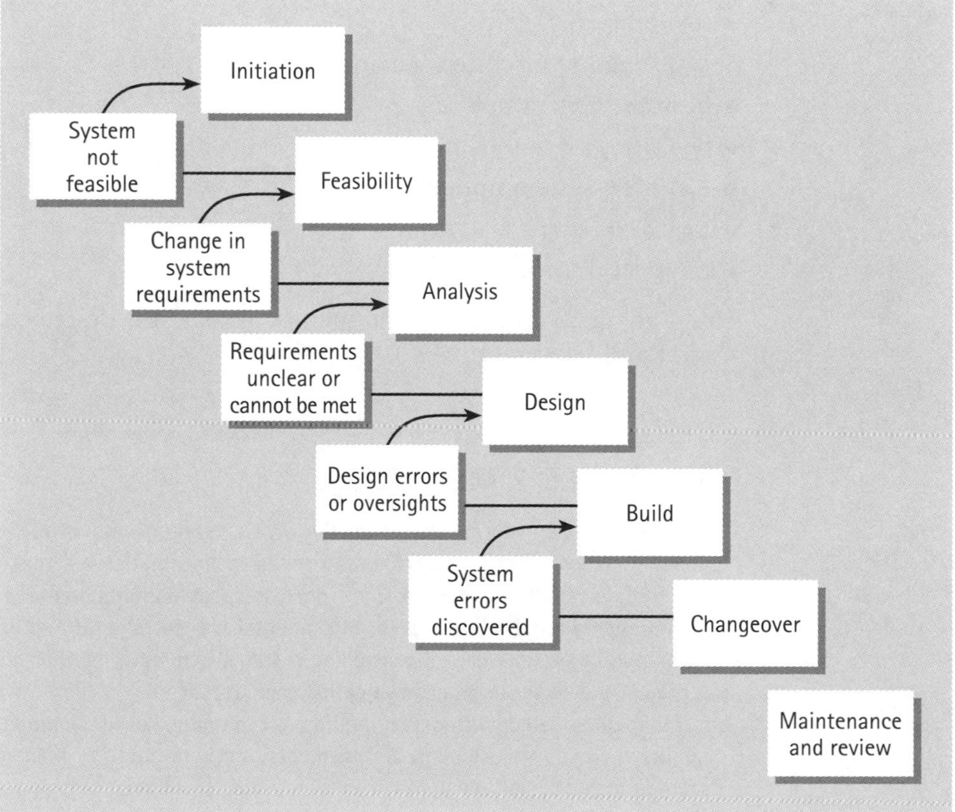

Figure 4.2 The traditional waterfall model of information systems development

- feasibility study;
- system investigation;
- systems analysis;
- system design;
- implementation;
- review and maintenance.

As Avison and Fitzgerald (1995) point out, 'these stages together are frequently referred to simply as "conventional systems analysis", "traditional systems analysis", "the systems development life-cycle" or the "waterfall model". The term "life-cycle" indicates the iterative nature of the processes – by the time the review stage came, the system was frequently found to be inadequate and it was not long before the process started again to develop a new information system with a feasibility study' (pp. 20–21). While this approach has many advantages and is still widely used, Avison and Fitzgerald observe that there are limitations to the approach, such as unambitious systems design, inflexibility and a failure to meet the needs of management (pp. 30–35). This encouraged designers to develop alternative approaches which attempt to overcome the observed weaknesses. These include the Structured Systems Analysis and Design Method (SSADM) which has seven stages:

- feasibility;
- investigation of current environment;
- business system options;
- definition of requirements;
- technical system options;
- logical design;
- physical design.

This and many other current methodologies are described in Chapter 6 of Avison and Fitzgerald (1995).

The PRINCE 2 Methodology

The method has been developed for the UK Government and is intended to be used for planning major projects, especially those based on information systems. The method applies three key elements to each project – processes, components and techniques.

The approach advocates seven 'fundamental processes': start-up, initiation, directing, managing stage boundaries, controlling a stage, managing product delivery and closing a project. All of these processes link to techniques.

Techniques listed within the method are product-based planning, change controls, quality reviews, project filing arrangements and configuration management. Finally the method includes eight components: organisation, planning, controls, stages, management of risk, quality, configuration management and change control.

Each of these aspects is specified in considerable detail, giving clear guidance on how major projects should be structured and managed. For example, the organisation component sets out the responsibilities of structures such as the project board, project support and the project support office. A PRINCE project is divided into a number of stages, each forming a distinct unit for management purposes. PRINCE defines the organisation of the project and its stages; the processes which drive the task; the structure and content of project plans; some basic project management techniques and a set of controls.

A different set of theories places more emphasis on the emergent rather than the planned nature of change. The next section summarises these ideas.

NOTEPAD 4.1

Using the project life cycle approach

If you are unfamiliar with this approach, you can gain some insight into it by using it on a practical task. For example:

- if you have a piece of work to do connected with your studies, such as an assignment or project, sketch out the steps to be followed, by adapting Figures 4.1 or 4.2;
- alternatively do the same for some domestic or social project.

After doing the assignment or project, reflect on how the life cycle approach affected the way you worked.

Planned or emergent projects?

Projects are the building blocks of organisational strategy, so they are likely to resemble the nature of that broader process. If managers develop strategy through following a logical, rational, planned process, then they are likely to do the same in the projects which give practical expression to strategy. What theories are there about the strategy process?

Early views of strategy saw it as essentially a planning activity, based on assumptions that people behave rationally and interpret events and information objectively. Writers such as Quinn (1980), Mintzberg (1994a, b) and Stacey (1994) believe these assumptions of rationality, objectivity and certainty rarely apply in the real world. They developed the view of strategy as an emergent or adaptive process. Mintzberg believed that strategic planning suffers from three 'fundamental fallacies', shown in Table 4.1.

Mintzberg's point is that managers should not expect rigid adherence to 'the plan'. Some departure from it is inevitable, due to unforeseeable changes in the external environment, the emergence of new opportunities, and other unanticipated events. He distinguishes between *intended* and *emergent* strategies. He acknowledges the validity of strategy as a plan, setting out intended courses of action, and recognises that managers will achieve some of their deliberate intentions. However, they

Table 4.1 Mintzberg's views on the fallacies of strategic planning

Fallacy	*Description*	*Counter-view*
Predetermination	'The prediction of... the unfolding of the strategy formation process on schedule... and the imposition of the resulting strategies on an acquiescent environment, again on schedule' (1994, p. 228)	Dynamic nature of the internal and external environments which ensure that in reality plans rarely unfold as intended
Detachment	'The prescription is that organizations should complete their thinking before they begin to act'	'Effective strategists are not people who abstract themselves from the daily detail but quite the opposite: they immerse themselves in it (and) abstract the strategic messages from it'
Formalisation	Analytical, scientific approach to strategy, with its prescribed series of steps or boxes, and array of checklists	Strategy requires insight, creativity and synthesis, all the things that formalisation discourages. It needs to function beyond boxes

will fail to implement some of their intentions (unrealised strategies), while implementing some changes that they did not expressly intend (emergent strategies). Nevertheless these emergent strategies resulted from 'actions taken one by one, which converged in time in some sort of consistency or pattern' (p. 25). The 'realised' strategy combines (some) intended strategies and other unintended, 'emergent' strategies. Figure 4.3 summarises this.

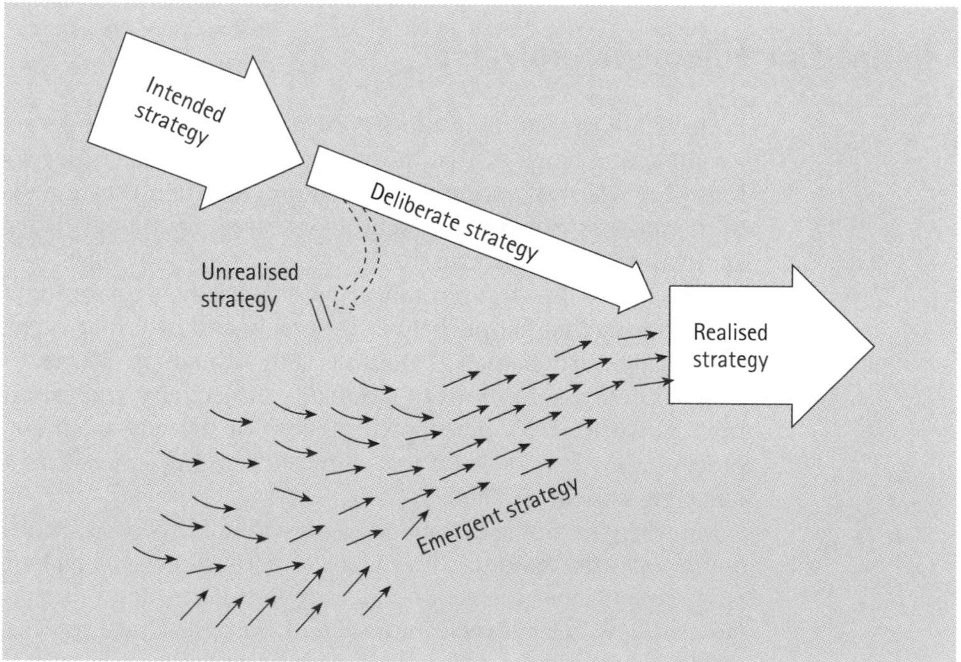

Figure 4.3 Forms of strategy

A flexible approach to strategy is one which recognises that 'the real world inevitably involves some thinking ahead of time as well as some adaptation en route' (p. 24).

The view of strategy as an emergent process is equally true of those managing projects in the public sector. In a classic work Charles Lindblom (1959) also concluded that the rational approach was unrealistic. He argued firstly that limits on the intellectual capacity of humans, sources of information and resources were such that comprehensive rational planning, involving extensive analysis and detailed evaluation of alternative strategies, was impossible. Moreover, the sectionalism or conflicting interests so characteristic of public policy frustrates attempts to reach agreement on objectives.

Lindblom concluded that strategy-making was not a scientific, comprehensive or rational process, but an iterative, incremental process, characterised by restricted analysis and bargaining between the players involved: 'Policy is not made once and for all but made and remade endlessly through a process of successive approximation to some desired objective.' Lindblom's analysis is close to the views on emergent strategy set out by Mintzberg.

Emergent strategy in the public sector

Lindblom's ideas find support in a contemporary account of project management in the public sector, based on research amongst a group of managers implementing major change projects: 'The powerful influence of the political process on organisational and cultural change is transparent for local authorities, but this may also be relevant in other non-elected organisations. Competing values and interests between different stakeholders are often less overt but none the less powerful factors championing or blocking processes of change' (Hartley *et al.*, 1997, p. 71).

The position taken by these authors applies to projects as much as it does to strategy. Projects are the means through which organisations deliver broad strategy. They take place in exactly the same volatile, uncertain environment as does the organisation as a whole. People with different interests and priorities try to shape both the ends and the means of projects. So while planning can undoubtedly help, the project manager is likely to experience an emergent rather than a planned project.

Participative approaches

The participative approach to management has become a familiar theme in the management literature. Some observers expect it to overcome resistance and win commitment to new ideas, through what Pettigrew (1985) described as the 'truth, trust, love and collaboration approach'. This is a key feature of much organisational development literature, and has also become an integral component of European and Scandinavian management thought and practice. The concept of establishing 'ownership' of change became central to this argument in the late 1980s. The term indicates feelings of personal involvement in and contribution to events and outcomes. The underlying, and wholly reasonable, assumption is that if people are able to say 'I helped to build this', they will be more willing to live and work with it, whatever it is.

Many texts offer advice on how to involve employees in implementing change effectively. This applies to the 'quality of working life' movement of the 1960s and 1970s, to the 'quality circle' movement of the 1970s and 1980s and to 'high involvement management' practices (Lawler, 1986).

A well-known example of the participative approach in the field of systems design is Mumford and Weir's (1981) ETHICS approach, summarised in Figure 4.4. Here the key ingredients include user involvement in system development, recognising the social issues in implementation and using socio-technical principles to redesign work. Several other methodologies are available for involving users in the system design process, for understanding users' needs more effectively, and for giving them wider influence in design decisions that will affect their work.

However, the approach has its doubters. For example Child (1984) explores the circumstances in which participation may be inappropriate or unworkable. While supporting the view that the involvement of those to be affected by change is ethically desirable, Child argues that it is not always appropriate. If

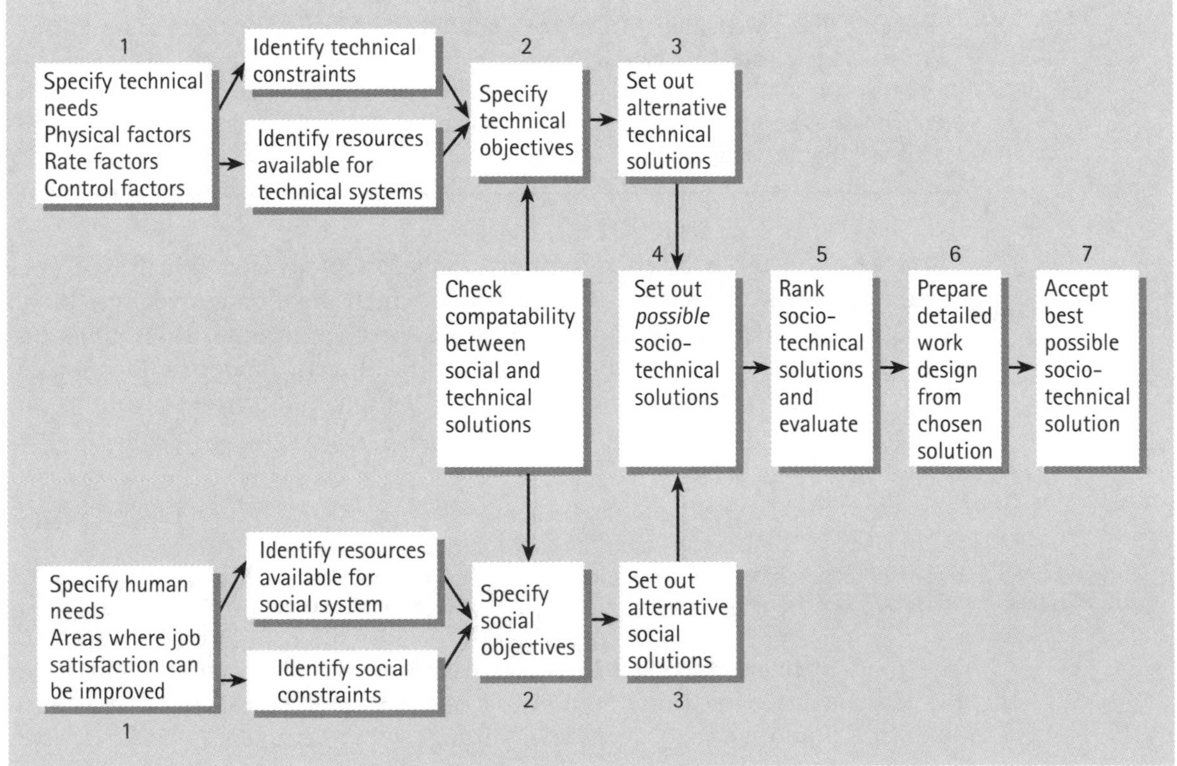

Figure 4.4 The ETHICS method – diagnosis and socio-technical systems design

there is full agreement on how to proceed, or where management is powerful enough to force changes through, extensive participation will be a waste of time. Similarly, where there is fundamental disagreement and inflexible opposition to change, opponents can use participative processes to obstruct implementation. Child also cites American research suggesting that it is wholly unrealistic to think of moving to consensus through participation in large public sector bureaucracies. These tend to have rigid hierarchies and competing political interest groups. Some large private sector companies have these bureaucratic and political characteristics too.

Participative approaches to change are consistent with democratic values and beliefs, and it is easy to agree that those managing change should seek to follow these prescriptions. However, because change projects regularly run into difficulties, there must be something wrong with the easy prescription. One possibility is that although the remedies sound easy, they are difficult and time-consuming to put into effect. The project manager able to handle all the dimensions of a participative change process is rare, especially when under pressure from a range of other demands on their time and energy.

A second reason is that in some situations participative approaches are inappropriate or unworkable. Where there is wide agreement on how to proceed, or where the practical scope for consultation to change matters is limited, then to go through the motions of participative management is dishonest and time-wasting. If there is wide and fundamental disagreement from some parties to the change, participation can lead to the change being blocked – in which case those pushing the change are unlikely to engage in it.

Successful projects that had little participation

Research reported more fully in Chapter 5 provides evidence of successful projects in which managers did *not* use participative techniques. A quantitative analysis of 46 successful and 54 unsuccessful projects showed that managers of successful projects showed a statistically significant tendency to **disagree** with two statements:

'Care was taken to ask people with different perspectives for their views on the change.'

'There was a lot of exploring and experimenting with ideas.'

This result was unexpected, as it showed that successful implementers had not used some common participative techniques. One interpretation is that the changes being studied were unfamiliar for most of the organisations. There would be little in-house experience, or perhaps even interest, in the project. Perhaps in those circumstances managers believed (correctly, on the evidence) that extensive debate would be counter-productive. More generally, it confirms the view that successful projects do not necessarily depend on participation.

Source: Boddy and Macbeth (2000)

In other words, participative approaches assume that a sensitive approach by reasonable people will result in the willing acceptance and implementation of change. For some changes, and in some organisations, that assumption will be correct. In such cases the approach will be a relevant source of guidance to the project manager. However, as with the project life cycle approaches, if the assumptions do not fit reality, the guidance will be misleading.

NOTEPAD 4.2

Reflecting on participation

Have you been involved with, or affected by, a change, either in your work or studies?

(a) If so:
- What evidence was there that those managing the change agreed with the participative approach?
- In what way, if any, were you able to participate?
- How did that affect your reaction to the change?

(b) If you have not been involved directly:
- Identify three advantages and three disadvantages for the project manager in adopting a participative approach.
- Suggest how they should decide when to use the approach, and when not.

Political approaches

Both the approaches outlined above work in certain circumstances. Where the project is relatively straightforward and uncontentious life cycle approaches provide a valuable way of organising the work to be done. Where the change is uncontentious, and people have ideas to contribute, participative approaches will bring benefits, although they may take longer to implement.

These methods are of little help in projects which challenge established interests, or where powerful players have opposing views. Whipp *et al.* (1987), for example, argue that change often involves a number of actors, representing different levels and sections of the organisation. They will probably be pulling in different directions, in the pursuit of personal as well as organisational goals:

> Strategic processes of change are now more widely accepted as multi-level activities and not just as the province of a . . . single general manager. Outcomes of decisions are no longer assumed to be a product of rational . . . debates but are also shaped by the interests and commitments of individuals and groups, forces of bureaucratic momentum, and the manipulation of the structural context around decisions and changes (p. 51).

Several sociological analyses of change implementation emphasise the political and cultural nature of the change process (Buchanan and Badham, 1999; Markus, 1983; Pettigrew, 1985, 1987; Pfeffer, 1992a,b). They show how the rational and political dimensions are intertwined.

Pettigrew (1985) was an early advocate of the view that decisions on strategic change combine rational, cultural and political factors. He also highlights the influence of historical and contextual factors on the process of change. The perspective takes issue with rational-linear models of change as being inadequate ways of theorising events and as oversimplified guides to management action. The managerial process in Pettigrew's view is a complex and untidy cocktail of ostensibly rational assessment mixed with differential perceptions, quests for power, visionary leadership, and the 'subtle processes' of marshalling support for ideas.

Central to Pettigrew's analysis of 'the processual dynamics of changing' is a concern with 'management of meaning' and with the processes through which people create a climate in which others accept a change as legitimate. He highlights the effect of the context into which managers introduce change, and how those involved in a project can use that context to support their approach.

Pfeffer (1992a) also argues that power is essential to get things done in organisations. His point is that decisions in themselves change nothing. It is only when someone implements them that anyone notices a difference. He proposes that projects require more than people able to solve technical problems. Projects frequently threaten the status quo: people who have done well in the past are likely to resist them. Innovators need to ensure the project is on the agenda, and that senior managers support and resource it. Innovators need to develop a political will, and to build and use their power.

Henry Kissinger on politics in politics

In another work Pfeffer (1992b) quotes Henry Kissinger:

> Before I served as a consultant to Kennedy, I had believed, like most academics, that the process of decision-making was largely intellectual and all one had to do was to walk into the President's office and convince him of the correctness of one's view. This perspective I soon realised is as dangerously immature as it is widely held (p. 31).

Many observers now stress the importance of power and political behaviour for project managers. Buchanan and Badham (1999, p. 11) consider why political behaviour occurs, and conclude that:

> Its roots lie in personal ambition, in organisation structures that create roles and departments which compete with each other, and in major decisions that cannot be resolved by reason and logic alone but which rely on the values and preferences of the key actors involved.
>
> Power politics and change are inextricably linked. Change creates uncertainty and ambiguity. People wonder how their jobs will change, how their workload will be affected, how their relationships with colleagues will be damaged or enhanced. Change in one organisational dimension can have knock-on or 'ripple' effects in other areas. As organisations become more complex, the ripple effects become harder to anticipate.

Reasonable people are likely to disagree about means and ends, and to fight for what they believe to be the appropriate line of action.

It is also possible that the importance of power and political behaviour arises from the way companies create the job of project manager. So, for example, Pinto (1998) argues that 'project management and politics are inextricably linked.

Successful project managers are usually those who intuitively understand that their job consists of more than simply being technically and managerially competent.' He offers three reasons for the influence of politics on projects:

- Project managers in many companies do not have a stable base of power (either high status or overriding authority), they must learn to cultivate other methods of influence.
- Projects often exist outside of the traditional line (functional) structure, relegating project managers to the role of supernumerary. Almost all resources (financial, human, informational, etc.) must be negotiated and bargained.
- Project managers do not have the authority to conduct formal performance evaluations on their project team subordinates, denying them an important base of hierarchical power (based on pp. 85–6).

NOTEPAD 4.3

Pinto's view

- Do you agree with Pinto's explanation of political behaviour?
- Do you have evidence that will support or contradict his theory?

The political perspective recognises the messy realities of organisational life. Major projects will not only be technically complex: they will often be a challenge or threat to established interests. The different interests involved may pull in different directions, and pursue personal as well as organisational goals. The practical implication of this is that political tensions are likely to arise in projects where people disagree about ends and means, and where resources are scarce. Managers will need political skills as well as those implied by rational or participative models of change.

Eastern Electronics

In 1998 the company had 150 staff who design, manufacture and sell various kinds of electronic equipment. It is part of the Asia Industrial Group (AIG), a major holding company in the sub-continent. AIG had had increasing problems in gathering financial data from units within the group as each company had adopted its own methods. Head Office wanted to control the financial system more closely so that it would reduce their workload and give more insight into group performance. They decided to introduce a Computer-aided Production Management system (CAPM).

Head Office decided to establish CAPM systems without consulting the group companies, which resulted in little response from them. The implementation has run into these problems:

1 CAPM is an integrated system which cannot simply replace the existing manual system. Other organisational changes are needed. These include changes in the way Eastern staff handle and process information and the way departments cooperate.

2 Eastern felt no ownership of the system because the decision had been imposed by AIG.

3 Eastern managers argued that their company was not big enough for such a sophisticated system.

4 Eastern had an organic management structure, with little definition of responsibilities, unclear tasks and a belief that change occurs at its own pace.

5 Departments within Eastern had different views of CAPM. The Purchasing Department disagreed strongly with the system. The Purchasing Manager had created the current manual system and believes that CAPM would serve group needs, rather than those of the companies. The Engineering Department did not at first see the value of the system. When they saw the functions it could provide, they rapidly became supporters. The Production Department was strongly in favour. Both the Director and Manager had previously worked in a computerised environment and could see the advantages.

After two years of work the company had still not implemented the system, though staff had done considerable work on the project.

Source: Personal communication from a manager in Eastern Electronics

NOTEPAD 4.4

Eastern Electronics

- Which of the models outlined in this chapter best describes the CAPM project?
- Which, if any, of the causes of political behaviour identified by Buchanan and Badham, or Pinto, may be present in this case?
- Have you experienced a similar situation?

In politically charged situations, effective management of the project is likely to require the exercise of political skills, as well as those of problem-solving and participation. Those managing the change will need to be sensitive to the power and influence of key individuals in the organisation, and to how the change will alter the pattern of influence. They will need to be able to negotiate and sell ideas to indifferent or sceptical colleagues. They may have to filter information to change perceptions, and do things which make the change seem legitimate within the organisation. The skills are in some ways similar to those prescribed in the participative approach. The difference is that the manager is using them to build credibility, gather support and block opposition on behalf of the project as a whole. This is separate from dealing directly with the individuals or groups affected by the change.

These views (life cycle, emergent, participative and political) are not necessarily competing with each other. Rather they are complementary in that successful large-scale change is likely to require elements of each. Each perspective can be linked to a series of management practices, which can help or hinder the implementation of change. Later chapters will discuss these. For the moment, the point to emphasise is that the political perspective has some major implications for the skills of project managers seeking to implement large projects. They have to produce a public, front stage performance of rationally planned change linked to convincing participative mechanisms. But they also have to pursue backstage activity. They have to exercise power skills – influencing, negotiating, selling, searching out and neutralising resistance.

CASE STUDY

Pensco

Pensco was a medium-sized life insurance business. Changes to pensions legislation brought new opportunities in the market for personal and group pensions, and also more competition. The industry changed and so did the company. A new General Manager (GM) arrived, who immediately began to move the organisation vigorously in the direction of a market-led, sales-maximising approach. He introduced a new pensions product which placed major demands on the Information Systems Division (IS). He also recruited a colleague from his previous company as head of IS, with a reputation as an autocratic and aggressive manager. The project to introduce new pensions products was closely linked to projects to develop the information systems to process the new business.

In response to new legislation, managers began developing new pensions products. The initial proposals came from the Actuarial Department (AD), though it later transpired that their proposals used very limited market research. Staff in Sales and Marketing (S&M) were dismissive of the AD proposals, criticising AD as a very conservative department. S&M had a different interpretation of market requirements, and actively lobbied for their view.

S&M also believed that IS were too powerful:

> IS has too much power in the organisation . . . We are working to change that. S&M should drive the organisation . . . But I can't get away from the view that IS still dictate what the company can and can't do (p. 187).

However S&M succeeded in overturning the original decision on new products, by 'asserting a particular view of the market, legitimised by an appeal to a change of opinion being expressed in the financial media' (p. 190).

For their part, IS had trouble finding out what the business requirements were – partly because of unresolved conflicts between AD and S&M over the product range. In part also the Head of IS was seen to be keen to curry favour with the GM. He did so by appearing to accept all requests for systems developments – which they were unable to deliver. Commenting on the development process one manager said:

> There is no standard process for specifying business requirements [at Pensco]. In particular, a 'top down' approach should have been adopted whereby the key requirements affecting system design were identified first . . . IS staff did not really analyse . . . they tended to ask the users what they wanted and then program it (p. 169).

As the authors of the case study comment, this surprisingly informal manner of operating might have been sufficient on a small, well-defined and stable project. However the pensions project was large and unstable.

The company maintained the public position that despite the many difficulties the project was successful. The authors of the case study reported different views from the clerical staff who were processing new proposals (without adequate IS support). As a team leader commented:

> They (the managers) don't have a grasp of what's going on. They just want the figures. They don't appreciate our problems. I wish they'd acknowledge there is one (p. 162).

Source: Based on Knights and Murray (1994)

Case study questions

1 What specific examples can you identify of managers in Pensco acting in ways that support the political view of project management?

2 What factors in the context may have encouraged this behaviour? Did the GM act to encourage or discourage political behaviour?

3 What evidence is there of Pensco managers using rational-linear or participative approaches when managing this project?

4 What do you think were the effects of the behaviour you identified in your answer to question 3?

5 Is the case an example of a company adopting the emergent approach to project management?

Summary

This chapter has outlined some contrasting theories about the nature of project management. Understanding these differences will enable the manager to identify more accurately the nature of the task, and the management skills that they are likely to need to use.

The key points from this chapter are:

- Life-cycle models recommend the use of techniques such as setting objectives, setting milestones, communicating effectively and keeping tight control, to ensure successful projects.
- Emergent models emphasise that major projects cannot be planned in too great detail in advance. Changing circumstances enable a high degree of learning and discovery to occur as they are implemented.
- Participative approaches emphasise the benefits of securing the willing commitment of those affected by the project, through extensive consultation and sharing information.
- Political approaches take the view that major projects are likely to threaten established interests, and are therefore likely to generate conflict and resistance.
- The four approaches are complementary, in that each may accurately describe some aspects of a major project.
- All of these points have major implications for the skills required by the project manager.

Chapter questions

1 List some of the practices associated with the life-cycle approach.

2 Is a participative approach always going to be worthwhile? What are the dangers and costs of taking this approach?

3 Do you agree or not with the view that even an effective use of participative methods may not ensure success?

4 Under what circumstances is a political perspective likely to be an accurate description of a project?

5 Compare the views of Mintzberg and Lindblom on the value of planned approaches to change. What conclusion do they reach about the nature of major change?

6 What evidence can you collect which supports or contradicts the views expressed here about strategy (and therefore major projects) having an emergent, rather than a planned, character?

Further reading

Buchanan, D. and Badham, R. (1999) *Power, Politics and Organizational Change: Winning the Turf Game*. London: Sage Publications. A modern approach to politics in organisations, offering a theoretical and practical guide, based on extensive primary research.

Kharbanda, O.P. and Pinto, J.K. (1996) *What Made Gertie Gallop? Lessons from Project Failures*. New York: Van Nostrand Reinhold. A highly readable (and sometimes contentious) account of a wide variety of classic project failures from around the world, leading to some valuable lessons.

Pfeffer, J. (1992) *Managing with Power*. Boston, MA: Harvard Business School Press. A clearly written argument for the view that managers of all kinds should take power seriously, and understand how to use it to enhance their position and satisfaction.

References

Avison, D.E. and Fitzgerald, G. (1995) *Information Systems Development: Methodologies, Techniques and Tools*. Maidenhead: McGraw-Hill.

Boddy, D. and Macbeth, D.K. (2000) 'Prescriptions for managing change: a survey of their effects in projects to implement collaborative working between organisations', *International Journal of Project Management*, 18, 297–306.

Buchanan, D. and Badham, R. (1999) *Power, Politics and Organizational Change: Winning the Turf Game*. London: Sage Publications.

Chaffey, D. (ed.) (1999) *Business Information Systems*. London: FT/Pitman.

Child, J. (1984) *Organisation: A Guide to Problems and Practice*. London: Harper & Row.

Hartley, J., Bennington, J. and Binns, P. (1997) 'Researching the roles of internal-change agents in the management of organizational change', *British Journal of Management*, 8, 61–74.

Knights, D. and Murray, F. (1994) *Managers Divided: Organisation Politics and Information Technology Management*. Chichester: Wiley.

Lawler, E.E. (1986) *High Involvement Management: Participative Strategies for Improving Organisational Performance*. San Francisco: Jossey-Bass.

Lindblom, C.E. (1959) 'The science of muddling through', *Public Administration Review*, 19, 79–88.

Lock, D. (1996) *Project Management*, 6th edn. Aldershot: Gower.

Markus, L. (1983) 'Power, politics and MIS implementation', *Communications of the ACM*, 26, 430–44.

Mintzberg, H. (1994a) *The Rise and Fall of Strategic Planning*. Hemel Hempstead: Prentice Hall.

Mintzberg, H. (1994b) 'Rethinking strategic planning Part I: Pitfalls and fallacies', *Long Range Planning*, 27, 12–21.

Mumford, E. and Weir, M. (1981) *Computer Systems in Work Design – The Ethics Method*. London: Associated Business Press.

Pettigrew, A.M. (1985) *The Awakening Giant, Change and Continuity in ICI*. Oxford: Blackwell.

Pettigrew, A.M. (1987) 'Context and action in the transformation of the firm', *Journal of Management Studies*, 24, 649–70.

Pfeffer, J. (1992a) *Managing with Power*. Boston, MA: Harvard Business School Press.

Pfeffer, J. (1992b) 'Understanding power in organisations', *California Management Review*, 34:2, 29–50.

Pinto, J. (1998) 'Understanding the role of politics in successful project management', *International Journal of Project Management*, 18, 85–91.

Quinn, J.B. (1980) *Strategies for Change: Logical Incrementalism*. Homewood, IL: Richard D. Irwin.

Stacey, R. (1994) *Managing the Unknowable*. San Francisco: Jossey-Bass.

Whipp, R., Rosenfeld, R. and Pettigrew, A. (1987) 'Understanding strategic change processes: Some preliminary British findings' in Pettigrew, A. (ed.) *The Management of Strategic Change*. Oxford: Blackwell.

Woodward, J. (1997) *Construction Project Management*. London: Thomas Telford Publications.

5 The job of project management: activities, skills and structures

Introduction

Earlier chapters have set out ideas about projects, their contexts and theories of change. What do these imply for the role of the project manager? In broad terms it is to influence people to support the project in a volatile context. In view of the many project features (Chapter 2) and contextual elements (Chapter 3), where do managers of successful projects focus their effort? Research into the work of project managers can offer some guidance.

The first section of this chapter explains the research which identified these essential project management activities. These clearly make a difference between successful and unsuccessful projects. The following sections describe and illustrate five key activities. Project managers perform these through personal activities and, where possible, with the support of formal structures.

Objectives

After reading this chapter you should be able to:

- describe and illustrate five activities that help produce a successful project;
- explain why the ability to influence others is an essential task in managing projects;
- understand why project structures can support individual effort;
- compare these perspectives with traditional views of project management.

What effective project managers do

Chapter 1 gave an overview of the nature of project management, and the conflicting demands of performance, cost and time. Chapter 2 presented eight distinctive features of projects and Chapter 3 seven elements of their context. Figure 5.1 illustrates these.

Clearly not all of these will be significant in any single project. They represent analytical tools, and the significance of any feature and any element varies between projects. Some may not matter at all, while others may be significant at some stage of a project's life.

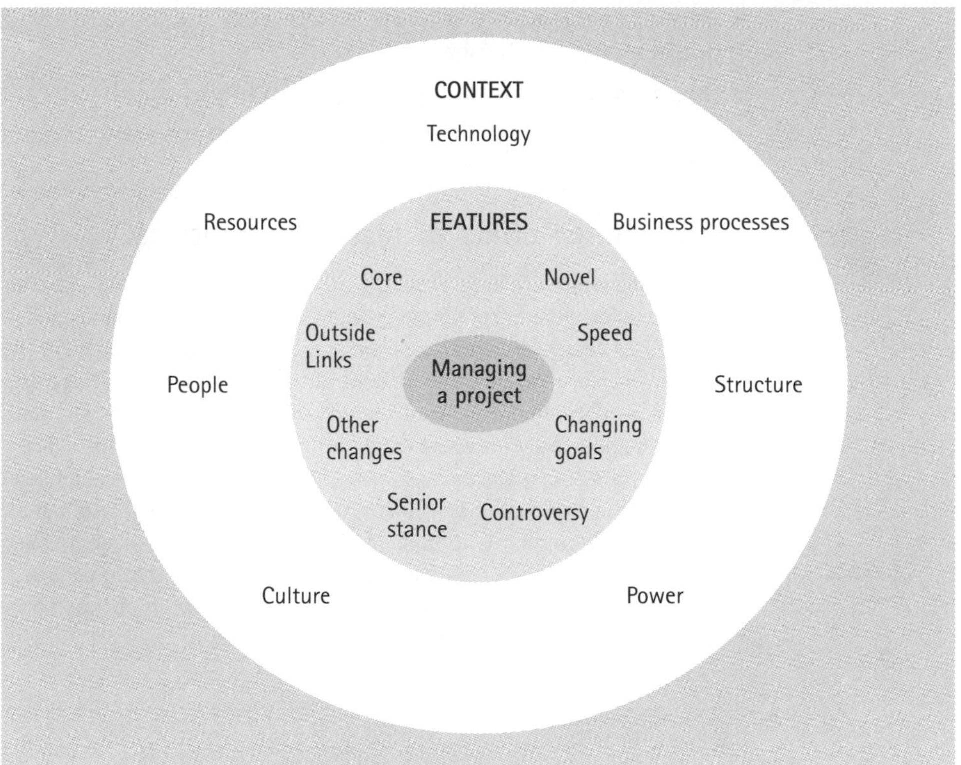

Figure 5.1 Summary of project features and context

Nevertheless, while acknowledging the uniqueness of each project, do people managing successful projects use a different set of practices from those managing less successful ones? Available research gives some guidance on this. It shows which aspects of the role are most likely to produce a successful outcome, and so where project managers may best concentrate their effort.

The earlier version of this book (Boddy and Buchanan, 1992) drew on well-known prescriptions about the work of managing projects. The authors used quantitative and qualitative data to develop these into a new list of the activities of project managers. This emphasised the interpersonal skills which made a difference to project outcomes. Since then the author (with colleagues) has conducted further research on the activities of project managers (for a summary see Boddy and Macbeth, 2000), including a quantitative postal survey of 100 project managers. Forty-six of the projects had been successful, 54 unsuccessful. This (and related) work both confirmed and extended the earlier account. It confirmed it by providing statistically significant support for the earlier conclusions. It extended it by stressing the role of formal structures, in support of interpersonal skills.

Respondents from successful projects showed a statistically significant tendency to **agree** with only five of the 45 statements of recommended practice. These were:

- The people affected by the change within my organisation agreed with the goals.
- Management created a clear structure within which to manage the change.

- Senior management accurately estimated the amount of resources needed to implement the change.
- The joint senior team created specific lines of authority and responsibility.
- A satisfactory system was developed to measure the progress of the change.

The limited effect of many prescriptions

In passing it is worth noting that the survey showed that several other commonly prescribed practices had little effect on project outcomes. For example, many authors recommend that successful change requires the public support of senior management. The responses showed that while this had occurred in 82% of successful cases (in line with received wisdom), it had also occurred in 60% of the unsuccessful cases. Replies to another question gave some support to the frequent recommendation that significant change needs to have the support of a strong champion – 74% of successful companies had had a strong champion backing the change. Yet 51% of the unsuccessful ones had also had a champion. Another common prescription is to prepare a detailed plan to manage a change. Replies showed that this occurred in 57% of successful cases, but also that it occurred in almost as many of the unsuccessful cases. Such results suggest that while common prescriptions may help a project, they do not in themselves ensure success.

Source: Boddy and Macbeth (2000)

Combining these results with those from the earlier work indicates five practices which should be the top priority for project managers. These are the areas on which they should focus to achieve a successful project. Table 5.1 summarises and explains these.

Table 5.1 Successful project management practices

Successful practice	*Description*
Ensuring agreement with goals	Setting or receiving overall objectives and directions, interpreting them, reacting to changes in them, clarifying the problem and setting boundaries to it
Obtaining resources	Identifying them, negotiating for their release, retaining them, managing their effective use
Monitoring and learning	Seeing the whole picture: taking a helicopter view, managing time and other resources, anticipating reactions from stakeholders, spotting links and unexpected events
Exercising influence	
Using individual initiative	Moving things forward by taking action and risks to keep the project going, especially through difficult phases
Creating appropriate structures	Clarifying and modifying their role, and those of other functions; creating teams, procedures and links to wider organisation
Ensuring effective communication	Linking the diverse groups or individuals contributing to the project, to obtain their support and commitment

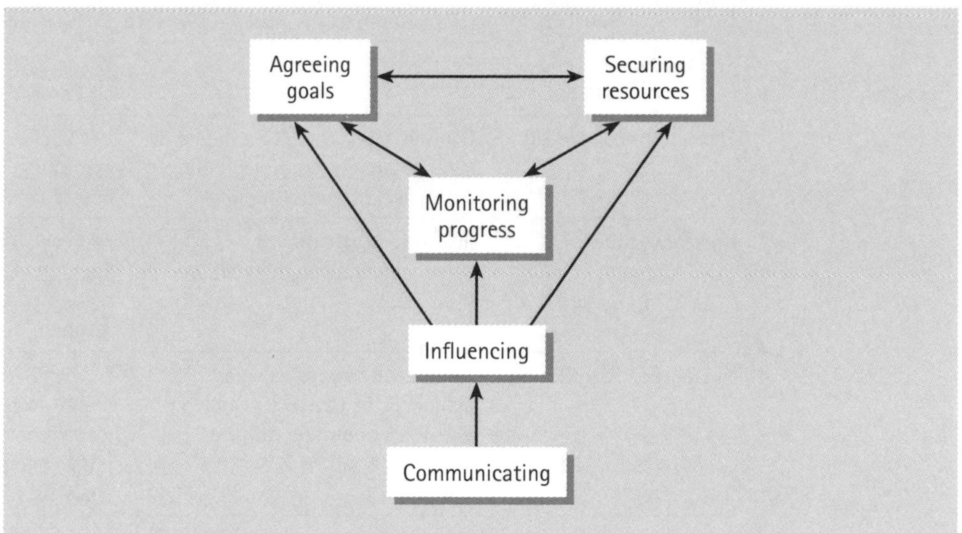

Figure 5.2 Key activities of project managers

Successful projects are most likely when managers put effort (and skill) into agreeing goals, securing resources and monitoring progress. To do this they need to influence other players, and to do that they need to communicate effectively. Figure 5.2 shows the relationship between these activities, and the following sections present them more fully.

Agreeing goals

Influencing the range of people connected with the project to agree a common set of goals is easier said than done. Many people find it difficult to set goals for an activity. It requires an ability to look to the future, and to identify a plausible future state at which to aim. Setting targets runs the risk of not meeting them, and suffering as a result. Many instinctively want to get on with the work, rather than spend time on the rather abstract activity of setting objectives.

The task is much more challenging in major organisational projects, where differences will arise over both ends and means. Players will interpret the environment differently, and so favour one end rather than another. They will interpret cause and effect differently, and so prefer one means to another. People will have different personal anxieties or ambitions about a proposal. The project features in Chapter 2 give some clues – the more novel the project, the more external links, the more controversial the idea, the harder it is to secure agreement on goals. The scope for simple misunderstandings and communication failures add to the challenge. Managers also need to sustain agreements as circumstances and preferences shift.

Table 5.2 Sources of goal problems and perspectives to ensure agreement

Status of project goals	*Reasons*	*Theoretical perspective to reach agreement*
Clear, defined, agreed	Routine, familiar project, agreed by senior management. People have put effort into agreeing goals	Life cycle. Clarify and operationalise goals. Allow time before moving to action
Unclear, vague	Insufficient attention by management, urge to act rather than plan	Life cycle and/or participative Seek ideas, encourage discussion among parties until agreement reached
Not agreed, conflicting	Disagreement within senior managers, or between senior managers and other groups	Political. Project manager's ability to resolve may be limited Identify most powerful players, possibly expose differences and what they imply for the project
Changing	Changing external demands or changes in other projects creating ripples Learning as a result of work done during the project to change elements of the context prompts review of options	Participative and/or emergent Encourage awareness that change is likely, and engage players in open review and revision Recognise that change is not a sign of failure

Table 5.2 indicates that project goals can have a different 'status'. It also suggests why each of these conditions arise. In some projects this is not an issue – where, say, the project is comparatively familiar, with few outside links, and threatens few interests. In other situations project managers work to meet goals that are vague, conflicting or changing.

Contrasting objectives for PRP

Kelly and Monks (1998) illustrate how people held different priorities for the objectives of a project to introduce performance-related pay (PRP) into a multi-divisional food company. The Human Resources Director intended the scheme to improve, amongst other things, performance, reward good performance, motivate staff, promote organisational change, reduce trade union influence and eliminate collective bargaining. A quantitative survey of 70 company managers asked them to rank the objectives of PRP in order of importance. While respondents mentioned the first two of the HR Director's objectives frequently, others scarcely featured. For example, 'only 2 per cent ranked the promotion of organisational change as the top objective, while 59 per cent ranked it among the bottom three objectives. The reduction of trade union influence . . . was ranked as a priority by only 1 per cent of managers' (p. 119).

Project goals in public sector projects

Achieving clear goals is also a challenge in local authorities. Research by Hartley *et al.* (1997) with internal change agents led them to observe that: 'In such organisations goals are often:

- comprehensive (i.e. concerned holistically with the needs of a complete population rather than a specific group or market niche);
- qualitative (i.e. concerned to balance a complex set of possibly conflicting values rather than measuring performance in terms of single quantitative outputs); and
- political (i.e. goals are inherently open to continuous public dispute and choice).'

They concluded that different stakeholders will have particular views on the goals of a project. Consequently 'the job of the change agent is to generate sufficient consensus across a range of very diverse departments, as well as diverse councillors and political parties' (p. 70).

Source: Hartley *et al.* (1997)

Changing goals may also be a positive sign, such as that people are discovering new possibilities during a project, and adapting goals accordingly.

Table 5.2 also suggests how managers can use the theories of change introduced in Chapter 4 to plan their approach. They need to adapt this to what they believe to be the source of the problem. If the issue is not controversial, then he or she may be able to achieve agreement by using life cycle or participative approaches. The technique described in Chapter 9 (pp. 139–45) may help. If the difficulty arises from basic conflicts of interest between powerful interest groups, then the manager will need to use political skills. In some cases they will be unable to do anything significant as the problem may be beyond the reach of individual action.

Obtaining resources

The second primary task for project managers is to influence people to release resources. Project managers frequently comment that senior managers seriously under-estimate the resources a project requires. They spend a great deal of time securing, and then retaining, project resources.

All of the elements in Figure 3.1 (p. 34) have implications for the resources a project requires. A project to implement some new technology or a new business process does not just require expenditure on hardware, software, infrastructure and the like. There will certainly be costs associated in such areas as information technology, structure and culture. The sooner the project manager anticipates these the sooner he or she can try to influence senior or other managers to make them available.

The difficulty managers face is that their project is a one-off activity. They are competing for staff who work for other managers. They have to persuade these to release them. Projects often need staff who are competent in the operational area concerned, *and* with relevant project skills. Such people are scarce, and equally valuable to their line manager's priorities. Projects inherently suffer from constraints, as they compete with other uses for the available resource-base. Writing about the product development process in the automotive industry, Cusumano and Nobeoka (1998) observe that:

> Most companies have more than one product, and many companies have more than one new product under development at the same time . . . (all such) projects compete for key engineers or financial resources (p. 7).

Table 5.3 indicates the main sources of resource problems, and, as in Table 5.2, suggests which theoretical approach will be relevant.

Resources (especially of people) are not, of course, fixed. Effective project managers can add to their resources by developing the capabilities of the staff they have. The resource-based view points out that any organisation has a collection of tangible and intangible *resources* available to it. They can use these to build distinctive *capabilities*, which could include the ability to handle projects effectively. These capabilities develop when resources work together in a complementary way, supported by organisational routines. These are 'regular and predictable patterns of activity which are made up of a sequence of co-ordinated activities by

Table 5.3 Sources of resource problems and perspectives to ensure agreement

Status of project resources	*Reasons*	*Theoretical perspective to reach agreement*
Adequate and available	Senior management has understood requirements	Life cycle. Clarify and operationalise resource allocations
Inadequate and causing delays	Insufficient appreciation by management of scale or type required	Participative or political, depending on the scale of the gap in requirements
Available, but allocated to other projects	Disagreement among senior managers over priorities, or between powerful sectional interests	Political. Project managers may have little ability to resolve problem. Identify most powerful players, possibly expose differences and what they imply for the project
Changing	Changing external demands or changes in other projects creating ripples Learning as a result of work done during the project to change elements of the context prompts review of options and resource requirements	Participative and/or emergent Encourage awareness that change is likely, and engage players in open review and revision Resource estimates can only be provisional when a project is a voyage of discovery

individuals' (Grant, 1991, p. 109). The same principle can apply at the level of the project, if the project manager devises ways to mobilise people into unusually effective project teams, or other aspects of project management.

Resources also shape goals. A manager who finds that resources are unavailable may try to adapt the goals to what is achievable. The manager of a Social Work Information System project in a local authority found that she could not raise the significant capital budget required in a single year. It was available over two years, pointing the way to a solution in which the goal for the first year centred on installing the infrastructure, and for the second year to applications.

Establishing whether the resources available are achieving the agreed goals depends, of course, on monitoring progress in a timely way.

NOTEPAD 5.1

Assessing the resources a project needs

- What resources have you needed to secure for your project?
- Do the elements in Figure 3.1 help to identify the resource implications?
- Which have been the most difficult to acquire?

Monitoring progress

All recommendations about managing projects include some means of monitoring actual progress against the original plan. This information can enable people to keep short-term control by making adjustments to project activities considering new circumstances. It can be equally valuable as a source of learning, to improve performance on future projects.

Short-term control

Managers regularly use formal techniques to help control large and complex projects. These derive from the familiar planning and control cycle, shown in Figure 5.3. They monitor events against a project plan, especially those that are relatively predictable and quantifiable. People exercise control by comparing where they are with where they expected to be, so that they can take corrective action if necessary. Are the agreed goals being met? Are resources being used effectively? Should goals and resources be adjusted? They continuously monitor events by gathering relevant information on which people can act. The intention is to keep variances acceptably small. Table 5.4 indicates some of the benefits of monitoring progress in good time.

Monitoring and control becomes more difficult when projects take place in a changing, linked context, and are difficult to plan. Drummond's (1996) study of the Taurus project to computerise many core functions of the London Stock

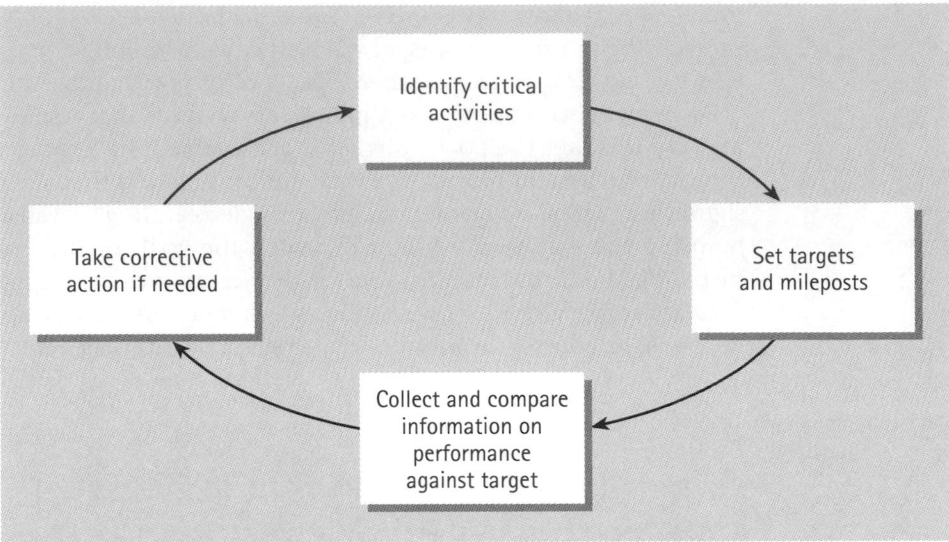

Figure 5.3 Elements in the control cycle

Table 5.4 Benefits from an effective project monitoring system

Benefit	*Description*
Track progress	Ensuring that the results expected are being achieved, in terms of time, budget, quality and acceptability – despite disruptive changes in direction and priorities
Take corrective action	The earlier people identify deviations from plan, the easier it is to put things right. It also helps to anticipate potential problems which would jeopardise progress later
Obtain acceptable performance	Are people meeting work targets, motivating their own staff, turning up to meetings, providing resources, releasing staff for training or answering queries? These can also be symptomatic of deeper issues
Assess attitudes	Are people on the project enthusiastic and committed? Are there signs or hints of resistance? Are staff becoming frustrated by delays, difficulties or changes to plan?
Monitor external changes	It is essential to take a 'helicopter view' to look beyond the immediate project and be ready to react to unexpected changes elsewhere in the organisation, or in the outside world. Projects with many external links in a volatile environment experience many such shifts

Exchange shows the dangers. She concluded that one (amongst several) factor in the failure was ineffective project control, which allowed requirements to change continuously throughout the project. Management also ignored repeated warnings about technical risks, as powerful interests pushed for the development to continue. This is an example of project escalation, in which people continue to increase their commitment to a project, against all the evidence. They ignore the fact that earlier resources have not produced results, and that the project is unlikely to achieve the objectives (Brockner, 1992; Keil and Robey, 1999).

Control systems only work if they reflect the task being controlled. To 'keep control', the project manager needs to receive and interpret information about progress. This will include:

- hard, structured, measurable information, such as: has the design been tested or not? how did it perform? how much did it cost? how many branches have been converted?
- soft, unstructured, intangible information such as: are staff agreeing with the proposals? how much commitment is there towards overcoming difficulties? are people having doubts about the wisdom of the project, but are not speaking out openly?

Stacey (1994) has pointed out the impossibility of using conventional control practices in volatile conditions. He acknowledges that day-to-day control of a business (or familiar project) requires comparison of progress against planned milestones, and the taking of corrective action. This requires a rational approach to control, through systems and rules familiar to any project manager. Effective control of an activity in the open-ended, unknowable long term (such as covered by many organisational change projects) requires a different approach. Above all, it depends on a degree of self-control by the people doing the work, and who control each other through a subtle variety of internal processes.

This implies that project managers can benefit from:

- seeing the project and the changing context together – taking a helicopter view and maintaining wide awareness helps to anticipate difficulties and opportunities;
- being receptive to 'unstructured' as well as unstructured information;
- allowing a high degree of self-control by those closest to the action, who know what the information means, and can interpret and use it responsibly.

Long-term learning

An increasingly common prescription for those implementing change is to use the activities of monitoring and review to learn lessons for future practice, because, 'if change is not monitored, how can the experience contribute to organizational learning?' (Doyle *et al.*, 2000). Despite the frequent advice to managers to use experience as a source of learning and development this is evidently difficult to achieve in practice. Doyle *et al.* (2000) found that of the respondents to their survey:

- 96% agreed that 'having responsibility for major change implementation can be an invaluable management development experience';
- 22% agreed that 'we use change projects systematically as a management development tool';

Table 5.5 Theoretical perspectives on control

Perspective	*View of monitoring and control*	*Implications for project manager*
Life cycle	Rational, objective activity	Non-controversial – decide data required and collect
Emergent	Evolving nature means that hard to specify what controls to use. Also stresses learning opportunities	Be wary of collecting only what is easiest to measure – may not be important. Seek opportunities to learn, rather than to keep on track. Share control information widely to encourage reflection and learning
Participative	Mutual gain from deciding what to monitor, and sharing performance information	Encourage critical debate amongst members about what controls will help. If they 'own' the information, more likely to use it
Political	Information can threaten interests and affect power and status of groups. Interests view information as a threat or resource	Expect disputes over monitoring from interests threatened. May have insufficient power to affect this

- 49% agreed that 'change has encouraged us to develop more explicitly defined procedures for learning from our experiences' (p. S64).

Such evidence of the practical difficulties does not diminish the point that project managers can interpret their role to include ensuring that people learn from the experience. Project staff inevitably have to cope with uncertainty, unforeseen implications, widespread ripples, conflicts and tension. These are not deviations from a norm – they are the nature of projects. Project managers can encourage people to learn from them.

Table 5.5 links the monitoring and control process to the theoretical perspectives on change, and draws some implications.

NOTEPAD 5.2

Critical reflection

This activity aims to encourage you to reflect critically on the previous three sections.

- What examples can you recall about the effects of these three activities (or the lack of them) affecting the progress of a project? Make notes summarising your evidence.
- Which seem to have caused the most difficulty, and how was this resolved?
- Are you confident that these are the three most critical activities of project managers? What evidence do you have about other activities that may be equally critical?
- What does this activity suggest about the areas you wish to focus on in developing your own skills as a project manager?

Influencing others – a new emphasis

Agreeing goals, obtaining resources, monitoring progress – to perform these functions the project manager needs to influence others. Tables 5.2 to 5.5 have shown that the scale of the influencing task will vary. People can deal with some issues by using life cycle or participative techniques, but many projects are highly political. The manager needs to use political as well as rational influencing skills.

So the work of the project manager does not look like that of the careful analyst, working out precisely the best solution to the project. It is closer to that of an entrepreneur, determined to get things done within an often hostile, indifferent or highly political setting. They are typically operating across established functional or departmental boundaries, and working with a wide variety of different people, who are pursuing their interests.

As Hartley *et al.* (1997) found, a 'recurring theme (amongst the internal change agents) was how best to mobilise programmes of organisational and cultural change . . . when they lack direct access to the traditional levers of line-management power . . . and the role depends on influence rather than direct command' (p. 67). Project managers usually have little formal authority, yet the key part of their job is to influence others to do certain things. To be successful, they have to be able to use political and interpersonal skills as well as those of rational problem-solving and participative management. Such skills are quite different from those which figured in the original training of most project managers.

It is also clear that relying on personal skills alone will often be insufficient. More formal structures and institutions need to support them.

Personal skills and energy

Without some human agency, without someone putting personal effort into the problem, nothing will change. In this vein, Kanter (1983) suggests the modern change agent needs a portfolio of 'power skills' to overcome resistance and apathy to new ideas. Boddy and Buchanan (1992) explored empirically the interpersonal and political skills project managers required and gave examples of personal initiative. Many respondents demonstrated both flexibility and persistent determination as they took advantage of opportunities or dealt promptly with delays.

The bigger the change, the more scope for delay and disappointment. Effective project managers refuse to give up in the face of technical problems, opposition or indifference:

> *'A lesson I received from this project was that it is essential to maintain one's stability and equilibrium, and not to give way to despair when things go wrong. One has to maintain a positive, outward face and smile at all times when things are deteriorating. If one perseveres then, eventually, things* **do** *get better.'*

Building roles and structures

There are, however, limitations to what people acting on their own to solve a problem or improve a process can achieve. These can to some extent be overcome by supporting individual action with appropriate structures and mechanisms. Sometimes the project manager can build their support structures, at other times senior managers need to ensure these are in place. Examples include clarifying the role of the project manager and creating project teams.

The manager's role

How well do other people understand the manager's role? It may have wide scope for interpretation and definition. An energetic project manager can turn this to advantage, by using the discretion to shape and extend the role. For others, especially when they are working with a range of other units and departments, an unclear role weakens their position. Webb (1994) points out that managers can gain power from having their role clearly legitimised, especially when they are managing across several departments.

Roles without and with formal authority

'My role was not properly set up, and clearly it was my mistake that I would be subordinate to the Board, and not a member of it. In hindsight I really needed to operate at the highest level to carry the necessary "clout", and to keep the Board itself properly informed.'

* * *

'A number of interesting things have happened. I personally have been legitimized by my division's management team as the Customer Service and Order Fulfillment Manager. I have also been legitimized as the European Programme Manager for order scheduling. The process of engagement has begun.'

Source: Boddy and Buchanan (1992)

The role of the sponsor of the project is also critical if the project is to get the sustained backing and support that it needs. The project manager needs to build and exploit a supportive relationship with whoever is in the role of sponsor. This includes ensuring that top management properly establishes the project – as illustrated by the second case in the box.

Project teams

As projects themselves become more complex, people give greater attention to the structures with which to manage them. Smaller projects occur within a single function or department. As they come to require additional expertise they need more formal structures.

Teams to support a supply chain project

A long-term study of two organisations developing supply chain partnering showed that as people in the two organisations learned to cooperate informally in their new roles, they also developed more formal institutions within which to conduct and support those relationships. These operated within and between the companies, and at several levels. They encouraged further cooperative behaviour and helped to embed this in the wider context of both organisations. The joint institutions included:

- *Weekly schedule review.* A meeting between a buyer–planner and sales coordinator to ensure that the supplier knew about recent changes in the (volatile) schedule.
- *Monthly quality meeting.* This reviewed any continuing quality issues that staff had not been able to resolve in informal discussion.
- *Monthly commercial review.* This was normally attended by the most senior people involved. It helped to ensure that the companies settled all outstanding commercial issues between them on a regular basis.

Source: Boddy *et al.* (2000)

Such project teams – within and between organisations – serve a variety of purposes in supporting individual effort. Ways of creating, structuring and developing them is the subject of Part 3.

NOTEPAD 5.3

Critical reflection on influencing

This activity is intended to encourage you to reflect critically on this section about influencing.

- What examples can you recall about the effects of project managers influencing (or failing to influence) other people? Make notes summarising your evidence.
- Are you confident that this emphasis on influencing others is such a key aspect of managing projects? What evidence do you have to support or contradict the argument put forward here?
- What does this activity suggest about the areas you wish to focus on in developing your own skills as a project manager?

Establishing good communications

Communication during change projects is widely recommended in the prescriptive literature (such as Kotter, 1996) and this is no surprise. Project managers need effective channels of communication to influence others. They need to be able to gather ideas in forming and transmitting the project goals, in securing resources, and in gathering information for monitoring and learning. To get things done with the cooperation of groups or functions over whom they have little or no formal authority they need to engage in an intense communication process.

Yet while the prescription is familiar, Doyle *et al.* (2000) found that communication remains problematic. This was especially notable in vertical and cross-functional communication – 64% replied 'No' to the question: 'Have cross-functional communication problems largely been resolved in your organisation?' Moreover, only 9% agreed that they would regard their organisation as a model of best practice in communication about change. This reinforces the notion of a high degree of discomfort with what might otherwise be regarded as a well-understood dimension of management and organisational practice. Project managers need to be able to use both interpersonal and formal means of communication.

Interpersonal communication

Project managers inevitably secure, send and receive most of their information through informal, face-to-face communication – through the grapevine. This is the spontaneous informal system through which people pass information and gossip. It happens throughout the organisation and across all hierarchical levels. It is in action as people meet in the corridor, by the photocopier, at lunch, on the way home. A grapevine develops wherever people meet or communicate with each other. The information that passes along the grapevine is usually well ahead of the information on the formal system. It is about who said what at a meeting, how that project is going, or about an idea being discussed in another department.

The grapevine passes qualitative information around at great speed – current ideas and proposals rather than agreed policies. It is a valuable source of advice and information about what is happening, which the project manager can use in their influencing activities.

The grapevine can be a source of early information about what is happening elsewhere in the organisation. This allows those affected, but not yet formally consulted or asked for their views, to begin preparing their position. Put the other way round, someone preparing proposals or plans can be quite sure that information about them will get out onto the grapevine sooner than they expect. The project manager can use this to advantage.

Formal communication processes

As projects grow, it is progressively more difficult to rely on informal channels of communication. Project managers find benefit in building formal means of passing and receiving information – to staff or users, to colleagues, and to senior managers. These help to ensure that all have a common set of information to work from, and at the very least ensures that the project manager's story is available, to counter whatever information is passing through the informal channels.

Many use regular newsletters to keep all players informed of progress and achievements. Intranets are another way of ensuring that people around the organisation are kept up-to-date with progress. It is especially important to ensure good communication with senior managers, and Chapter 12 contains some ideas on how to do that.

CASE STUDY

Fountains and deadlines at Ericsson Japan

At the time of this case study Ericsson was a leading company in providing cellular telephone systems. Their products included developing, producing and installing complete telephone systems for companies offering telephone services. The company had experienced rapid growth, especially in Europe and North America. They had not had a presence in the Japanese market. In the early 1990s that market began to be deregulated, and the company decided to establish a Japanese subsidiary. To protect its dominant position in the market, the company believed that it was strategically important to win a contract with one of the newly established operators in Japan.

In early 1992 the 'Japanese Division', the unit responsible for activities in Japan, secured a contract to provide a system for Tokyo Digital Phone (TDP). That company expected to receive a licence to begin operating commercially on 1 April 1994. Ericsson had to have the system ready by that date: a time schedule that presented the project management team with a difficult task.

They estimated that the customer would need two months for user testing, by which time the company would need to install and test the whole system. Testing would take two months, and installing the 147 radio base stations three months – 'they just had to work perfectly from the start'. The base stations would be produced in Sweden, and packaged to be easy to unpack and install in Tokyo:

> *'If we were supposed to ship all the equipment in August, we had to start production in June. We saw that we had only 13 months for the development work. The first prototype of the radio base station had to be ready by 1 May 1993. I would not exaggerate if I said that we were a bit worried at this point in time.'* (Division Manager)

Encouraged by the Division Manager the project management team decided that they had to manage the project in a new way. The traditional sequential model would not allow them to meet the deadline. On earlier projects they had used the 'waterfall' model, in which the activities of the project occur sequentially, with specified exit and entry criteria. Later stages cannot start until earlier ones are complete. They decided to use instead what they called the 'fountain' model, to express the idea of water flowing simultaneously from many sources. They would perform many activities concurrently.

Implementing this model implied many distinct project management practices, such as:

- having development and design work driven by downstream phases;
- providing high levels of feedback, based on frequent and specific milestones;
- providing feedback in public sessions, to make it obvious to everyone how a delay in one part of the project would affect the others;

- using a network-like organisation, based on tight integration between functions;
- new integrating mechanisms such as the 'systems emergency ward' which was a forum for problem-solving on all aspects of the project;
- ensuring that everyone knew how critical the project was, and that it had very senior support;
- having definite and unambiguous deadlines:

  'If we said it was to be ready by Friday, we did not accept anything else. If it did not work, we hunted the person responsible for delivery, no matter where he was. You have to get people to understand that next week is too late. Trying hard is not enough. It is only success that counts – nothing else.' (project leader)

After two years of intense work, the system was installed and accepted for commercial operation by the deadline. The company had secured further business from the client, and was becoming an established player in the Japanese market.

Source: Based on Lindkvist *et al.* (1998)

Case study questions

1 What features of this project made the waterfall approach unsuitable?

2 Are there any benefits of the waterfall approach which the company has foregone by using the fountain approach?

3 Use the performance dimensions in Figure 2.1 to evaluate the success of the project.

4 What does the fountain approach imply for the work of the project manager? Use the four main sections of the chapter to identify these.

5 Identify the main communication processes which the company used in the project.

6 What does the case suggest as being the main challenges in using the fountain approach?

Summary

This chapter has outlined evidence from original empirical research about the job of managing projects. It has shown that in addition to the traditional aspects of the work, many project managers now work in relatively political settings, and need to exercise a variety of influencing skills.

The key points from this chapter are:

- Empirical, quantitative research has shown that successful projects are more likely to have used a limited number of specified practices than unsuccessful ones.
- Ensuring agreement with goals is especially important in uncertain, ambiguous projects where different players will have different views about what those goals should be.

- Any significant project competes for resources with other uses, and effective project managers influence senior managers to ensure adequate resources.
- The more uncertain a project, the more it depends on adequate monitoring for both control and learning. Ambiguous projects may be most susceptible to the phenomenon of project creep, or 'escalation'.
- All these activities depend on influencing others – above, across and lower down the organisation.
- Some influence is exercised by managers using their individual bases of power.
- Their activities can be supported by appropriate structures, such as clarifying their role and creating project teams.
- Effective communication is an essential tool for helping to achieve all these activities, yet research continues to show this is a source of difficulty.

Chapter questions

1 What did the survey described at the start of the chapter find were the project management practices followed in successful companies?

2 What was the conclusion reported by Kelly and Monks (p. 66)? What are the implications for other project managers?

3 Is securing agreement on goals likely to be harder in public sector organisations than in private ones? If so, why?

4 How would a lack of clarity about goals affect the ability of a project manager to secure adequate resources?

5 What benefits can a project manager gain from an effective method of monitoring and control? What are the main difficulties they experience in implementing such a system? Relate your consideration to the life cycle, emergent, participative and political theories of change (Chapter 4).

6 Does your experience (or other evidence) support or contradict the view that influencing is the core skill of project managers?

7 What forms of structural support are suggested as ways of supporting individual attempts at influence?

Further reading

Cusumano, M.A. and Nobeoka, K. (1998) *Thinking Beyond Lean*. New York: The Free Press. A thorough discussion, based on empirical work within Toyota, of the way the automobile industry uses cross-functional product development teams to ensure a rapid flow of new models. A specialised interest, but worth reading if you work on projects to develop new products.

References

Boddy, D. and Buchanan, D. (1992) *Take the Lead: Interpersonal Skills for Project Managers*. Hemel Hempstead: Prentice Hall.

Boddy, D. and Macbeth, D.K. (2000) 'Prescriptions for managing change: a survey of their effects in projects to implement collaborative working between organisations', *International Journal of Project Management*, 18, 297–306.

Boddy, D., Macbeth, D.K. and Wagner, B. (2000) 'Implementing collaboration between organisations: an empirical study of supply chain partnering', *Journal of Management Studies*, 37, 1003–17.

Brockner, J. (1992) 'The escalation of commitment to a failing course of action: towards theoretical progress', *Academy of Management Review*, 17, 39–61.

Cusumano, M.A. and Nobeoka, K. (1998) *Thinking Beyond Lean*. New York: The Free Press.

Doyle, M., Claydon, T. and Buchanan, D. (2000) 'Mixed results, lousy process: the management experience of organisational change', *British Journal of Management*, 11, Special Issue, S59–80.

Drummond, H. (1996) *Escalation in Decision-Making*. Oxford: Oxford University Press.

Grant, R.M. (1991) *Contemporary Strategic Analysis*. Oxford: Blackwell Publishers.

Hartley, J., Bennington, J. and Binns, P. (1997) 'Researching the roles of internal-change agents in the management of organizational change', *British Journal of Management*, 8, 61–74.

Kanter, R.M. (1983) *The Change Masters*. London: Allen & Unwin.

Keil, M. and Robey, D. (1999) 'Turning around troubled software projects: an exploratory study of the deescalation of commitment to failing courses of action', *Journal of Management Information Systems*, 15, 63–87.

Kelly, A. and Monks, K. (1998) 'View from the bridge and life on deck: contrasts and contradictions in performance-related pay', in Mabey, C., Skinner, D. and Clark, T. (eds) *Experiencing Human Resource Management*. London: Sage Publications.

Kotter, J.P. (1996) *Leading Change*. Boston, MA: Harvard Business School Press.

Lindkvist, L., Soderlaund, J. and Tell, F. (1998) 'Managing product development projects: on the significance of fountains and deadlines', *Organization Studies*, 19, 931–51.

Stacey, R. (1994) *Managing the Unknowable*. San Francisco: Jossey-Bass.

Webb, A. (1994) *Managing Innovative Projects*. London: Chapman & Hall.

6 Influencing stakeholders

Introduction

Project managers need to identify and influence the stakeholders who have an interest in the task. The primary targets of such influence are the project team itself, managers higher up the organisation, managers in other departments or organisations, and staff. How effectively project managers can exercise influence over these groups depends on developing and using recognised sources of power. They must then apply that through suitable techniques of influence.

This chapter begins by presenting some ideas on stakeholder theory, followed by a method for conducting a stakeholder analysis for a project. It then develops the idea that project managers are likely to be influencing in four directions, and considers the implications of this. The sources of power available to a manager are summarised, followed by the forms of influence they can use in managing stakeholders. The final section describes a method for preparing to influence any of the target groups identified.

Objectives

After reading this chapter you should be able to:

- conduct a stakeholder analysis for a project and explain the likely benefits;
- identify some problems the project manager faces when 'managing in four directions';
- identify four sources of power, and give examples of personal and institutional forms;
- summarise each form of influence described, and give examples of how it is being used;
- evaluate a manager's sources of power;
- prepare a systematic approach to influencing identified stakeholders in a project.

Stakeholders and interest groups

Stakeholder theory

A long-established view amongst many managers and commentators (notably Friedman, 1970) is that the primary function of business organisations is to maximise the financial returns to their owners. On this view, managers should only engage in activities and projects that would increase profits. They should not take account of other interests such as communities or suppliers, so long as they acted legally. In contrast, those who advocate a stakeholder theory of organisations maintain that business needs to consider the interests of a wider range of groups. Carroll (1993) defined such stakeholders as 'those groups or individuals with whom the organisation interacts or has interdependencies' and 'any individual or group who can affect or is affected by the actions, decisions, policies, practices or goals of the organisation' (p. 60). Supporters base their views on a variety of arguments that are far beyond the scope of this book. Some take a normative view, that it is morally right for corporations to consider stakeholder interests in setting strategies and creating projects to realise them.

Others argue that how a company takes account of stakeholder interests will affect its performance. This view has attracted much support (see Donaldson and Preston, 1995) on the grounds that 'an economically successful firm will . . . necessarily be one in which senior management adopts corporate governance strategies and policies that facilitate the maintenance of an appropriate balance between different stakeholder interests' (Ogden and Watson, 1999, p. 527). These authors point out that demonstrating empirically that 'corporations whose managers adopt stakeholder principles and practices will perform better than those who do not' involves formidable challenges (p. 527). Nevertheless they take on the challenge, and use data from the privatised UK water industry to show that improving relative customer performance brings positive returns to shareholders – consistent with the instrumental view of stakeholder theory.

The same principles are likely to apply at the level of specific projects within the firm, although they are equally difficult to demonstrate empirically. The instrumental view of stakeholder theory is that successful projects will be those in which management adopts policies that maintain a reasonable balance between different stakeholder interests. As at the corporate level, project stakeholders are the people and groups with an interest in the project, and who can affect the outcome. They may be active promoters or supporters of the change, keen to have it succeed. It may affect them, though some will not be aware of it. Stakeholders have an interest in the substance and results of change, and in how the change is managed. They can make a difference to the situation, and for instrumental reasons, if for no other, project managers need to gain and keep their support. They represent a primary focus for the project manager, as he or she attempts to influence the behaviour of the main stakeholders in a way that helps the project.

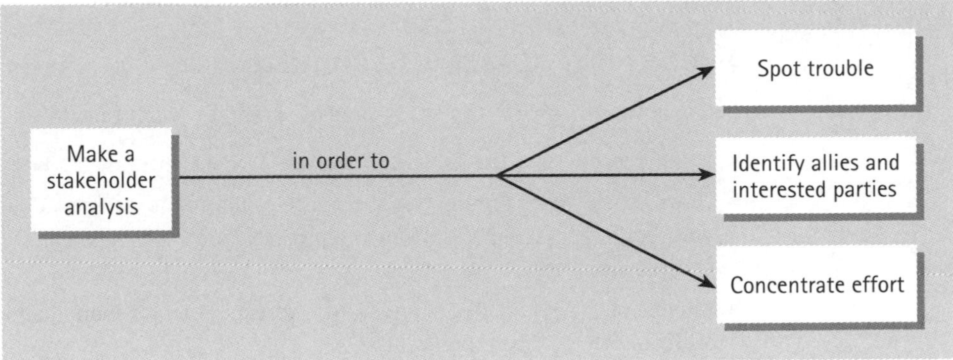

Figure 6.1 Benefits of a stakeholder analysis

Making a systematic plan to secure stakeholder support avoids unexpected difficulties. Spending time to anticipate reactions makes the project less vulnerable to unexpected snags. It helps the project team to spot potential allies and coalitions (Figure 6.1). It helps the project team to understand the various interested parties in the project:

> *'If we had carried out a stakeholder analysis during the early stages of the project, and presented it to the team, it would have resolved a tremendous amount of confusion in a single document.'*

It concentrates time and energy on the most critical groups – those whose attitude will make or break the project – rather than dissipating them over a wide range of interested parties.

Important tasks for the project manager therefore include:

- identify stakeholders in a project;
- assess their commitment;
- assess their power to help and hinder the change;
- assess their interests, and how this will affect what they think and do about the change;
- manage relations with them – to gain their support, minimise opposition and generally create a climate favourable to the change.

Identify stakeholders in a project

In a big project it is useful to take a few minutes to identify stakeholders whom the work will affect. They will include external as well as internal interests. This will help alert the project manager to possible difficulties, and perhaps to discover possible allies whose help may be useful during the project.

NOTEPAD 6.1

Prepare a stakeholder map

A simple way to visualise this is to prepare a map showing the stakeholders in a project.

- Write the name of the project in a circle at the centre of a sheet of paper.
- Draw other circles around the sheet, each identifying an individual or group whom you regard as having a stake in the project. Place the most significant nearer the centre; others around the edge.
- Check you have included all relevant interests – senior management, colleagues, staff, people in other organisations.

Stakeholders vary in their power to affect the project, and the project manager needs to be aware of the pattern. Strong stakeholders need more attention than weak ones, so thinking of this allows them to decide where it is most useful to concentrate effort.

Figure 6.2 shows the stakeholder map prepared for the Freight Connect project (see p. 96).

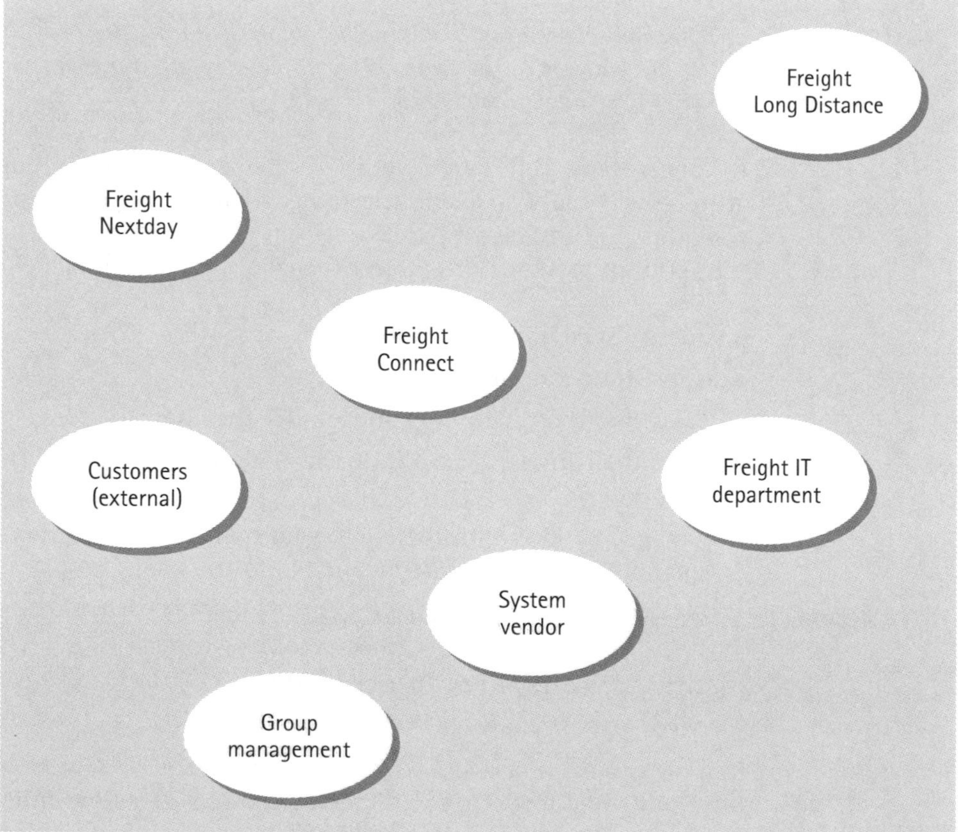

Figure 6.2 Stakeholder map for the Freight Connect project

Key stakeholder	Vigorous opposition	Some opposition	Indifferent towards it	Will let it happen	Will help it happen	Will make it happen
Freight				✗		Y
Overnight						
Freight IT				✗	Y	
Freight			✗		Y	
Group						
Board						
Vendor				✗		Y
Customers		✗	✗		Y	

Figure 6.3 Stakeholder commitment at Freight

Assess their commitment

The next step is to assess the degree of commitment of the main stakeholders to the project. This can range from vigorous opposition to vigorous support – a determination to 'make it happen'. The project manager can assess the present commitment of each stakeholder on a scale such as that shown in Figure 6.3. A manager involved in the Freight project compiled this. They can use the same scale to assess what level of commitment they hope each stakeholder will have towards the project. Mark both current and desired levels on the scale for each stakeholder – such as 'present' = X, 'hoped for' = Y.

Assess their interests

The next step is to assess the interests of the main stakeholders – those on whom you want to concentrate. This involves considering questions such as:

- What are their priorities, goals, interests?
- What is the tone of our relations with them – cooperative, antagonistic or neutral?
- What specific behaviour do you expect of them, on this project?
- Are they unlikely to see this as positive or negative for them?
- What is their likely action to defend their interests?
- What actions does this suggest we should consider to influence them?

You can do this on a grid like that shown in Figure 6.4.

Stakeholder	Their goals	Current relationship	What is expected of them?	Positive or negative to them?	Likely reaction?	Ideas for action

Figure 6.4 Grid for summarising stakeholder interests and reactions

NOTEPAD 6.2

Assess stakeholders' commitment and interests

- Using a grid like that in Figure 6.3, assess the current and required commitment for the main stakeholders in your project.
- Using a grid like that in Figure 6.4, write the key stakeholders down the left-hand side of a sheet.
- Summarise in each column your answers to the questions above for each stakeholder.

Considering the project from the stakeholders' point of view is likely to identify some practical steps a project manager can take to influence the stakeholders to support the project. This includes asking what benefits the project team can offer to stakeholders that they will value, and how best to sell those benefits.

Stakeholder commitment at Freight

Freight Nextday were clearly the project owners. However, poor project management had resulted in a lack of control and direction. Key stakeholders therefore slipped to a relaxed 'will let it happen' mode instead of the proactive 'will make it happen'. Other business priorities had encroached on the other divisions. The key stakeholder had not pressed them, so the project slipped in priority and focus.

The company gave little information to customers about the new product. They did not explain additional benefits – such as that the customer would be able to use the product for all dealings with the Freight Group. Customers were therefore unclear about the benefits to them, and were reluctant to release staff for training (even though Freight would provide this, and the product, without charge). The software vendors too had not been convinced of the value of the project, and took an indifferent approach to it.

Source: Commentary by a Freight manager

Johnson and Scholes (1999) introduce the idea of analysing not only the power of stakeholders, but also their interest in an organisation's strategy (see Figure 6.5). This idea is also relevant at the level of the project, as it indicates what kind of relationship the manager needs to establish with each group. Clearly the acceptability of the direction of a project to key players (segment D) should be a major consideration. The manager needs to devote much time and effort to key players. Less effort, or a different kind of effort, will be acceptable to those in other segments. A major hazard to be aware of is that players may suddenly change their position – such as from Segment B to D. The project manager needs to adapt their approach accordingly.

Managing stakeholders

The project manager can then take some practical steps to manage the stakeholders. Questions to work on include the following:

- How can we influence them to support the project?
- What benefits can we offer which they will value?
- How can we sell those benefits?

Note your ideas for action in the last column of the grid.

The project manager can do this assessment and action planning on their own or with members of the team.

Finally, consider three other points – relationships, gatekeepers and sleepers.

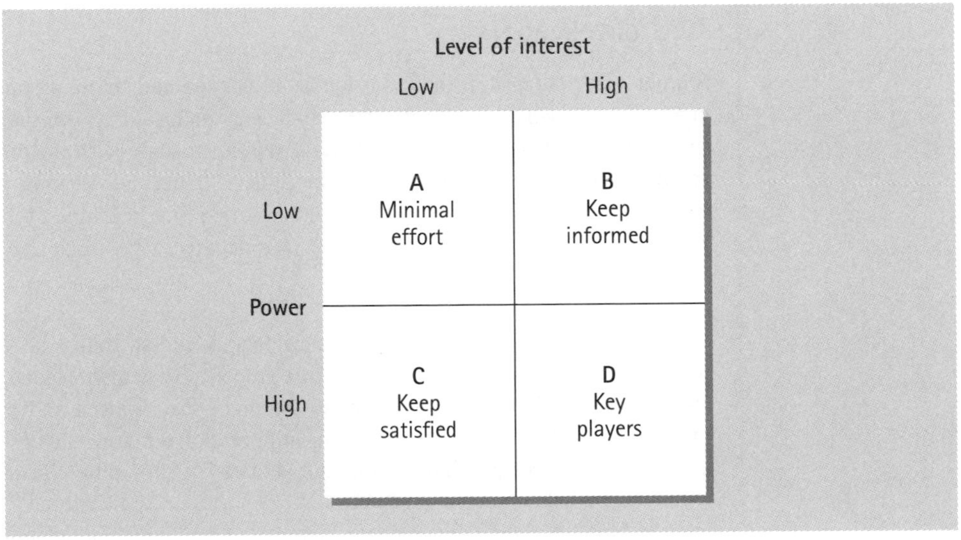

Power \ Level of interest	Low	High
Low	A Minimal effort	B Keep informed
High	C Keep satisfied	D Key players

Figure 6.5 Stakeholder mapping: power/interest matrix

Source: Johnson and Scholes (1999)

Relationships

What links are there between stakeholders? There may be close links between some of these interest groups – or links may rapidly develop during the project. This refinement of the stakeholder map may indicate how actions to deal with one group can affect others – either in favour of or against the project. Stakeholders talk to each other, and will pass bad news as well as good round the grapevine.

- How do they presently relate to each other, and will the change make that better or worse?
- During the project, will the reactions of one group of stakeholders change the attitudes of others? For example, will concessions given to one group affect the expectations of others?
- If two groups have to work together during the project, are they able to do so effectively?

These ripple effects become increasingly speculative, and it is pointless to anticipate too far. But stakeholders will be talking to each other, seeing what others are getting, and asking what it means for them.

Gatekeepers

Communication between a project manager and stakeholders may take place through another person. This could be the manager of a department whose members have an interest in the change; or the representative on the project team of another group, such as senior management.

Two gatekeepers

A group attempting to introduce a significant change had set up a team consisting of the heads of the main departments affected. It was important to the success of the project that staff in each of the departments were kept up-to-date with the proposals. It was also essential to secure their support for the project. It became clear to the person leading the activity that not all the necessary information was reaching staff in one area. This was creating dissatisfaction and leading to a negative view of the proposals.

* * *

The manager of a project to build a new facility for an industrial chemicals business relied on his boss briefing the Board about progress. They also needed to understand the business implications of any changes to the plant specification as the team worked out the design. It later became clear that this information did not reach the Board. They were unaware of significant changes in design, and of the difficulties facing the project.

Both examples show how someone filtering the flow of information affects communication between the project manager and stakeholders.

Sleepers

Not all stakeholders will be obvious at the start. Project staff may not anticipate their interests, and they themselves may not realise that the project will affect their position. They may still emerge later in the project to protect their interests.

Should the project manager ignore potential difficulties, only dealing with them if they arise; or is it better to seek them out? One advantage of the latter approach is that the project manager takes the initiative. He or she can choose when and how to raise the issue, rather than have it crop up at an awkward time.

Sleeping directors

A national travel agent introduced a new branch accounting system. This used a networked computer system to transfer reservation details automatically from the retail outlets to head office. This system also enabled a great deal of management information, about the trends in business, and the relative performance of branches, to be provided to management at the centre.

Regional directors of the company had previously been the main source of this information, based on their local knowledge of the branches. They took little interest in the project to install the networked accounting system until, very late in the project, they realised its implications for their status and security within the company. They then tried, unsuccessfully, to modify the proposed system to maintain their control over branch information.

Source: Boddy and Gunson (1996)

Timing

The attitudes and actions of stakeholders may change as the project takes shape, and at different phases. For example, a project to introduce a time-recording system into an insurance company involved three principal stakeholders. One had positive attitudes to the change throughout – they gained status and rewards at each stage. Another group was negative at first, but became positive later on, while the opposite happened to the third group. For them, initial high expectations disappeared when they became aware of the increased control they would experience.

The significance of this is that it emphasises the dynamic nature of the relationship between the project and the stakeholders. Outside events, as well as the actions of the project manager, affect how interest groups view the project. Sometimes this will bring them round as supporters – at other times the shift will be the other way. The project manager has to be vigilant, not take the current position of a stakeholder as certain, and be alert to external changes which may shift that position.

NOTEPAD 6.3

Are you up-to-date with what stakeholders think?

- When did you last discuss the change with the key stakeholders?
- Who are the sleepers and the supporters?
- Is there any evidence of gatekeepers interrupting, or enhancing, the flow of information?
- What external events might alter the views of particular stakeholders, and how?

Influencing in four directions

It is clear from discussions with many project managers that they have to work in several directions at once. Project management is not about managing subordinates. It is about managing in each of the directions shown in Figure 6.6.

Managing the team

Project managers usually depend on a range of others to help achieve the change – sometimes a rather loosely connected set of individuals, at others a formally established project team. Whatever the particular status, the team is potentially the primary resource available to anyone managing a significant project. Therefore a primary task is to gain and keep the motivation and commitment of the project team, whether they work on the project part-time or full-time. The temporary nature of such teams, their varied knowledge, interests and backgrounds, and the competing demands on their loyalty, make managing such a group difficult. Part 3 of this book examines the benefits and hazards of project teams, the way teams develop, and how best to improve their performance.

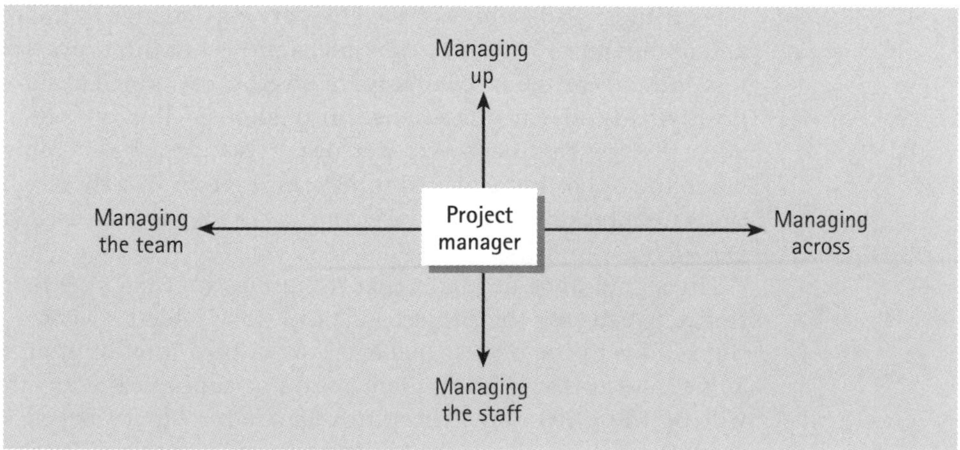

Figure 6.6 Managing in four directions

Managing across

Most projects depend on the cooperation of other departments or external organisations, such as suppliers, customers or joint venture partners. They too have a stake in the project. Managers call on them to provide advice on functional operations. They may need them to provide members for a project team or to change the way they operate. Given different backgrounds and interests, this was often difficult. Partly the problem lay in ensuring departments knew what the project manager required. They also needed to remain committed as changes elsewhere strained their resources:

> *'That site is a very important partner in this enterprise, and we have to make sure that their management team understands what we are trying to do. They also need to be resourced in such a way, and their objectives set in such a way, that they can support this programme. This is additional work, but has to be done before we can even start to get them doing what we need to support our project.'*

Managers need to resolve conflicts and disagreements amongst the key stakeholders and work to maintain their sense of ownership in the project. Project managers need to build, use and maintain a network of contacts. These help ensure that they are up to date with changes elsewhere. Chapter 10 deals with ways of managing people in other departments and organisations.

Managing staff and users

Project managers also need to ensure the commitment of staff upon whom the success of the project change ultimately depends. Some may need to change how or where they work. Others have to cope with additional work for the change, while still using the old system. The project team may also depend on them to understand the way a system works now, and as a source of ideas on how to design the new approach. Managers can easily take staff support for granted, unaware of the contribution which those closest to events can make.

The techniques for doing this are well known, including involving those people who will be affected by the change in its planning and implementation, as far as this is practical. It also includes training staff on the new system and providing support and back-up during the changeover. All of these activities depend on commitment and motivation. This is primarily the responsibility of the manager of their department – but project managers can affect this by the way in which they deal with users and other staff. Chapter 11 present ideas and approaches to this task.

Managing up

A stakeholder analysis usually reveals that senior managers, perhaps in several departments, have an interest in a project, if only because they provide the resources. Project managers frequently have to influence the attitudes and actions of senior managers, including Boards of Directors and the heads of other functional areas. They generally need to exert influence in this direction in the processes of shaping goals, negotiating for adequate resources, or seeking other forms of commitment and support:

> *'This is the second time we have been to the management team to pose the problem of how we wish to move forward. We need them to authorise the resources needed to move us forward. It is, however, worth taking the time up front to get all the members fully supportive of what we are trying to do. Our aim is that by pressure and other means they can try to move plant X into a more positive attitude.'*

Project managers often need to educate senior managers about what a project may achieve, and what expectations they may reasonably hope to attain. Chapter 12 presents ideas and techniques about managing up.

Sources of power and methods of influence

The argument of this book is that to manage significant projects in a volatile environment, people need influencing skills. The skills of analysis, definition and control – the essence of project life cycle approaches – are still valuable. Indeed they are necessary: but they are not sufficient. Equally managers need to use participative skills to encourage a sense of ownership and commitment to the change. This is necessary, but again may not be sufficient. For, in addition, they need to use political skills to influence people in situations where opposition is strong, or where political considerations are high. They need, in short, to exercise influence based on using their power.

Sources of power

What is the basis of one person's ability to influence another? It is their power, which has several sources. Hales (1993) identified four types of power, each of which can come from personal and positional sources: 'Each of these power sources are, to varying degrees, available to managers – either as personal possessions or, more especially, by virtue of their . . . position as managers' (p. 22). The list is:

- **Physical power** – the capacity to threaten, harm or restrict the actions of another, which others desire to avoid.
- **Economic power** – possessing, or having access to, scarce and desired rewards (such as money or promotion).
- **Knowledge power** – possessing, or having access to, scarce and desired knowledge and skills, of either an administrative or technical nature.
- **Normative power** – possessing scarce and desired qualities, ideas, beliefs, values (charisma or attractive personality at the individual level; being able to invoke the prevailing culture to influence someone's behaviour at the organisational level).

Table 6.1 summarises the model.

Table 6.1 Personal and positional sources of power

Power resource	*Personal*	*Positional*
Physical	Individual strength or forcefulness	Access to sanctions or punishment
Economic	Individual wealth or income	Access to or disposal of organisational resources
Knowledge		
– Administrative	Individual experience	Access to or control over organisational information
– Technical	Individual skill or expertise	Access to or control over technological information and technology
Normative	Individual beliefs, values, ideas, personal qualities	Authority to invoke norms and values of the organisational culture

NOTEPAD 6.4

Reflecting on sources of power

- Which of the sources of power in Table 6.1 have you seen used by a manager?
- Write a sentence or two indicating the situation and how people reacted to it.
- Which of these sources of power may someone managing a project find most difficult to acquire and use (apart from physical)?

Forms of influence

To be useful managers have to exercise their power through some form of influence. Charles Handy (1993) identifies four forms:

1. **Force or the threat of force.** This derives from physical power, and is rarely used in business life – although the scope for intimidation and barely concealed threats should not be underestimated.
2. **Exchange.** Often called negotiation or bargaining, this is when A agrees to do something for B in exchange for some reward. It usually flows from a person's position, or from the economic resources to which they have access.
3. **Rules and procedures.** This occurs when A establishes, or enforces, a procedure that obliges someone in B's position to act in a particular way. It usually derives from administrative power, backed up by economic power.
4. **Persuasion.** This relies on the power of argument and the presentation of convincing evidence. It derives from a person's acknowledged technical knowledge of the issue.

Front or back stage?

Managers can try to influence other people by 'front stage performance' or 'back stage activity' (Buchanan and Badham, 1999; Buchanan and Boddy, 1992).

Front stage performance

Visible projects within organisations have to conform to organisational 'theatre' to be successful. People have to be convinced that they are genuinely involved in the change and have some influence on its outcome. Top management and expert staff have to be convinced that the change is technically rational, logical and also congruent with the strategic direction of the organisation. Established project management techniques such as network planning and control techniques, cost–benefit analysis and technological appraisals are useful in themselves (see for example Lock, 1996). So are bar and Gantt charts, cumulative spend curves and scheduling tools. Such techniques are widely recognised as appropriate tools for managing change projects. They are also valuable in sustaining the image of the project manager. They reassure senior management that the right things are being done in their name.

There may also be an element of theatre in user-involvement. Management aims to convince people that genuine user-involvement, as well as technical elegance, is part of the change process. Many involvement mechanisms may be symbolic acts or rituals which those using them hope will create a feeling of participation in the change processes.

Backstage activity

The literature on participative management consistently advises that manipulation and threats as project management techniques are counterproductive. Nevertheless in large complex projects management resorts to them due to lack of time, resources and expertise, as well as the scale and complexity of the project. It is also necessary to confront the political realities of managing projects that are both core to the business and novel in form – those in Quadrant 4. Keen's (1981) solution to this paradox is a political approach, a 'counter-counter-implementation' strategy which establishes who can damage the project. It recommends co-opting likely opposition early, providing clear incentives and benefits from the new system and creating a 'bandwagon' effect. This is a 'backstage' political strategy that few technical staff have the skills to operate. The method depends heavily on the presence of a 'fixer' with prestige, visibility and legitimacy. Boddy and Gunson (1996) cite several examples of such moves based on negotiation and on mobilising coalitions. Some led from the front and put strong political pressure on sometimes reluctant managers to push through a project.

The role of someone managing a major project is inherently manipulative and political. While the front stage activities of technical and strategic logic and user-participation strategies provide credibility, the backstage activity is key to success or failure. If a project manager intends to use backstage techniques successfully he or she must have access to the backstage politics of the organisation. A change agent who has little insight into internal power politics will be unable to operate this type of strategy successfully.

Using these ideas in the book

These theoretical frameworks will guide the discussion throughout the book. As it examines how project managers seek to influence the four targets, it will do so with these frameworks in mind. However, it will not do so mechanically – it will use them as appropriate, to show how managers can develop personal and institutional methods to influence others. Their aim is to encourage others to act in ways that support the manager's intentions for the project.

Planning the approach

Power itself is only a latent resource. To get things done people have to deploy it effectively, so that others see and respond to it. This chapter concludes by outlining a well-established technique for exercising influence, which is common to all the target groups. It enables project managers to make the best use of their position whichever target group is being addressed and whatever method of influence is being used. All of these methods will benefit from time spent planning as indicated below.

The starting point is to focus on the particular event being planned, and to concentrate on specifying very clearly what is to be achieved *by the end of the event*. There will be long-term goals to which this event should contribute, but in planning the exchange, it is essential to concentrate on that event, and on specifying what is to be achieved by the end.

Set the objective. Define as clearly and exactly as possible what is being looked for by the end of the event. Set this out as what the other person or group will do or say, as a result of the meeting. Examples could be as follows:

- 'The team will have agreed to start work on the new project tomorrow, and have agreed a plan of work.'
- 'The manager of department X will have agreed to release a named member of staff to work on the project, and he will tell him this later today.'
- 'The manager of department Y will have agreed in principle to stop developing their new system independently, and to set up a meeting next week to look at ways of developing a joint system.'

These are examples of objectives for forthcoming influencing attempts that are clear, unambiguous and which describe intended outcomes that will be observable.

Set measures of success. Express what you hope to achieve from the event more precisely by setting some measurable targets. These can refer both to the end result itself and how people achieve it. The box shows some possible measures of success for the first of the objectives above.

An objective and some success criteria

Objective: *'The team will have agreed to start work on the new project tomorrow, and have agreed a plan of work.'*

Possible success criteria:

- The team members will themselves set out the timetable.
- At least three proposals for ways of solving the problem will have come from them.
- Two members will have volunteered to work late to finish off the current project while the new one begins.
- There will be a clear allocation of tasks, with each member's name allocated to one or more of these.
- We will agree within two hours.

These give more specific 'sub-objectives' to aim for, and help provide a clear measuring-rod against which to check progress, and what else needs to be done. Not all of them may be achieved, but at least achievement can be compared with targets.

Plan behaviour. Once there is a clear picture of objectives and targets, it becomes easier to decide what to do, and where to concentrate energies. These will depend on the understanding of the situation, the balance of power, and the arguments to use. The following chapters give some ideas on how to do this when dealing with each of the target groups.

CASE STUDY

Freight Connect

The Freight Group is a large European transport and logistics company. It grew rapidly during the 1990s, mainly by mergers and acquisitions. Most of these businesses brought legacy systems with them, resulting in a diverse range of purpose-built applications in operation throughout the business.

An IT development strategy formulated in late 1998 identified the core information system requirements for the group to meet its business goals. These included a single freight management system, warehouse management systems, financial, human resource and executive information systems.

In October 1998 Freight acquired Nextday, a parcel delivery business. The deal included an arrangement whereby Nextday's previous owners would maintain a proprietary freight management system until December 1999. This system enabled customers to enter their freight pick-up and delivery requirements to the Nextday system. Freight did not currently have a system able to do this, though e-commerce functions such as this had been identified within the IT development strategy.

Freight proposed to develop a proprietary e-commerce system for use within the Nextday business and then across the entire Freight Group. A secondary objective of this system was to eliminate the divisional boundaries caused by the many existing systems. The system therefore needed to be able to handle all kinds of freight requirement, from single parcel pick-ups to large container loads.

The December 1999 requirement to be off the Nextday system resulted in a re-prioritising of projects and the commencement of the e-commerce project. The e-commerce project was known as 'Freight Connect'. The objective was to develop a PC-based application which would allow customers to enter consignment information on-line. The documentation and labels are generated automatically to provide printed consignment information. Drivers then receive the pick-up information and the movement of the parcel commences. Customers can use the Internet to track parcel deliveries. Proof of delivery documents are scanned and can be viewed by customers. Freight Connect also allows customers to analyse and report on their shipments with Freight. The system shifts the responsibility of data entry for pick-up and delivery details from Freight to the customer.

The project commenced with a brief user needs analysis, which developed a base specification for functionality of the required new system. One key objective was to differentiate, i.e. develop something that was not available to competitors. The designers used a prototype development method to build the system in an exploratory way. Having sought the views of users on their needs, developers then set about building a model of the proposed system. This model was then put to users for feedback regarding functionality, screen design, layout and ease of use. Responses were incorporated into a final product.

In late 1999 software development was largely complete, and management was putting pressure on systems staff to clear the product for roll-out to customers. However, other managers were concerned that little time had been devoted to product testing, in particular user acceptance testing.

Source: Communication with Freight staff

Case study questions

1. What particular problems would face the project manager leading this project?
2. Why do you think the analysis of stakeholder commitment produced the pattern shown in Figure 6.3?
3. Which stakeholders would the project manager be dealing with in terms of 'managing up, across and staff'?
4. Who do 'the users' work for?
5. Identify one issue that should be at the top of the project manager's agenda for each of the three target groups.
6. What factors in the wider context could the project manager use to support his or her influence attempts?

Summary

This chapter has introduced ideas about identifying and managing those with a stake in the project. It has shown how the widely used stakeholder idea is just as relevant to projects as to the whole organisation. It has presented and illustrated a method for identifying and analysing stakeholders and their interests. Managing stakeholders is essentially a matter of developing and using power to influence their behaviour in a way that balances the various interests in the project. The chapter has identified the forms of power and methods of influence that a manager can use to influence any of the target groups.

The key points from this chapter are:

- The stakeholder idea is widely used to analyse how the interests affected by a change will view it.
- There is some (albeit limited) evidence that achieving an acceptable balance between stakeholder interests benefits performance as well as satisfying democratic preferences. This is even more likely to be the case at the level of the project than of the whole company, as project teams can more easily identify and manage them.
- For sound instrumental reasons, project managers will benefit from using the techniques presented to identify stakeholders and analyse their interests.
- Such an analysis will show that the project manager needs to work in four directions – the team, up, across and staff.
- In exercising influence, managers can draw on four power sources – physical, economic, knowledge and normative, each having both personal and institutional sources.
- They can also draw on four methods of influence – force, persuasion, negotiation and charisma, all depending in turn on effective personal and formal communication practices.
- The manager can plan an attempt at influencing a stakeholder group using the steps outlined.

Chapter questions

1 Can you identify a recent public case in which management have shown either effective or ineffective practices in managing stakeholders?

2 Why should managers pay attention to the interests of a wide range of stakeholders? What are the practical limits to this?

3 If stakeholders appear to have widely contrasting interests, how should the project manager try to reconcile these?

4 How might the process of managing up differ from that of managing across, or managing staff?

5 Why are the sources of power available to a manager likely to change during a project?

6 How might the relative power of the project manager and the people he or she is trying to influence be affected by the wider context of a project? Try to identify one specific, empirical example.

Further reading

The major sources on the stakeholder concept are:

Freeman, R.E. (1984) *Strategic Management: A Stakeholder Approach*. London: Pitman.
Mitroff, I.I. (1983) *Stakeholders of the Organisational Mind*. San Francisco: Jossey-Bass.

The Journal of Business Ethics is a useful source of articles on stakeholder theory. Note however that most deal with the topic at company level, rather than individual projects.

References

Boddy, D. and Gunson, N. (1996) *Organizations in the Network Age*. London: Routledge.

Buchanan, D. and Badham, R. (1999) *Power, Politics and Organizational Change: Winning the Turf Game*. London: Sage Publications.

Buchanan, D. and Boddy, D. (1992) *The Expertise of the Change Agent*. Hemel Hempstead: Prentice Hall.

Carroll, A. (1993) *Business and Society: Ethics and Stakeholder Management*. Cincinnati: South Western Publishing.

Donaldson, T. and Preston, L.E. (1995) 'The stakeholder theory of the corporation: concepts, evidence and implications', *Academy of Management Review*, 20, 65–91.

Friedman, M. (1970) 'The social responsiblity of business is to increase its profits', *New York Times Magazine* (September 13).

Hales, C. (1993) *Managing Through Organization*. London: Routledge.

Handy, C. (1993) *Understanding Organisations*. Harmondsworth: Penguin.

Johnson, G. and Scholes, K. (1999) *Exploring Corporate Strategy*. Hemel Hempstead: Prentice Hall.

Keen, P. (1981) 'Information systems and organization change', in Rhodes, E. and Weild, D. (eds) *Implementing New Technologies*. Oxford: Blackwell/Open University Press.

Lock, D. (1996) *Project Management*, 6th edn. Aldershot: Gower.

Ogden, S. and Watson, R. (1999) 'Corporate performace and stakeholder management: balancing shareholder and customer interests in the UK privatised water industry', *Academy of Management Journal*, 42, 526–38.

Part 3

Managing the project team

7 Project structures and project teams

Introduction

As projects grow and involve a wider range of players, they need some form of management structure within which people can work. This usually means a project team, which can add value to individual effort. They are not free, however, as they require time and skill to deliver worthwhile performance. Creating a project team is an investment that deserves a conscious decision.

This chapter begins by outlining how steering groups link the project to the organisation, and then considers three ways to structure a project – as a functional, matrix or semi-autonomous team. It then indicates some distinctive features of project teams, which have implications for managing them. After a section considering the advantages and disadvantages of project teams, the final section invites the reader to evaluate the assumption that teams are always worth the investment.

Objectives

After reading this chapter you should be able to:

- explain how a team can add value to a project;
- describe three types of project team structure, and when each is appropriate;
- recognise some distinct features of project teams and the challenges these pose;
- summarise the disadvantages of team work, as well as the advantages;
- evaluate systematically the amount of effort to put into developing a project team.

Creating a project structure

Because a project is there to do something new or unusual, people almost inevitably see it as something apart from their normal job. If the project is at all significant, it will require some deliberate structure. Unless management creates such a structure, signalling it as a separate task, it will remain entwined in regular activities. The project then faces the risk of being nobody's problem and is likely to fail.

Project managers need the support of other people, often in different units or departments. Yet they operate outside the established structure of responsibility and authority. For other units to provide support projects need to be visible and recognised. They need some kind of structure linking them to the rest of the business. The structure should also help their internal operation. Options include steering groups, functionally-based projects, matrix structures and semi-autonomous projects (Webb, 1994).

Steering groups

A steering group usually undertakes the overall direction of large, long-term projects. This typically consists of senior managers, often with some external or non-executive members. It meets relatively infrequently, monitors progress and serves as a link between the details of the project and the wider activities of the enterprise. The project manager will usually be a member of this group, and reports to it. It is one of the ways in which project managers 'manage upwards'. Organisations using the PRINCE project methodology, for example, establish a Project Board as the ultimate authority for the project. This is normally appointed by senior management to take overall responsibility and control. It includes three senior roles, each representing major project interests:

- Executive – to represent the interests of the business;
- Senior User/Customer – to represent users;
- Senior Supplier – representing those with specialist knowledge or responsible for committing supplier resources.

Steering groups for library projects

In her guide to managing information systems projects in libraries, Liz MacLachlan illustrates a typical Project Board (or steering group) for a small project (see Figure 7.1).

She recommends that the board should be big enough to represent all the major interests, but small enough to work. The roles of the members include:

- *Chair* – to take overall responsibility, and to resolve conflicts between interests.
- *Users* – representing possibly several communities in a large project.
- *Technical* – ensuring the system works, and fits with other systems and larger plans.
- *Financial* – monitoring costs and benefits, and other financial aspects in larger projects.
- *Project manager* – to get the work done, and to ensure regular reports to the Project Board.

Source: Based on MacLachlan (1996)

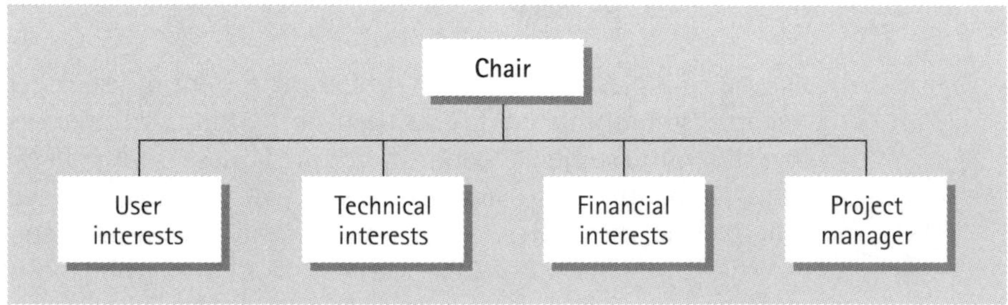

Figure 7.1 A typical project board structure for a small project

Functionally-based projects

These are projects in which the project manager coordinates and directs a change within a single department or unit. He or she will probably report to the head of the unit, and draw on other staff in the unit for their expertise. There may be some limited involvement with other units, or with people in other organisations. The manager needs to set up channels of communication with other functional heads, and form alliances with them. The scale of the task may mean that people only work part of the time on the project. Project managers in this structure experience conflicts of interest if other managers need the same resources to meet their objectives.

This form of project structure is, however, economical, and fits the existing hierarchy. For relatively small projects informal arrangements for securing co-operation are probably adequate. There is a danger that if several parts of the same function become involved, the project manager has to ensure that they work together effectively, as they may have different priorities to fulfill. As projects become larger, and with more complex links, they need more structures to support them – either matrix or semi-autonomous forms. Table 7.1 summarises some of the differences between functional and cross-functional teams.

Matrix management – cross-functional teams

In this structure, a designated manager leads the project and draws staff from functional departments. Staff spend a proportion of their time (often all of it) on the project. The project manager gives day-to-day direction on matters relating to the project. The functional head is mainly responsible for the quality of work and the longer-term professional development of staff. The project manager may strengthen the identity of the team by bringing them together in one location. This enhances communication and visibility within the project team, but at the expense of staffs' relationship with their functional department.

Table 7.1 Comparing functional and cross-functional teams

	Functional teams	*Cross-functional teams*
Skills and expertise	Similar	Varied
Work processes of leaders and members	Compatible because of similar backgrounds	Incompatible – leaders lack expertise to guide all members
Communication	Not inhibited by structural constraints	More potential conflict from diverse perspectives
Leaders	Have technical or professional authority – can act as supervisors	Lack technical authority – act as coaches, coordinators and facilitators
Problem-solving	Technically supervised, can be guided by leaders' expertise	Requires interdependent work processes and personal commitment of team members

Source: Based on Uhl-Bien and Graen (1998)

Internet procurement at IBM

A project to implement IBM's Internet procurement strategy at one of their UK sites illustrates the benefit of a single location. It involved intense working between a range of staff, including those who worked for Information Systems Global Services (another division of the company) on a separate part of the site. This physical separation led to lengthy communication processes within the team. The project manager pressed for seven ISGS staff to move into the procurement area for the duration of the project.

> *'We wanted a war room approach – get everyone in the one place – and we brought them in here. Being closer together got more teamwork activity, we could be up-to-date with what they were doing, and whether they were meeting targets. They worked much more effectively as a team, and were not distracted by other activities.'*

Source: Communication to the author

The project manager's status is clearer than in the functional structure. The risk is that the manager is more vulnerable to the failure of the project, even if the reasons are beyond their control. A difficulty for junior staff working on such a structure is that they are responsible to two bosses. On the other hand, they benefit from being able to identify with the project, and gain a broader experience than they may get within their function.

Product development at Toyota – Part 1

Until 1992 Toyota organised its product development in a matrix form. Then the product planning division employed about 7000 people working on 16 current projects. Each represented a new model being developed. Each project had a chief engineer and several hundred staff. At the same time, there were 16 functional engineering divisions. 'A chief engineer had to co-ordinate people in 48 departments in 12 divisions to launch a new product... In addition, relatively young chief engineers did not always get sufficient co-operation from senior functional managers... For their part, functional managers found it difficult to spend the time on managing details on so many projects. Most of these managers had to oversee work for about 15 different projects at the same time.'

Source: Cusumano and Nobeoka (1998), pp. 22–4

The semi-autonomous project group

This form resembles a small company within the larger one. Senior management allocate to the group the resources for the project. Staff have no other responsibilities and work only on the project: that is their job. The project manager may have a status similar to that of a managing director, with complete discretion over expenditure within the agreed budget. They direct all the relevant functional areas within their small organisation, contracting for other resources as they require them. Some use the term 'product management' to describe this structure, reflecting responsibility for all phases of a product's life. The team manages the product from conception to profitability.

Product development at Toyota – Part 2

Faced with the organisational problems outlined in Part 1, Toyota management changed the product development structure. They divided all new product development projects into three development centres (see Figure 7.2).

Each centre employed about 1800 people and focused on about five projects with similar vehicle platforms – such as rear-wheel drive models. The number of functional engineering divisions within the development centres fell from 16 to 6.

Source: Cusumano and Nobeoka (1998), pp. 29–34

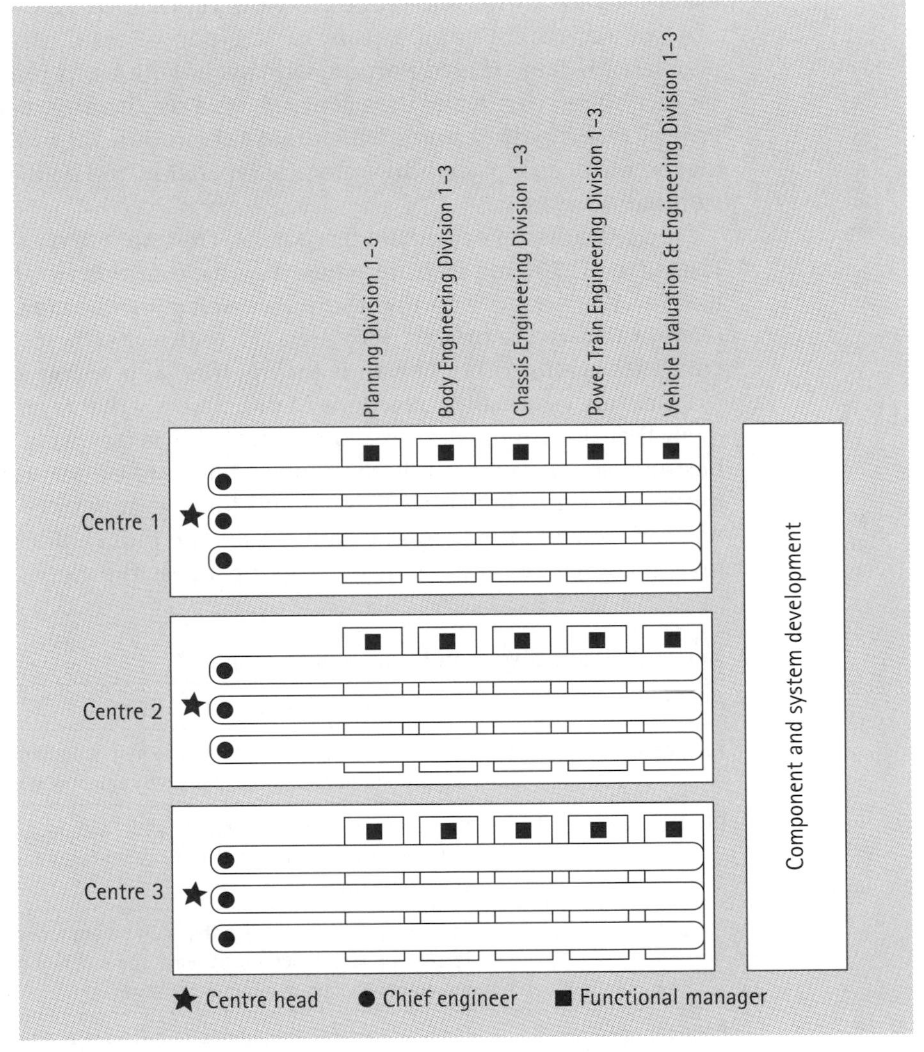

Figure 7.2 Toyota's project development organisation in 1992

The joint venture group is a derivative of this arrangement. Managing a matrix structure across two companies is very complex. A solution is to create a separate company jointly owned by the two or more businesses which have agreed to work together on a joint project. Each will be represented on the Board, usually in proportion to their financial stake in the company. The Board then creates a management structure to deal with the project, and appoints the necessary staff.

Features of work in project teams

Managers create many variations of the project structures set out above, to suit local circumstances. In themselves they are groups or teams, and in turn they usually create further sub-groups to work on defined aspects of the project.

A familiar definition of a team is: 'A group or team consists of two or more people with some shared purpose who assume different responsibilities, depend on each other, coordinate their activities, and see themselves as part of the group.' Project teams have features which make them difficult to manage – temporary, diverse membership, (possibly) physical separation and political agendas. Table 7.2 summarises these.

Project teams are essentially temporary. They are often called task forces (as in Hackman, 1990) and disband when they have completed the task. Members are likely to have one eye on the next job as well as on the current work. The project team or task is a temporary job; their career lies elsewhere. The project manager competes against other demands for the time and energy of team members.

Teams are essentially collections of differences – that is one of their advantages – but that diversity is not easy to manage. This is especially the case as changing business practice means it is common to have project teams with members from more than one company. Alliances and joint ventures between companies and nations – such as the European Airbus – require multi-cultural teams representing several companies and countries working across the globe.

Table 7.2 Distinctive features of project teams

Features	*Description and implications*
Temporary assignment	Career future lies elsewhere, and may work with that in mind, rather than the project. Project manager competes with other calls
Diverse membership	Brings different working habits and styles into the team. Such cultural differences inhibit progress until team faces them and members set common norms
Physical separation	Lose the personal contact that can smooth working relationships. Need to seek opportunities for at least some personal contact early in the project and when possible after that
Political agendas	These will reflect the inevitably different positions of stakeholder groups. Not necessarily disruptive, although will be if taken to extremes. Manager needs to recognise and learn political skills to cope with this

Cultures and teams

Geert Hofstede reported how students from Germany, France and Britain analysed a case concerning conflict between sales and production departments. The majority of French students recommended referring the problem to the next level in the hierarchy. The majority of British students recommended training programmes so that the two departments would be better at dealing with interpersonal communications. The majority of German students recommended establishing a clearer written policy.

Diversity brings great benefits if the team can handle the management issues. For example, staff from different professions or national backgrounds, or even simply from different operations of the same company, operate in different ways. People from some cultures tend to be open and creative in solving problems. Others tend to stay within their area of special expertise. Some may not be able to cope with the speed and intensity of the work, or with the forward-looking, often 'conditional' and unpredictable nature of project work. Others may not be natural team players, so that when difficulties arise in the team, as they inevitably do, they withdraw rather than come forward.

Physical separation of project teams is also more common. As companies operate internationally, face-to-face interaction becomes costly and so less frequent. Developments in technology such as voice and video-conferencing, E-mail, groupware and desk-top video systems make it feasible to exchange information without a physical presence. While these technologies make it easier, they do not make it *easy* for a project team to work without face-to-face interaction (see Boddy *et al.* (2002) for a fuller discussion of this). Informal, social contact around the formal business contribute to team performance and technology cannot realistically replace that.

Political agendas are likely to be evident when a team draws members from several departments or functions. Members are not there as individuals, but as representatives. Whatever their personal inclinations, and however close their working relations with other team members, they have an 'invisible committee' behind them, representing the interests of their unit. There is tension between the interests of those committed to the project, and those committed to the interests of separate departments. Such local interests will always be part of the team members' thinking. They will influence what they do and say more than the wider interests of the project as a whole.

How teams can benefit a project

Projects are a step into the unknown. If the step is small and in familiar territory it will probably not need a team. As the scale and novelty increase, the project will require a wider range of skills and perspectives. As that happens, people will usually begin forming project teams to do the work. There are good reasons for this, including complementary skills; wider perspectives; creating a recognised forum; ownership of solutions; a sense of challenge; and learning.

Business and social problems are often complex, and bound up with related issues. They are often beyond the capacity of a single person or profession. A project team creates a structure within which people from different backgrounds can consider the issue from their perspective, express their views and work together on a solution. Teams can combine complementary skills beyond those of any of the individual members.

Members can test their ideas on others. They consider them against this wider knowledge – and then develop or discard them. So good teams are collections of differences. There is little point in having a team made up of people from similar backgrounds. A team usually benefits not only from different knowledge and technical skills to work together, but also from radically different positions. They can challenge the accepted wisdom and propose new ways of working on the problem. Kettley and Hirsch (2000) found that organisations sought to gain synergies (the ability of team members to accomplish more working together than they could have done alone) from cross-functional teams. Table 7.3 indicates four kinds of synergy which companies reported.

Teams provide a mechanism or a forum in which people can raise issues or problems. They can then deal with them – rather than leave them unattended. It may be that in doing so they encourage people to recognise a problem, and to help find a solution. If people take part in a project team or task force they will know more of the constraints and limitations. The group work can build a sense of ownership, and a willingness to overcome implementation problems. A motivational benefit comes if people see that a project offers a challenging and interesting task. It is a change of routine. People see the chance to work on

Table 7.3 Projects gain synergies from cross-functional teams

Synergy	*Description*
Decentralisation	The common practice of creating autonomous business units has reduced the scope for sharing ideas. Some organisations were deliberately creating teams from separate functions to improve communication and reduce the divide between units
Differentiation of functions	Separate functions and business units develop unique ways of working. These gradually build barriers between departments, often reinforced by physical separation. Organisations saw cross-functional teams as a chance to develop collaboration and cooperation
Value of constructive conflict	Conflict between opposing views can be a better route to adaptation and renewal than order and equilibrium. Organisations in the study recognised that functions had different views, and saw this as potentially productive if properly managed
On-going process improvement	The companies in the study expressed a sense of continuing change, and saw cross-functional teams as part of the continuing search for better ways of doing things

Source: Based on Kettley and Hirsch (2000), pp. 12–13

a team developing a new service or product as a way to be more visible, and to advance their career.

Teams can promote learning. As people work together to solve problems, they not only deal with the present task. They can also reflect on what they can learn from the experience, and perhaps see how to do the job differently next time. People often use tacit, taken for granted knowledge to reach solutions. Working in a team exposes those assumptions to challenge from other perspectives.

A project team as a learning opportunity

Senior management in a semiconductor business decided to launch a new product. Management of their UK plant created a team to develop expertise in the new product, and to support a European design network. The local manager arranged for four of his engineers to participate in the project. He was excited about the possibility of getting his team involved in this advanced design development. The strategy proposed would make the local group stronger, enhance their skills and result in even more challenging and rewarding tasks for the engineers. The team members had each been chosen for their ability to assimilate the skills quickly. Each agreed enthusiastically to participate.

To sum up, Katzenbach and Smith (1993, p. 19) claim that:

> When teams work, they represent the best proven way to convert embryonic visions and values into consistent action patterns because they rely on people working together. They are also the most practical to develop a shared sense of direction among people throughout an organization. Teams can make hierarchy responsive without weakening it, energize processes across organizational boundaries, and bring multiple capabilities to bear on difficult issues.

How teams can damage a project

For all the undoubted benefits that a team can bring, they can also be a source of danger. The project manager who is alert to these can take steps to avoid them.

By taking on their own purpose

Some groups take on a life of their own, and become too independent of the organisation that created them. As members learn to work together they generate enthusiasm and commitment – and become harder to control. The team may divert the project to meet goals that they value, rather than those of the sponsor. As experts in the particular issue they can exert great influence over management, by controlling or filtering the flow of information to the organisation as whole, so that their goals become increasingly hard to challenge. Their work becomes relatively isolated from other parts of the organisation, and focus on what they see to be key issues. The case study in Chapter 12 is an example of this. The group at Chem Ltd believed that their approach benefited the organisation – senior management saw it differently.

By using too much time

The benefit of wider perspectives comes from discussion. This inevitably takes longer than if an individual made the decision. Time spent in discussion may encourage participation and acceptance – but only if the group manages this well. If discussion strays over unrelated issues, or goes over matters that they have already dealt with, the team loses time. This can also be an opportunity for members opposed to the project to prolong group discussion and to use the search for agreement as a blocking tactic. Some members will complain about the time spent. In fast-moving situations, they may simply not be able to afford the time and so withdraw their support.

By allowing an individual to dominate

Some teams allow one member to dominate. This may be the formal leader of the group in a hierarchical organisation, where people do not challenge those in a position of authority. It may be a technical expert who takes over, when others hesitate to show their lack of knowledge, or to ask for explanations. In either case, the group will not draw on the experience available, and will probably be a dissatisfying and unproductive experience. It may produce a worse result, and be more costly, than if one person had dealt with the issue.

By slipping into conformity and groupthink

Teams can become too cosy. The close-knit ideal can go too far. This happens when a team becomes complacent and inward-looking, with people unwilling to challenge the prevailing direction of the group. People come to value their inclusion in the group so highly that they are reluctant to voice criticism, in case this is seen as disloyalty, leading to isolation. This means that they ignore counter-propositions or inconvenient evidence – which may lead the group to the wrong conclusion.

Irving Janis (1971) offered an influential analysis of groupthink, which he defined as:

> A mode of thinking that people engage in when they are deeply involved in a cohesive in-group, when the members' striving for unanimity overrides their motivation to realistically appraise alternative courses of action.

So despite their potential benefits, teams may damage a project. People can reduce the risk by effective management effort and training, but this is not free. Project teams require investment to be effective – are they *always* worth it?

NOTEPAD 7.1

Critical reflection on project teams

This activity is intended to encourage you to reflect critically on the previous two sections.

- Which of these advantages and disadvantages have you observed or experienced in project teams? Make notes summarising your evidence.
- Does your experience suggest that project teams have always performed well? What have been the reasons for any difficulties?
- Before reading the next section, do you agree that project teams are always worthwhile?

Are teams worth the investment?

Groups and teams

In normal conversation people use the words 'group' and 'team' interchangeably. This book reflects that usage. However the words mean different things to different people. Some think that any group of people that works together is a team, or that teams inevitably work cooperatively together. Some see them as a waste of time, an excuse for talking rather than doing. Others create them at every opportunity.

The essential point to recognise is that some groups (or teams) work a great deal better than others. Katzenbach and Smith (1993) use the 'team performance curve' to make the point clear (see Figure 7.3).

They define a team as 'a small number of people with complementary skills who are committed to a common purpose, performance goals, and approach for which they hold themselves mutually accountable' (p. 45). Their central point is that while many groups call themselves teams, most put too little effort into clarifying their common purpose, goals and approach. They do not achieve their true potential. In many situations what they call a working group (see Table 7.3) is a perfectly adequate arrangement. It relies on the individual contributions of its members, and is well suited to situations which stress individual accountability.

The team makes sense *only* when the task needs more than individual effort – where there is benefit in group discussion, debate and decision. In so doing, members are able to deliver 'collective work products' – something more than the sum of individual effort. In such circumstances it is worth investing the time and effort required to move up the team perfomance curve. Having, for the purpose of their argument, distinguished between working groups and teams, they emphasise that they do not advocate particular labels. They recommend (and this author agrees) that people should use the terms with which they are comfortable. It is what teams do that matter, not what they are called. Table 7.4 describes the five points on the curve.

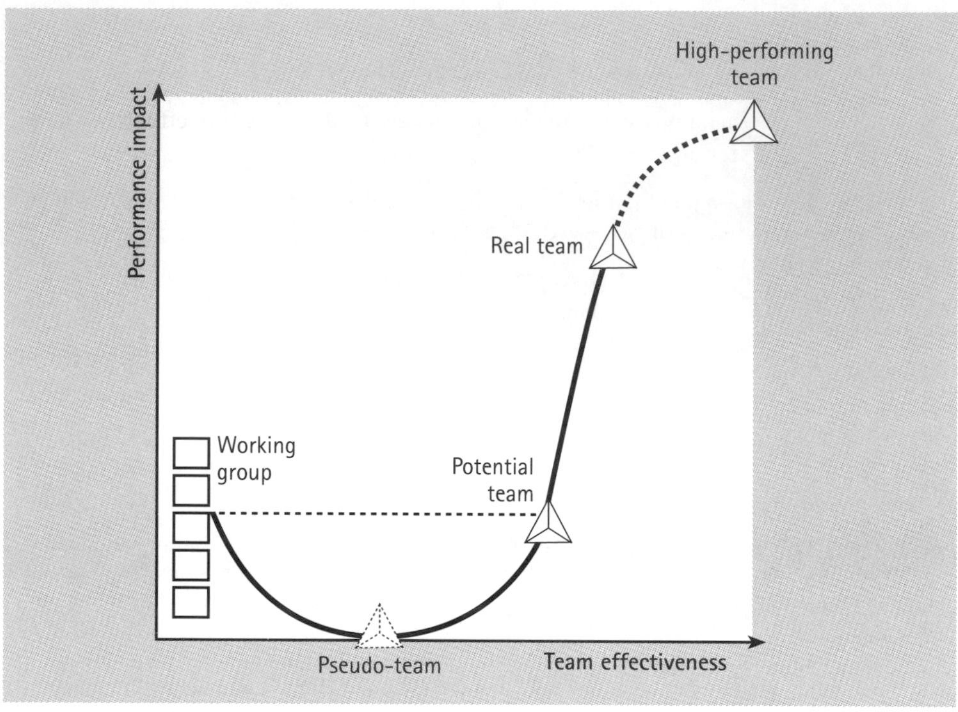

Figure 7.3 The team performance curve

Table 7.4 Description of the points on the team performance curve

Working group	There is no significant need to become a team. The focus is on individual effort. Members interact mainly to share information and best practices. They help each other to perform within their area of responsibility. There is no strong common purpose or joint work product for which they are all accountable
Pseudo-team	There are opportunities for collective performance, but members have not focused on trying to achieve it. No interest in shaping a common purpose or set of performance goals, although it may call itself a team. Time in meetings detracts from individual performance, without any joint benefits. Whole is less than potential sum of parts
Potential team	There are opportunities for collective performance, and members are trying to achieve these. They still need to develop clarity over purpose, goals or joint work products. They may need more discipline in working out a common approach or to establish collective accountability
Real team	A small number of people with complementary skills who are equally committed to a common purpose, goals and working approach for which they hold themselves mutually accountable
High-performance team	Meets all the tests of a real team, and in addition members are deeply committed to one another's personal growth and success

Source: Katzenbach and Smith (1993), pp. 90–2

Working groups or real teams?

Katzenbach and Smith (1993) raise the question of whether teams as they have defined them are always necessary for effective performance. Individuals can handle many tasks as well as a group – and perhaps better. An example is where a task requires someone to use their expertise on a narrowly defined technical issue with no wider implications. For such purposes someone who is part of an effective working group can meet the performance required. There is no need to invest the extra effort needed for team performance. Indeed it could be counter-productive. Off-site team development activities can be exciting and motivating. If members then find that the task to be done involves little real interaction, beyond normal interpersonal cooperation, they will feel let down by the wasted effort.

In other projects the task clearly requires people to work together to create joint work products besides individual contributions. Then the risk and cost of creating a team will be worthwhile.

Critchley and Casey (1984), two British consultants specialising in developing teams at senior level, raised the same dilemma. Reviewing the many teams with which they had worked they concluded that teams were not always necessary, and may have represented an expensive solution to simple problems. They concluded that the expense of developing a high level of skill in team working is often unnecessary. The answer depended on the nature of the task being undertaken:

- *Simple puzzles of a technical nature* – could be done quite effectively by members working independently of each other, on the basis of their technical expertise, with a reasonable degree of polite social skills;
- *Familiar tasks with moderate degrees of uncertainty* – some sharing of information and ideas required, but main requirement is reasonable cooperation between the people concerned using skills of negotiation and coordination;
- *High degree of uncertainty and relatively unknown problems affecting all concerned* – requiring high levels of information-sharing, and of deeper interpersonal skills to cope with the 'shared uncertainty', implying a high level of team skills.

NOTEPAD 7.2

Reflect on a team of which you have been a member

- On balance, where on the scale between working group and high-performance team would you place it?
- Was a working group appropriate for the task? In other words would any more intense type of team activity have been counter-productive? Could one person have done the job better?
- Do your conclusions support the two views above, or not?

CASE STUDY

Consulting Engineers

Consulting Engineers employed 600 people. The company consisted of five divisions based on broad professional disciplines, and each of these contained several groups of staff in separate sub-disciplines. The information system used to control project costs had serious defects. The software was difficult to support because the people who had developed it had left the company. They had left no documentation; the old hardware often failed; and the information produced by the system was of doubtful accuracy.

Management decided to install a new system to satisfy their need for flexibility, detail and accessibility of information. The system would streamline administration and provide a more effective tool for managing the core consultancy activities. It would provide information on project costing and charging and would affect accounting, personnel and marketing departments.

Top management created a steering committee to represent and coordinate the departments affected by the system. The committee had nine representatives from user groups and had powers to co-opt specialist expertise. The committee met regularly during the early stages of the project to prepare the specification for the new system and to choose a supplier. The committee would eventually transfer the running of the system to a system manager.

A manager from one of the technical departments chaired the committee, and he tended to dominate the group. He actively invited comment from other members, but in a way that some found intimidating. He did not always get a balanced and considered view from the committee.

The representative from the accounting function was young, unfamiliar with the kind of system planned, and was reluctant to voice his views. He limited his contribution to expressing satisfaction with progress, and gave assurances that his part of the project would be successful. Not surprisingly, other members lacked confidence in him. The system would integrate the accounting modules with other components so they had to be there from the beginning. Others depended on accounting, which the team could not treat in isolation. It emerged during system tests that the system designers had fundamentally misunderstood the internal procedures of the accounting function.

Members had different degrees of commitment to the project. The system manager supported the project and devoted all his time to it. The senior manager representing consultants and project leaders was less enthusiastic and often failed to do things to which he had agreed. There were other demands on his time and he gave low priority to this project. But another representative might not have carried the same seniority.

No one person had a clear overview of how the company's functions related to each other or how the internal functions of the information system related to each other. This made it difficult to establish a balance between the sometimes conflicting requirements of different functions.

While the system did provide significant benefits once it was in operation, many users said the project was a lost opportunity to make more radical use of IT.

Source: Research by the author in the company

►

Case study questions

1 Of the four structures outlined, which does this team correspond most closely to?

2 What were the potential advantages of creating the team?

3 Which of the disadvantages of teams are evident in this case study?

4 Would management have been better not to have set up a team for this task?

Summary

This chapter has discussed the kind of structures, especially project teams, which companies often create to support the work of project managers. While small projects can be handled informally, projects soon require some visible structure if people are to take them seriously. The chapter has outlined three main structures – functional, matrix and semi-autonomous, each of which is suitable for different conditions. Teams have both advantages and disadvantages, and project managers need to be aware of the potential costs of team-working. Finally the chapter raised the question of whether it is always worth the time and effort of investing heavily in teams, when many tasks do not require the added benefits that teams can bring.

The key points from this chapter are:

- Projects beyond the smallest enterprise require some form of structure.
- Structures usually correspond to functional, matrix or semi-autonomous types.
- Teams have advantages as well as disadvantages.
- High-performing teams are expensive to develop.
- Management needs to consider whether the cost of team-building outweighs the benefits.

Chapter questions

1 What are the alternative project structures, and what are their relative merits?

2 What are the advantages of creating a team to work on a project?

3 Identify some of the distinctive features of project teams.

4 What are the disadvantages of teams?

5 Katzenbach and Smith distinguish between working groups and real teams. Summarise the differences between them.

Further reading

The books by Hackman (1990) and Katzenbach and Smith (1993) contain many good examples of the use of teamwork.

Cusumano, M.A. and Nobeoka, K. (1998) *Thinking Beyond Lean*. New York: The Free Press. A thorough discussion, based on empirical work within Toyota, of the way the automobile industry uses cross-functional product development teams to ensure a rapid flow of new models. A specialised interest, but worth reading if you work on projects to develop new products.

References

Boddy, D., Boonstra, A. and Kennedy, G. (2002) *Management Information Systems: An Organisational Perspective*. Harlow: Financial Times Prentice Hall.

Critchley, B. and Casey, D. (1984) 'Second thoughts on team building', *Management Education and Development*, 15, Part 2, 163–75.

Cusumano, M.A. and Nobeoka, K. (1998) *Thinking Beyond Lean*. New York: The Free Press.

Hackman, J.R. (1990) *Groups That Work (and Those That Don't)*. San Francisco: Jossey-Bass.

Janis, I. (1971) *Groupthink: Psychological Studies of Policy Decisions*. Boston, MA: Houghton Mifflin.

Katzenbach, J.R. and Smith, D.K. (1993) *The Wisdom of Teams*. Boston, MA: Harvard Business School Press.

Kettley, P. and Hirsch, W. (2000) *Learning from Cross-functional Teamwork*. Brighton: Institute for Employment Studies.

MacLachlan, L. (1996) *Making Project Management Work for You*. London: Library Association Publishing.

Uhl-Bien, M. and Graen, G.B. (1998) 'Individual self-management: analysis of professionals' self-managing activities in functional and cross-functional teams', *Academy of Management Journal*, 41, 340–50.

Webb, A. (1994) *Managing Innovative Projects*. London: Chapman & Hall.

8 Project teams – motivation, composition and process

Introduction

Creating a project team does not ensure that it works effectively. Managers who wish to influence the performance of a project team can draw on a wide range of knowledge about teams. This helps them have an accurate mental picture of the factors that affect team performance, including internal and external factors. They can then influence team development in a confident and coherent way.

This chapter outlines some major areas of knowledge about teams, which is then continued, and used to make practical suggestions, in Chapter 9. People use different criteria to judge how effectively a team is operating, and the chapter begins by presenting one set of criteria. It then introduces a theory of the factors which affect these criteria – team motivation, composition and performance strategies. This provides the structure for the rest of the chapter. The second section considers the motivation of team members, while the third outlines team role theories which give an insight into composition. The chapter then explains the idea of team processes. It ends by looking beyond the team to external influences on performance.

Objectives

After reading this chapter you should be able to:

- compare three alternative measures of group effectiveness;
- explain how theories of individual motivation can guide project managers;
- identify the different roles that people take in teams;
- understand the importance of group processes (or performance strategies) and explain some elements;
- outline the wider organisational factors which affect group performance.

A model for improving team effectiveness

Table 8.1 summarises three long-term measures of team effectiveness. These are necessarily subjective, and a team may succeed on some and fail on others. Judgement must also reflect the conditions in which the team is working.

What models of team development can managers use to build a team that moves towards meeting one or more of these measures of success? Based on research with 27 teams of different types (including 'task forces' – equivalent to project teams), Hackman (1990) and his colleagues developed a framework which integrates several theoretical perspectives.

To perform well, the group must surmount three hurdles (see Figure 8.1). First, members must be willing to exert sufficient effort to accomplish the task to an acceptable level of performance. Second, members must bring adequate knowledge and skill to the task (otherwise effort will be used wastefully). Third, they must use group processes – how a group goes about its task – that are appropriate to the work and the setting. These hurdles can be used to assess how well a group is doing as it proceeds with the work, and for diagnosing possible sources of difficulty if things go wrong.

To overcome each of these hurdles, Hackman argues that a team needs both internal and external support. The project manager cannot rely on internal team practices (or their personal enthusiasm) alone. They should also attend to wider organisational conditions. If both are in place, it is more likely that the group will put in the effort, have the skill and use good team processes. Table 8.2 summarises these points.

Securing adequate effort is partly a matter of the tasks that people are expected to do, and factors in the wider organisation, such as the reward system. The same combination of internal and organisational factors affect the team's knowledge and skill, and their working processes. This approach matches the theme of this book, i.e. that individual, interpersonal effort can be supported by appropriate

Table 8.1 Criteria for evaluating team effectiveness

Criteria	*Description*
Has it met performance expectations?	Is the group completing the task managers gave to it – not only the project performance criteria, but also measures of cost and timeliness?
Have members' experienced the development of an effective team?	Is it enhancing their ability to work together as a group? Have they created such a winning team that it represents a valuable resource for future projects?
Have members developed transferable teamwork skills?	Are members developing teamwork skills which they will take to future projects? This represents a further level of effectiveness. Team meets business needs and needs of the team members

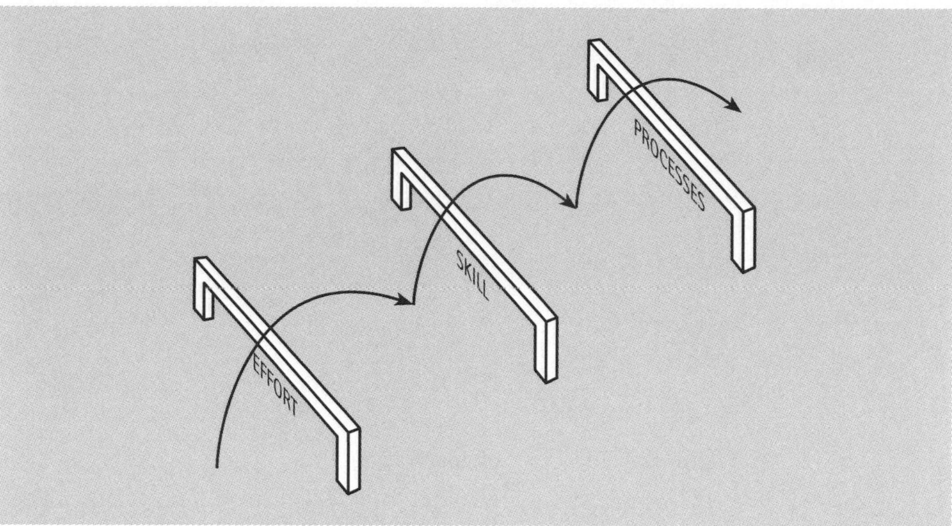

Figure 8.1 Three hurdles that teams need to surmount

Table 8.2 Points of leverage for enhancing group performance

Requirements for effectiveness	*Internal conditions*	*Organisational context*
Effort	Motivational structure of group task	Remedying coordination problems and building group commitment, e.g. rewards
Skill	Group composition	Available education and training, including coaching and guidance
Processes	Norms that regulate behaviour and foster review and learning	Information system to support task and provide feedback on progress

Source: Based on Hackman (1990), p. 13

structures. The following sections examine the contribution of motivation, composition and process to project team performance. A final section outlines the role of external factors.

Motivating team members

Employment is essentially an exchange relationship. Team members will be assessing whether the rewards match the effort they put into the project. It is up to the project manager to ensure that team members view the exchange as being in their interests, and so be willing to make the effort.

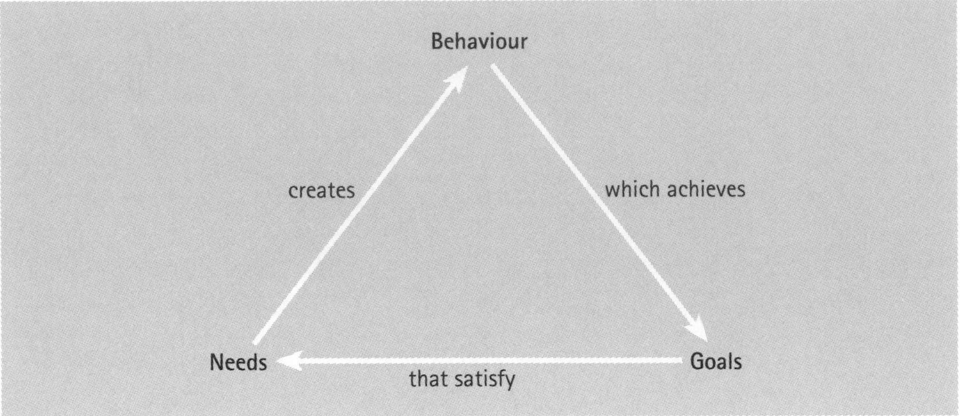

Figure 8.2 The cycle of motivation

Understanding individual motivation is the basis for understanding team motivation. People will be willing to do things for the project manager if they feel they are acting in their best interests, and that they are achieving their personal goals. Project managers need to establish what these interests are, and present their proposal in a way that people believe will meet them. People will then respond positively, as in doing so they will meet their needs – they are doing themselves a favour.

Motivation is a decision process through which an individual chooses desired goals, and sets in motion behaviours that will help achieve those outcomes. Figure 8.2 shows this.

Psychologists disagree over 'needs'. Research shows these are complex – yet the manager needs some practical guidelines. The project manager, as Huczynski (1996) observes, 'requires a theory of motivation which is understandable, portable and practical, even if it lacks sophistication. Influencers are seeking only to "nudge up the averages" of their successful influencing attempts, not get a doctorate in the subject' (p. 100).

Abraham Maslow

One such usable theory is, of course, that put forward by Abraham Maslow in 1943. Despite its age, the theory is still useful for those trying to influence others in the workplace. He proposed that individuals experience a range of needs, and will be motivated to fulfil whichever need is most powerful at the time. What he termed the lower-order needs are dominant until they are at least partially satisfied. Once they are, Maslow predicted that the normal individual would then turn their attention to satisfying the needs at the next level, and so on, so that the higher-order needs would gradually become dominant. He referred to these needs as being arranged in a hierarchy, although later research suggests it is more useful to think of these as a set of needs which people focus on at different times and circumstances.

Physiological needs are those that are essential for survival, such as food and water particularly. *Safety* needs represent the search for security, stability and a freedom from anxiety. People have a need for some degree of structure and order in their lives. They also have what Maslow called *belongingness* needs – friends, affectionate relations with others, incuding a place in a group. People want to be part of a congenial team, and to be able to work closely with others. They will object to new work patterns that threaten established relationships.

Maslow then argued that most people need a (realistic) high evaluation of themselves – the *esteem* need. He identified two aspects in this evaluation: self-respect, and the respect of others. Self-respect referred to a need for a sense of achievement, competence, adequacy, confidence in the face of the world, for independence and freedom. In addition, he believed people would seek the respect of others, what he called a desire for reputation in the eyes of other people – prestige, status, fame, recognition, attention, appreciation. Finally he identified the need for *self-actualisation*. Maslow used this term to refer to the desire for self-fulfilment, for realising potential, for becoming what one is capable of becoming. This implies that people seeking to satisfy this need will look for personal meaning and growth in their work. They may value new responsibilities that help them realise their potential or discover unknown talents.

Frederick Herzberg

Frederick Herzberg (1959) provided another perspective on motivation which is frequently cited. He developed the theory following interviews with 200 engineers and accountants about their experience of work. The interviewers first asked them to recall a time when they had felt exceptionally good about their jobs. Further questions probed for the events that had preceded those feelings. The research team then asked the respondents to recall a time when they had felt particularly bad about their work. Again the interviewers probed for the background to these negative feelings. When the team analysed the interviews they observed that when the respondents had talked about good times, five factors appeared frequently. These were:

- achievement;
- recognition;
- work itself;
- responsibility;
- advancement.

These factors appeared much less frequently when people were describing the bad times. When the team analysed the events preceding times of dissatisfaction an entirely different set of factors emerged:

- company policy and administration;
- supervision;

- salary;
- interpersonal relations;
- working conditions.

These factors appeared much less frequently when the respondents were recalling work experiences that had been satisfying.

Herzberg concluded that the factors associated with satisfaction seemed to describe people's relationship to what they were doing. They included factors like the nature of the task, responsibility carried or recognition received. He called these 'motivators' because they influenced the individual to superior performance and effort. The second set, associated with dissatisfaction, related to the circumstances surrounding the work – he labelled these the 'hygiene' or 'maintenance' factors. They served primarily to prevent dissatisfaction, rather than to foster positive attitudes.

In summary, he concluded that the factors that produce job satisfaction are separate and distinct from those which lead to job dissatisfaction, hence the term 'two-factor' theory. He suggested that satisfaction and dissatisfaction are not opposites of each other, but separate dimensions. They are influenced by different factors.

When people were feeling satisfied, it was because they were experiencing feelings of psychological growth, and gaining a sense of self-actualisation. So a 'hygienic' environment with fair policies can prevent discontent and dissatisfaction but will not in itself contribute to psychological growth and hence satisfaction. Such positive feelings could only come, he argued, from the nature of the task itself, and the opportunities for growth that it offers.

The dissatisfiers (the hygiene factors), included working conditions, salary, company policy – topics based in the context within which they worked rather than in the work itself. Positive ratings on the hygiene factors did not lead to satisfaction, but simply the absence of dissatisfaction. Dealing with them does not in itself create satisfaction. Herzberg's ideas encouraged management in many organisations to redesign jobs as a way of enhancing performance.

A key idea in Herzberg's work is the distinction between intrinsic and extrinsic rewards. Extrinsic rewards are those that are outside the job and separate from the performance of the task, such as pay, security and promotion possibilities. Intrinsic rewards are those which people receive from the performance of the task itself – the use of skills, a sense of achievement, work that is in itself satisfying to do. Recall that a central element in Frederick Taylor's doctrine of Scientific Management was the careful design of the 'one best way' of doing a piece of manual work. This was typically arrived at by carefully analysing how people normally did the job. Experts then identified the most efficient set of tasks, usually by breaking the task down into many small parts which people could learn quickly. Jobs of this sort are boring to many people, and were often criticised for leading to dissatisfaction, absence and carelessness.

As the limitations of mechanistic designs became clear, researchers began to seek ways of making jobs more interesting and challenging – in the belief that this would tap into the higher-level sources of motivation. The work of writers such as Maslow, Herzberg and McGregor (1960) prompted many experiments aimed at increasing the opportunities for people to satisfy their 'higher' needs at work. The idea was that staff would work more productively if management offered intrinsic rewards (motivators in Herzberg's terms) as well as extrinsic ones (Herzberg's hygiene factors). A series of research projects indicated the potential of this approach, and led to the development of the job enrichment model.

The job enrichment model

The job enrichment model extended the work of earlier motivation theorists by proposing that managers could change specific job characteristics to motivate employees and promote job satisfaction. Doing so would enable staff to satisfy more of their higher-level needs and so lead to greater motivation and performance. Richard Hackman and Greg Oldham (1980) did extensive research on the topic, and their model is widely quoted (see for example Boddy (2002) or Huczynski and Buchanan (2001)).

Central to the model are five key job characteristics – skill variety, task identity, task significance, autonomy, and feedback – all of which contribute to the motivational potential of a job:

- *Skill variety* – the extent to which a job makes use of a range of skills and experience.
- *Task identity* – whether a job involves a relatively complete and whole operation.
- *Task significance* – how much the job matters to others, or to the wider society.
- *Autonomy* – how much freedom a person has in deciding how to do their work.
- *Feedback* – the extent to which a person receives feedback on performance.

Figure 8.3 summarises the model, which was developed in the context of work on established, regular tasks. However, the same principles are likely to apply to project work. Projects also have the advantage that they are created from scratch, with fewer constraints from past practice. So they offer good opportunities to arrange the tasks in a way that enhances team motivation. How much responsibility and autonomy does a team have in deciding how to go about the task? How much feedback does it get? Wickens (1995), argues that: 'A team begins with individuals whose contributions are recognised and valued, and who are motivated to work together to achieve clear, understood and stretching goals for which they are accountable.' The evidence is clear that, alongside appropriate extrinsic rewards, the intrinsic aspects of the job will affect the motivation of team members.

Project managers may be unable to do much directly about the important extrinsic rewards, if these are more heavily influenced by a person's functional head. They can however do a great deal to offer intrinsic rewards. The job enrichment model implies, in the present context, that project managers can increase the motivating potential of jobs by using five implementing concepts. Table 8.3 summarises some options.

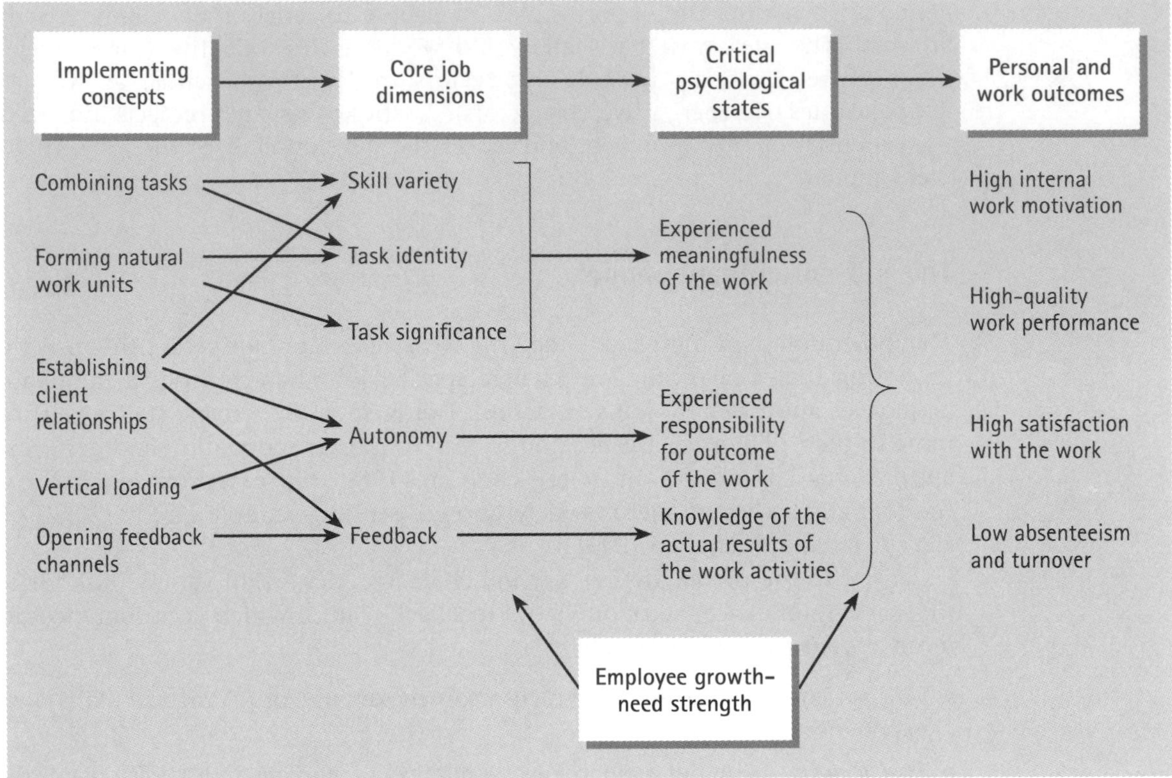

Figure 8.3 The job characteristics model
Source: Adapted from Hackman *et al.* (1975)

Table 8.3 Some applications of the job enrichment model to project work

Implementing concept	*Practical example*
Combining tasks	Rather than divide the project task into small pieces, combine them so that staff use more skills and complete more of the whole task
Form natural work groups	Give team responsibility for a significant project task, and construct it so that members can build strong working relations with each other
Establish customer relations	Ensure that project team members understand what the client expects. Link team members to specific customers, encourage visits, direct communication
Vertical loading	Where workers take on responsibilities traditionally taken by supervisors. Make team responsible for more of the scheduling, planning, budgeting, client liaison, etc.
Opening feedback channels	Passing information from customers. Invite project staff to customer meetings. Ensure positive as well as negative messages. Encourage more internal review and evaluation of perfomance

Team composition

In a mechanical sense, team composition includes questions of size and membership. Is it too large or too small? Is there an acceptable balance between part-time and full-time members? Do members have the right skills? Are they too similar in outlook, or so diverse that they are unlikely to agree a solution? Are all the relevant functions represented? These are important questions, but even more important is the question of whether members have the right skills and ways of working to form an effective team. Research by Uhl-Bien and Graen (1998) for example led them to warn that: 'Although cross-functional teams may be highly effective if implemented correctly (for instance, staffed with strong team players), if implemented incorrectly (staffed with independently focussed self-managing professionals) they may. . . . harm organizational functioning' (p. 348).

As people work together in teams they behave in different ways. This is bound to happen, as a major benefit of creating teams is to bring together people with different perspectives, skills and interests. Members tend to take on a relatively distinctive role within the group. A group needs a balance of such roles, so a task for the project manager is to do what they can to shape the composition of the group to enhance performance. Two ideas that project managers use are the distinction between task and maintenance roles and Meredith Belbin's research on team roles.

Task and maintenance roles

Some people focus on the project task, on getting the job done, on meeting deadlines. Other put most of their energies into keeping the peace, and ensuring the group stays together, i.e. they help to maintain the project team. Teams need both roles and skilful project managers try to ensure this happens. Table 8.4 summarises the typical activities of people in the two roles.

Table 8.4 Summary of task and maintenance roles

Emphasis on task	*Emphasis on maintenance*
Initiator	Encourager
Information seeker	Compromiser
Diagnoser	Peacekeeper
Opinion seeker	Clarifier
Evaluator	Summariser
Decision manager	Standard setter

Meredith Belbin – team roles

Meredith Belbin, of Oxford University, conducted a series of studies in which colleagues systematically observed several hundred small groups while they performed a task. From these observations he concluded that each person working in a group tends to behave in a way that corresponds closely to one of nine distinct roles. The balance of these roles in a group affects how well or badly it performs.

Belbin's research method

The research arose from the practice at the Henley School of Management of basing much of their training on work done by managers in teams. Groups of up to 10 managers worked on exercises or business simulations. The organisers had long observed that some teams achieved better financial results than others – irrespective of the abilities of the individual members as measured by standard personality and mental tests. The reasons for this were unclear. Why did some teams of individually able people perform less well than teams that appeared to contain less able people?

Belbin therefore undertook a study in which carefully briefed observers, drawn from the course members, used a standard procedure to record the types of contribution which members made. Team members voluntarily took the psychometric tests, and the researchers recorded quantifiable results of the team performance in the exercises. They tested and refined the conclusions in other settings as results from the exercises accumulated. These included individual companies and a similar training establishment.

Some clues as to the eventual results occurred when the researchers formed teams of members with well above average mental abilities, and compared their performance with the other teams. The 'intelligent' teams usually performed less well than the others. Of 25 such teams observed, only three were winners, and the most common position was sixth in a league of eight teams. The explanation seemed to lie in the way such teams behaved in carrying out the task. Typically they spent much time in debate, arguing for their point of view to the exclusion of other opinions. Members in these teams of highly intelligent people were typically good at spotting flaws in other members' arguments. They then became so engrossed in these arguments that they neglected other tasks. Failure led to recrimination. The lesson was that behaviour (rather than measured intelligence) affected group performance.

Source: Belbin (1981)

The researchers identified the types of behaviour which people displayed in teams – their preferred team roles. Some were creative, full of ideas and suggestions. Others were much more concerned with detail, ensuring that the team had dealt with all aspects of the situation and that quality was right. Others again spent most of their time keeping the group together. Table 8.5 lists the nine roles identified in Belbin (1993). Belbin and his colleagues observed that the composition of teams was crucial to their success, as members played a range of roles. Winning teams had members who fulfilled a balance of roles that was different from the less successful ones.

Winning teams had an appropriate balance. Losing teams were unbalanced. The box indicates some contrasts.

Table 8.5 Belbin's team roles

Role	*Typical features*
Implementer	Disciplined, reliable, conservative and efficient. Turns ideas into practical actions
Coordinator	Mature, confident, a good chairperson. Clarifies goals, promotes decision-making, delegates well
Shaper	Challenging, dynamic, thrives on pressure. Has the drive and courage to overcome obstacles – likes to win
Plant	Creative, imaginative, unorthodox – the ideas person who solves difficult problems
Resource investigator	Extrovert, enthusiastic, communicative – explores opportunities, develops contacts, a natural networker
Monitor–evaluator	Sober, strategic and discerning. Sees all options, judges accurately – the inspector
Teamworker	Cooperative, mild, perceptive and diplomatic. Listens, builds, averts friction, calms things – sensitive to people and situations
Completer	Painstaking, conscientious, anxious. Searches out errors and omissions. Delivers on time
Specialist	Single-minded, self-starting, dedicated. Provides scarce knowledge and skill

Source: Based on Belbin (1981, 1993)

Belbin on successful and unsuccessful teams

Particularly successful teams were those that had:

- a capable coordinator;
- a strong plant – a creative and clever source of ideas;
- at least one other clever person to act as a stimulus to the plant;
- a monitor–evaluator – someone to find flaws in proposals before it was too late.

Ineffective teams usually had a severe imbalance, such as:

- a coordinator with two dominant shapers – because the coordinator will almost certainly not be allowed to take that role;
- two resource investigators and two plants – because no one listens or turns ideas into action;
- a completer with monitor–evaluators and implementers – probably slow to progress, and stuck in detail.

Belbin and his colleagues did *not* suggest that all teams should have nine people, each with a different preferred team role. Rather, their point was that the composition of the team should reflect the task in hand (Belbin, 1981, p. 77):

> The useful people to have in a team are those who possess strengths or characteristics that serve a need without duplicating those that are already there. Teams are a question of balance; what is needed is not well-balanced individuals but individuals who balance well with one another. In that way human frailties can be underpinned and strengths used to full advantage.

Trainers use the model widely to enable members to evaluate their own preferred roles. They also consider how the balance of roles within a team affects performance. Some managers use it when filling vacancies. For example, a personnel director had recently joined a fairly new organisation, and concluded that it employed very few 'completer–finishers'. Management often started initiatives and programmes but left them unfinished as they switched their attention to something else. She resolved that in recruiting new staff she would try to bring in at least one more 'completer–finisher' to the senior team.

However, there is little evidence that companies deliberately use the Belbin model when forming teams from existing staff. Managers typically form teams on criteria of technical expertise, departmental representation, or who is available. How the team processes will work is a secondary consideration. A team where members are capable and committed to the mission will ignore individual status or ego issues. People will be able and willing to cover roles if one seems to be lacking.

However, whether widely used or not, there are some clear hints that a manager responsible for a team may find the work goes better if they put effort into securing the most suitable mix of members.

NOTEPAD 8.1

Team composition

This activity is intended to encourage you to reflect critically on this section about team composition.

- Select one of the lists of the roles a project team's members should ideally have.
- Evaluate the team you are working in at the moment against these characteristics.
- Which roles are well represented, and which are missing?
- Has that affected the way the team has worked?

Now consider Belbin's model specifically, and make notes on these questions:

- Which of these brief descriptions most closely matches your own preferred role when working within a team?
- Can you identify any of the other roles being taken by other members of teams you work in regularly?
- What happens if some of the roles are missing?
- What are the strengths and weaknesses of Belbin's model for the manager?
- Have you any evidence of managers using it to help them manage project teams? If so, in what way was it used, and with what effect?

Team processes

This element in group performance follows from the difference between content and process. *Content* refers to the task of the project group. This is the substantive deliverable work it must produce – design a product, agree a new organisation structure or set up a web site. When a group is sharing ideas about some aspect of the job, they are dealing with content issues. These are often to do with immediate, tangible questions, such as where to place the machinery, what software package to use, who will be responsible for checking quality?

Process refers to the way the group goes about the task. Content refers to *what* the group does, process refers to *how* the group does it. This is what Hackman called performance strategies. There are many dimensions to the processes in a group. They include the pattern of contributions to the discussion and whether members listen or constantly interrupt. Do members speak in a competitive, aggressive way or is the style one of mutual cooperation? Process covers both the verbal and non-verbal behaviour of members, how they solve problems and how they reach decisions.

Effective project teams have developed effective processes. Members bring, or develop, norms about behaviour that will contribute to the task. They develop ways of dealing with different degrees of commitment. They will have learned how to deal with the task, and with their internal working relationships. Effective teams will have developed the habit (or culture) of encouraging members to review tasks, to reflect on how the team worked on them, and how they could improve the way they work on future tasks. Techniques relevant to this are examined in Chapter 9.

Edgar Schein, team culture and team processes

Edgar Schein (1985) believes that teams that work together develop a distinctive culture, which he defined as the:

> pattern of basic assumptions . . . developed by a . . . group . . . that has worked well enough to be considered . . . as the correct way to perceive, think and feel in relation to . . . problems (p. 9).

Culture develops as group members share enough experiences to form a view of what works, and what does not. This view then shapes how members expect each other to behave: the common assumptions and beliefs can exert a profound influence on how the group performs. One aspect of team culture is the set of norms it develops about how the group should work. This includes:

- *Developing a common language* – a mutually understood terminology.
- *Group boundaries* – who is in, and who is beyond the margin?
- *Power and status* – how these are allocated within the group – by success or rank?
- *Relationships* – how authority and peer relationships should be managed.

Schein believed that these cultural assumptions provide members with a common set of guidelines on how to contribute. The more clearly members work through these issues to develop a common understanding the better the group will perform.

Organisational context

So far the emphasis has been on internal factors. Hackman (1990) also proposed that teams will be more effective if relevant elements of the wider context also support its development. First is the appropriateness of the *reward system*, especially whether this recognises group performance. Does it provide incentives to members to work as a team, or is the emphasis on rewarding individual performance? Some argue that individual pay discourages team work, and suggest instead that rewards should relate to what the team is achieving, and support team performance. A survey by the UK Institute of Personnel Development (IPD, 1996) identified many examples of such schemes in operation. Some were confident that team pay had encouraged closer team-working and cooperative behaviour. Others were sceptical, citing examples where team pay had reduced the motivation of high performers.

Another external matter is whether the *training and coaching system* in the firm provides assistance to help members develop the skills they need to deal with project problems.

Finally he drew attention to the *information system*. Does this provide the information the group needs to do the work, by indicating current perfomance in good time, enabling them to devise appropriate strategies?

The project manager will be unable to do much directly about these contextual factors. However, they are examples of the issues which they may need to include on their agenda when seeking to influence senior management, as discussed in Chapter 12.

CASE STUDY

The Credit Analysis Team

The head of a branch within a Government agency created the Credit Analysis Team to prepare a series of reports on aspects of credit policy. The project was politically important, and the sponsor expected that the team's final report could influence policy recommendations of the Credit Policy Working Group. (This was a senior political group to which the team would report.) The team members were mainly from the agency itself, appointed to work part-time on the project for about six months. They were highly competent professionals, expert in their respective fields. The team leader was Cynthia, a more junior member of the agency, who worked full-time on the project.

The output was to be a series of six integrated reports, the final one being a synthesis of the issues, and unbiased recommendations. The head of the branch believed strongly in using teams as a way of working, and they did most tasks within the branch. How any team operated was up to the team and its leader. In this case:

> Cynthia decided not to use the group as a group to develop strategies for accomplishing the work, to coordinate members' activities or to manage relations between the team and the Credit Policy Working Group. Instead she personally developed the grand design of the reports and then met individually with team members to assign them portions of the report to write. She also personally coordinated the efforts of those who wrote the reports, those who reviewed them, those who physically produced them, and those who received them . . . generally individual team members worked independently under Cynthia's direct supervision . . . The team structure was as clear an example of a hub-and-spokes model as one is likely to find' (pp. 136–7).

The team's preliminary report was well received by the Working Group. Their final report was over a month late, and did not influence policy because the political group had by then made the major decisions. The report also met internal agency quality standards. Many team members expressed dissatisfaction with their experience of working on the team. Complaints included excessive attempts by Cynthia to control members, and disagreements with Cynthia over the content of the reports. Cynthia resigned shortly before the final report was produced, noting that her morale had 'reached an all-time low' (p. 130).

Source: Based on Hackman (1990), pp. 126–45

Case study questions

1 Was the Credit Analysis Team, on balance, an effective team?

2 Evaluate Cynthia's decision to use a hub-and-spokes structure, rather than a more integrated team approach, for this project. Was it necessarily an unwise decision?

3 Having made that decision, what could she have done to reduce the risks?

4 Suppose that her successor decides to use teams more fully – what plans should he or she make, based on the ideas from this chapter?

Summary

This chapter has introduced some theories about the development of teams, and the factors that help them to succeed or to fail. Effective teams depend on sufficient effort, relevant knowledge and skills, and the use of suitable work processes. These are each affected by factors internal to the team, namely the motivating quality of the project tasks, the composition of the team and a culture which encourages reflection and learning about team processes.

The key points from this chapter are:

- Creating a team does not in itself ensure that the benefits of team-working are achieved.
- There are at least three measures of team effectiveness – performance of the task, members' experience, and developing transferable skills.
- Hackman's model links team effectiveness to effort, skill and suitable team processes.
- These are affected by internal team factors and wider organisational factors.

Chapter questions

1 Why would a single measure of team performance not necessarily be enough?

2 Describe and illustrate the three hurdles in Hackman's model of team effectiveness.

3 What Belbin roles would you want to be represented in your ideal team?

4 What combinations of roles would you expect to find in a less effective team?

5 If wider organisational factors affect team performance as Hackman predicts, what does that imply for the role of the project manager?

6 Give at least two examples from your experience of events which seem to support, and two which contradict, elements of the theories presented here.

Further reading

Belbin, R.M. (1993) *Team Roles at Work*. Oxford: Butterworth-Heinemann. A readable book that reports the original research on which the now widely used model of team roles is based.

Hackman, J.R. (1990) *Groups that Work (and Those That Don't)*. San Francisco: Jossey-Bass. Empirical study of 27 teams of many different types, including project teams. Types studied include top management teams, performing teams and human service teams. Linked by the theoretical model described in this chapter.

References

Boddy, D. (2001) *Management: An Introduction*. Harlow: Financial Times Prentice Hall.

Belbin, R.M. (1981) *Management Teams: Why They Succeed or Fail*. Oxford: Butterworth-Heinemann.

Belbin, R.M. (1993) *Team Roles at Work*. Oxford: Butterworth-Heinemann.

Hackman, J.R. (1990) *Groups that Work (and Those That Don't)*. San Francisco: Jossey-Bass.

Hackman, J.R. and Oldham, G.R. (1975) 'Development of the Job Diagnostic Survey'. *Journal of Applied Psychology*, 60, 159–70.

Hackman, J.R. and Oldham, G.R. (1980) *Work Redesign*. Reading, MA: Addison-Wesley.

Herzberg, F. (1959) *The Motivation to Work*. New York: John Wiley.

Huczynski, A.A. (1996) *Influencing Within Organizations*. Hemel Hempstead: Prentice Hall.

Huczynski, A.A. and Buchanan, D. (2001) *Organizational Behaviour: An Introductory Text*. Harlow: Financial Times/Prentice Hall.

IPD (1996) *The IPD Guide on Team Rewards*. London: Institute of Personnel and Development.

Maslow, A.H. (1943) 'A theory of human motivation', *Psychological Review*, 50, 370–96.

McGregor, D. (1960) *The Human Side of Enterprise*. New York: McGraw-Hill.

Schein, E.H. (1985) *Organizational Culture and Leadership*. San Francisco: Jossey-Bass.

Uhl-Bien, M. and Graen, G.B. (1998) 'Individual self-management: analysis of professionals' self-managing activities in functional and cross-functional teams', *Academy of Management Journal*, 41, 340–50.

Wickens, P.D. (1995) *The Ascendant Organisation*. Basingstoke: Macmillan.

9 Developing the project team

Introduction

Some teams work to very high standards, achieve more than people expected them to, and are conspicuously successful. Others work without much enthusiasm or commitment, waste their members' time and fail to achieve anything worthwhile. The case study in Chapter 7 describing the efforts to design a new management information system is an example of a team that failed, whereas that described in the case study at the end of this chapter is an example of a successful team. These differences in performance are not due to chance or to forces of nature: they reflect how people, including the members themselves, have managed the team.

Putting people together as a team does not in itself ensure that it either meets business goals or satisfies members. Creating a team (or 'group', 'task force' or 'working party') is only the start; members then need to learn how to work together to meet their objectives. This chapter provides some ideas to help them do that.

The chapter begins with ideas about the stages of team development, a theory about how teams evolve. It then outlines some of the specific problems which teams need to overcome if they are to complete the task and develop members' skills. These include setting objectives, using resources effectively by using high-performance methods, and monitoring the teams' own processes in order to improve and learn.

Objectives

After reading this chapter you should be able to:

- outline a theory about the stages of a team's development;
- use a technique to clarify a team's objectives;
- outline a set of practices that should help motivate a well-composed team;
- recognise some team-working processes that help group performance;
- understand why observation is essential to team performance;
- use a technique for observing how a team works, and recommend areas of improvement.

How teams develop

Before a team performs well it needs to go through stages of growth. Some never perform well. Tuckman and Jensen (1977) developed a theory that groups potentially pass through five stages of growth and development (see Figure 9.1).

Teams need the chance to grow and to develop trust amongst the members, which is not likely to exist when a team first comes together. As members work together people have the chance to learn about each other and to develop productive ways of working collaboratively. That depends, however, on passing successfully through the early stages of team development.

Forming

This is the stage at which members choose, or are told, to join a team. Managers may select them for their functional and technical expertise or for some other skill they bring. They come together and begin to find out who the other members are, exchanging fairly superficial information about themselves, and beginning to offer

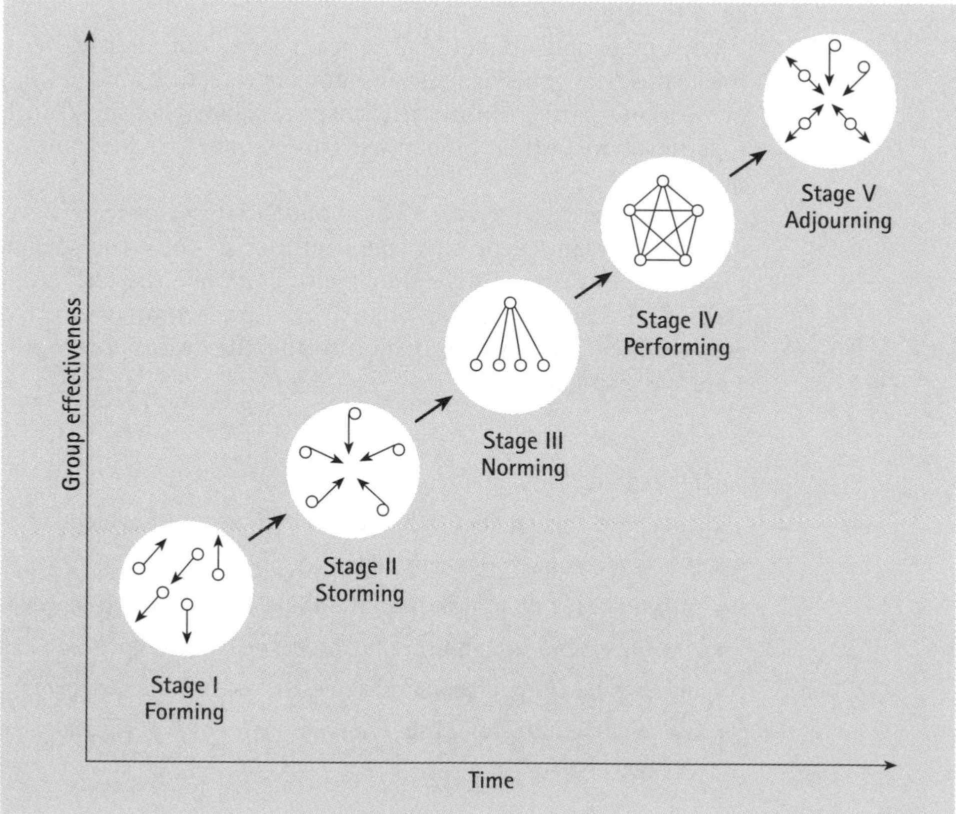

Figure 9.1 Idealised stages of group development

ideas about what the group should do. People are trying to make an impression on the group, and to establish their identity with the other members. At this stage, especially if they are inexperienced at teamwork, they may have few ideas about the processes the team should use to complete the task. A project manager may be able to help the process by initiating some exploratory discussions here about how members expect or want the team to work, or about previous experiences of team working from which this team can learn.

Storming

Conflicts may occur at this stage, which can be an uncomfortable one for members. As the group gets down to the actual work, members begin to express differences of interest that they withheld or did not recognise at the forming stage. People realise that others want different things from the group, or have other priorities – and perhaps hidden agendas. Members may express contrasting views on how the group should work, with some expecting the formal leader to give clear directions, while others perhaps expect a more participative approach. Some may experience conflicts between the time they are spending with the group, and other calls on their time. As they work, differences in the values and norms which people have brought to the team become clear.

Some groups never satisfactorily pass this stage, especially if they accommodate or repress differences, rather than acknowledging and discussing them openly. Movement to the next stage of development only happens when one or more team members do or say something that leads the group to the next stage. If the group does not surface and confront disagreements it will probably remain at the forming or storming stage. It will probably do no significant work, and fall further behind more successful teams. The project manager (or other skilled members) play a critical role here, in helping the team to face these difficulties, and so begin to move to the next stage.

Norming

Here the members are beginning to accommodate differences constructively, and establish adequate ways of working together. They develop a set of shared norms – expected modes of behaviour – about how they should interact with each other, how they should approach the task, how they should deal with differences. People create or accept roles so that responsibilities are clear – either when the leader formally establishes them, or as members accept or create them during early meetings. Members may establish a common language to guide the group and allow members to work together effectively.

Performing

Here the group is working well, gets on with the job to the required standard and achieves its objectives. Not all groups get this far, especially if they failed to pass the storming phase.

Adjourning

The group completes its task and disbands. Members may reflect on how the group performed, and identify lessons for future tasks. Some groups disband because they are clearly not able to do the job, and agree to stop meeting.

A project group which survives will go through these stages many times in the course of its life. As new members join, as others leave, as circumstances or the task change, new tensions arise which take the group back to an earlier stage. A new member implies that the team needs to revisit, however briefly, the forming and norming stages. This ensures the new member is brought psychologically into the team, and understands how they are expected to behave. A change in task or a conflict over priorities can take a group back to the storming stage, from which it needs to work forward again. The process will be more like that in Figure 9.2 than the linear progression implied by the original theory.

This model is a valuable reminder of the broadest stages through which a team progresses, and the stage a particular team has reached. That affects how well it can contribute to its purpose of supporting the project management process. If we combine the key project activities outlined in Chapter 5 with Hackman's model

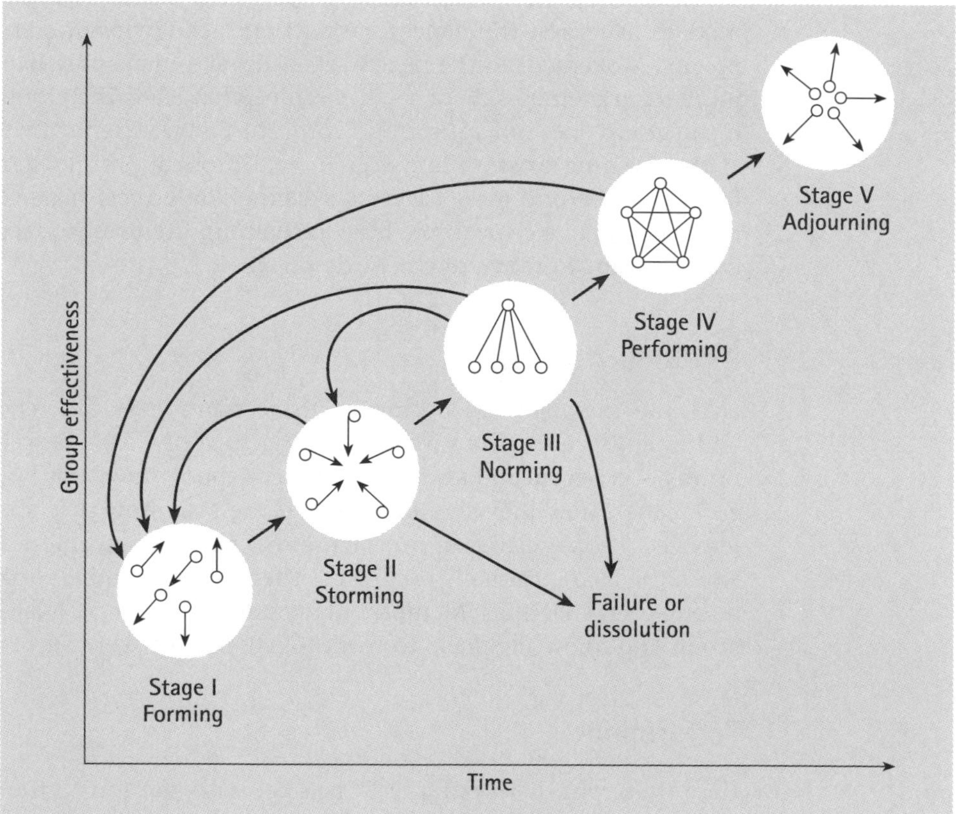

Figure 9.2 Stages of group development in practice

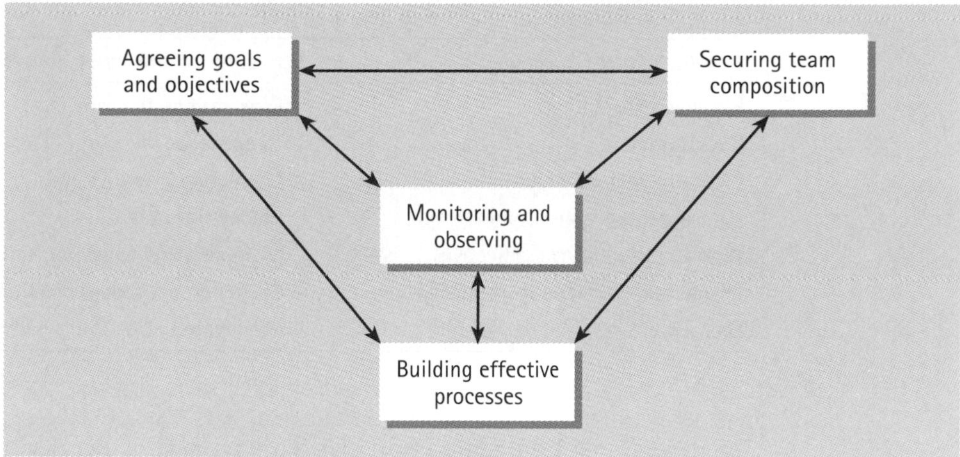

Figure 9.3 Key dimensions of group performance

of team effectiveness, we can suggest Figure 9.3 as a way of analysing a team's contribution. It asks to what extent it is agreeing goals and objectives, securing and motivating the right members and using effective working methods. At the centre of these is the critical process of monitoring or observing how the team performs on these dimensions, in order to take corrective action if necessary. Figure 9.3 shows these dimensions, while the following sections offer some practical suggestions to project managers on how to deal with each of them.

NOTEPAD 9.1

Monitoring the stages of a team's development

This exercise is intended to help you use the stages theory by applying it to a team of which you have been a member (whether socially or at work).

- Identify the team you are using, and recall its main function.
- Which stages did it pass through? What behaviours indicated the stage it had reached at different times?
- What did people do or say that helped the group move to the next stage?
- Were there occasions when it went back to a stage it had passed earlier?
- Does the evidence support or contradict the Tuckman and Jensen model?

Clarifying objectives

A common problem which teams face is that of clarifying and agreeing their objectives. Chapter 5 showed that this is a major task for project managers. Teams are unlikely to work well towards achieving their common purpose unless

Table 9.1 Benefits of clarifying team objectives

Benefits of clear objectives	*Hazards of unclear objectives*
Realistic expectations	Expectations that are too high or too low
Clear targets	Targets that are vague
Clear problem definition	Conflicting priorities
High acceptance and commitment	Hidden agendas
Work achieves several objectives	Multiple goals appearing to be inconsistent
People take initiative to meet objectives	Confusion and poor commitment
Focused effort	Misdirected effort

members spend time and effort clarifying what it is. Because the project team is probably drawn from people with different backgrounds, they will have different expectations of what the project is intended to achieve. Take time in the early stages to ensure common understanding of the remit.

They need to express the objectives in clear and measurable performance goals. The two go together – balancing the broad, longer-term vision that sets the tone and aspiration levels with more immediately achievable goals. Clear purposes and goals help to focus the energy of the group on activities that support their achievement. They also help communication between members, because people can interpret and understand their contributions better if they share the same aims. Clear and measurable goals can themselves have a positive effect on the effort which team members make. This works even better if the team uses small wins to show progress.

Table 9.1 summarises the advantages of clear objectives, and the disadvantages of unclear ones.

The potential benefits of spending time on objectives are evident, although some find the task frustrating. They want to get into action, not spend time debating the task. The more open and uncertain the task, the greater the pay-off from spending the time. Effective teams also review and perhaps revise their objectives several times during the project, as they gather new information about what is feasible.

The task can be organised by following the five steps shown in Figure 9.4.

Gather ideas

Most problems benefit from getting ideas from several points of view, especially when the project is novel and uncertain. A task that is novel to one manager may be familiar to another. Asking around for ideas and comments usually uncovers relevant experience about what is achievable. It reduces the uncertainty in the project manager's mind by providing information and ideas – about what others have done, what might be achievable, what areas to avoid, etc.

By mentioning the possibilities of the project to interested parties, to the stakeholders, their ideas can be sought about what is proposed, and whether it is sound.

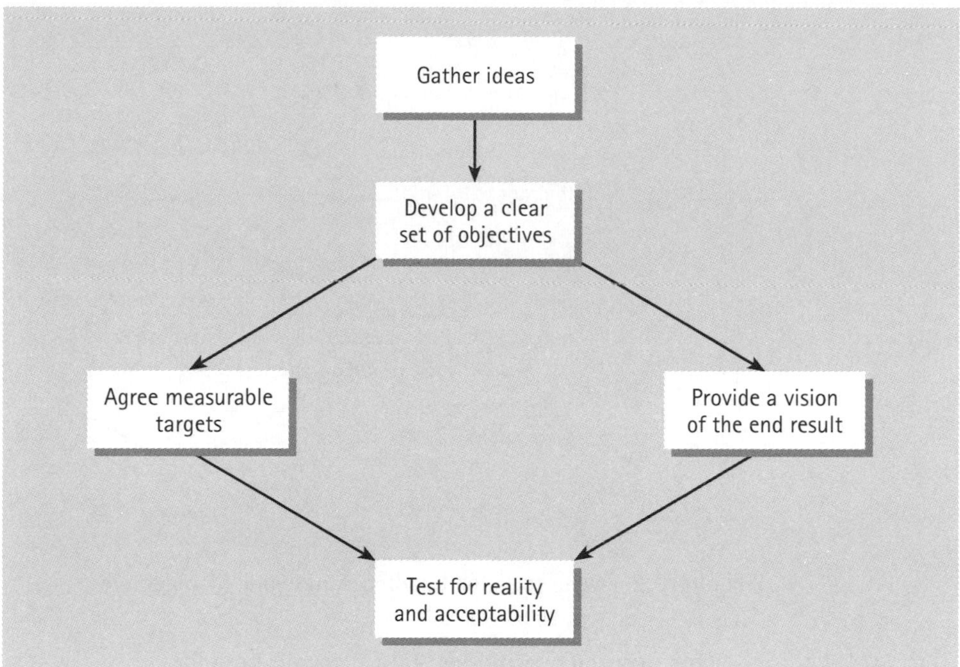

Figure 9.4 Steps in setting objectives

They can be asked what it might achieve in their area and how it could relate to their objectives.

Take care to ensure that expectations are not raised too high – emphasise the provisional nature of the discussion, and that the project is still in its early days. As ideas firm up, it may be appropriate to have a more formal discussion with key groups to begin setting a clear set of objectives for the project.

Develop a network of objectives

A technique for doing this is to use a 'why/how network'. This makes it easy to see how several objectives fit together and support each other. Start by writing the name of the project in the middle of a large piece of paper, and then ask 'why?'. Answer by one or more sentences beginning with the phrase 'in order to . . .', and write these answers above the project task. For each of these answers, repeat the process of asking 'why?', and answering with 'in order to . . .', writing your answers on the sheet. Repeat this several times, until it makes sense to stop – usually when the objectives become very broad and long-term. Figure 9.5 shows the method.

The diagram will need to be worked over several times to ensure all the main benefits are included, and that the right links are drawn between them. The method can be used with other people working on the project, as this may help to make the diagram clearer.

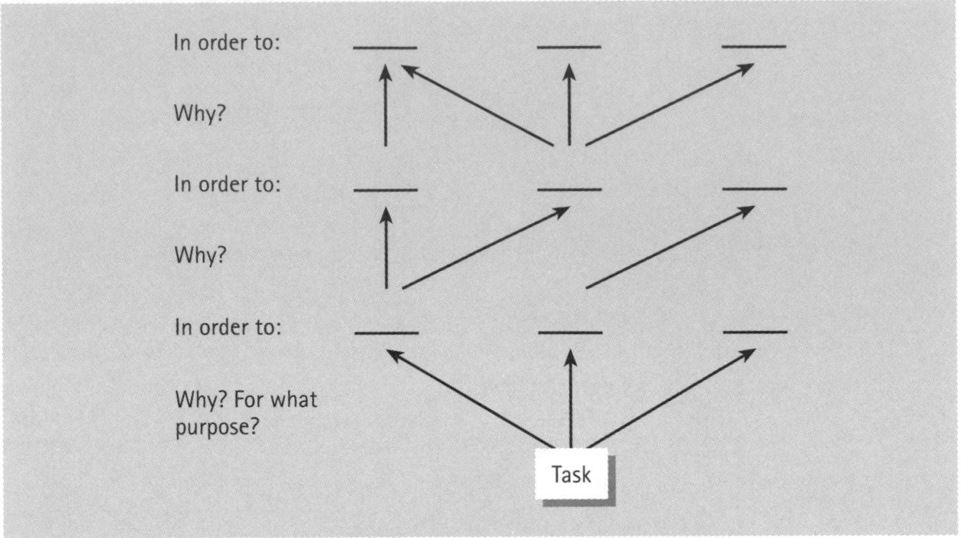

Figure 9.5 Framework for building a network of objectives

This approach provides the following benefits:

- It shows how different objectives can be met – they may be complementary, rather than competitive.
- It demonstrates that short-term objectives (those near the bottom of the sheet) can help to achieve longer-term ones (those nearer the top).
- It tests whether the project objectives support wider organisational objectives.
- It gains commitment by showing how the project can meet several interests.

The diagram can be used in that form as a guide, or rewritten into a more conventional form, listing the short-term objectives of the project, and then the longer-term ones to which it will contribute.

Set measurable targets

It makes sense to ensure that reasonably measurable or observable targets are set. Phrases such as 'reduce waste' or 'improve decision-making' are not precise enough, and are useless as a guide to progress. People are reluctant to make specific commitments in this area. That is understandable if a very novel project is being undertaken in a volatile business; in those circumstances it will be hard to know what is achievable, and there are risks in going public with an objective that could make failure visible. A natural urge to get into action will also cut down the time people are willing to spend. Setting any sort of objective is difficult enough – having to set measurable targets for them looks like an added burden.

The project manager must persist on this point. Targets will let him or her provide clear and unambiguous information on progress or the lack of it, information which will be vital to credibility with senior management. Clear evidence of measurable progress can bring its own rewards to the manager. Equally, clear evidence of delay or difficulty can be used to make the case for additional resources, or for other supportive action by top management. It can also help to motivate a team or group of staff if they see results being unambiguously achieved.

Examples of quantifiable targets:

- Deal with 95 per cent of claims within three days.
- Reduce departmental costs by 5 per cent within six months.
- Increase the proportion of repeat business to 60 per cent by 2003.

It is not always possible to quantify all the benefits, and some very important ones may be of this less tangible variety. These should be listed as well.

Examples of unquantifiable targets:

- Avoiding duplication of effort.
- Maintaining a reputation for innovative service.
- Improve staff commitment to the organisation.

Having a list of quantitative and qualitative targets dramatically reduces uncertainty on the project, by giving people something to aim for, and a measure with which to assess their progress.

Provide a vision of the end result

If the project is going to introduce significant changes, the project manager needs to help people to have a clear picture of what the changes will mean. Specific statements and examples are more useful than general impressions, and pictures or diagrams are more useful than words. Aim to give as clear a picture as possible of how the new situation will look to the people affected by it, or using it in some way.

For example, if the project concerns the introduction of a computer-based system, staff will probably want to know:

- what the screen will look like;
- what the terminal will look like;
- how the work area will be laid out;
- where information will come from, and in what form;
- where papers will be filed;
- how many others in the office will have the system;
- whether they will be linked together.

Most of these can be shown in simple diagrams or pictures, and will give those concerned a much better picture of what the system could look like.

The same principle can be used in more intangible organisational and business development projects. The box reports how The Royal Bank of Scotland initiated a radical change in their business in the early 1990s, and the role played by a shared vision.

Project Columbus: shared vision

Project Columbus' mission was clear – to Build the Best Retail Bank in Britain. This simple message was repeated in posters and mouse mats throughout the Programme Offices. The phrase was used in countless proposal documents and stated regularly in project meetings:

> *'If we want to build the Best Bank in Britain, then our staff have to have the best system in the market.'*
>
> *'It is the opinion of the study group that this proposal will be a significant step forward in our target of building the Best Bank in Britain.'*

This created a shared vision amongst the many project teams made up of people from many different departments of the Bank, and from external organisations. It helped to gel disparate staff by focussing them towards a common goal.

It did not matter that no specific measures were ever stated for what 'best' really meant, or that the goal was never officially or formally reached. What mattered was that staff had something to strive for, and to guide them in their day-to-day activities.

Source: Boddy *et al.* (2002)

If people have a clear picture of the goal, they will be able to come up with their own ideas as the project proceeds. This improves project decisions, as well as commitment and ownership.

What makes a good set of objectives? They should:

- Use clear and explicit words and phrases.
- State targets, and be easy to imagine.
- Make a clear contribution to wider organisational objectives.
- Be a realistic result of this project.
- Be seen as feasible and attainable.
- Be accepted by stakeholders and interested parties.

Test for reality and acceptability

Throughout this difficult process, keep testing ideas both for reality and acceptability. The enthusiasm of those closest to the project has to be tempered by wider considerations in the business – competition from other projects, changes in business priorities, difficulties that turn out to be larger than expected.

Objectives only energise commitment if people accept them. In the early stages of a project, not all the interested parties will have come on the scene, and may not even be aware that the change is being planned. The danger here is that if a group has worked in relative isolation on the objectives, they may not be acceptable to others. Early exposure to a wide range of interests, with the opportunity to influence them, will usually pay off.

NOTEPAD 9.2

A method for clarifying objectives

The value of this approach to setting objectives only becomes clear from trying it on a real project. To do so take a recent or current project with which you are familiar.

- How clear are you about the objectives of the change?
- Use the method described above to work out how you think the objectives of the project could have been expressed.
- Ideally, work through the approach with someone else, to see where and how you differ.
- More broadly, do you agree with the view expressed above that teams often spend too little time on objectives? If so, why do you think this is?

Securing and motivating the right members

A continuing issue throughout a project is to secure the right people to contribute to the work, and then to retain their enthusiasm and commitment.

Securing team members

Chapter 8 presented Meredith Belbin's theory that a team's performance is affected by the balance of preferred roles present amongst the members. The difficulty is that the project manager may not have the luxury of choice. The team may already be in place; there may be existing staff who cannot be moved; a department's nomination may be unchangeable. As well as skills, members also need the time and commitment to do the work. Project managers, if they have a say in the matter, can face a dilemma between those with the skill and those with commitment. A similar dilemma is between someone less skilled in the content or subject matter of the project, but makes up for that in their ability to exercise process skills.

Another consideration is the size of the group. This arises in discussing whether to include some of the key stakeholders in the team especially from outside the organisation, such as banks, customers or suppliers. It depends on the scale of the project how best to relate the range of stakeholders to the project team – too many makes the team unwieldy. Groups of more than about 12 people find it difficult to operate as a coherent team. It becomes harder for them to agree on a common purpose. The logistical problems of finding a place and time to work together become steadily greater as numbers increase. So most teams have between two and 10 people, with between four and eight probably being the most common range. If larger groups are formed, they are more likely to divide themselves into sub-groups.

Numbers can be kept down by rotating membership, with people moving in and out of the team as relevant. Another possibility is to invite them to join the broader steering group. The danger then is that if the steering group has to satisfy too many interests it will also work too slowly.

A fundamental team management skill is therefore that of negotiating, and reconfirming, enough time for the team from their departments. This is essential, as otherwise people will divert their energy to problems in their department rather than in the project. Awkward problems will be ignored, and will then get worse. This area of securing the right membership depends on 'managing across' and 'managing up', as described in Chapters 10 and 12 respectively.

Motivating team members

Chapter 8 argued that a major influence on motivation would be the nature of the work being done. The project manager's task will only become feasible if team members feel they are working on a task which is in their interests – whatever these are. Some may value the intrinsic aspects of the work, while others place more emphasis on tangible extrinsic rewards. If that condition is met, then progress can be further enhanced by the practices of taking staff concerns seriously, generating excitement and publicising success.

Take staff concerns seriously

Changes or uncertainty caused by wider changes in policy, or changes elsewhere in the organisation, sap the morale of project staff, and the project manager needs to be active in keeping commitment high. One manager realised his team of engineers were frustrated by delays to a project they were keen to work on, which meant they were having to do less challenging jobs. They were likely to leave if nothing was done, so their manager negotiated a separate set of tasks for them, to maintain their interest.

If problems arise, show that they are being taken seriously, take visible action to try and solve them – and let everyone know they have been solved:

> *'The director has visited the UK three times in the year, which serves to demonstrate to the local staff his obvious interest, and the fact that their services are required and are valued.'*

Acceptance is easier to obtain if the people involved have something to gain. One manager running a project that needed the support of other managers took care to identify deliverables that were of personal significance to each of them. He ensured each was dominant in the project at the time when that manager's support was most required.

Generate excitement

Try to get the project team's efforts off to a strong start. If they are from distant parts of the company, working on a high-profile project, arrange a special event with a top management presence, to generate a sense of excitement and indicate top management commitment. Boddy and Buchanan (1992) reported the case of a development group that had experienced several setbacks in the projects it had worked on, and morale was low. Changes in corporate policy and structure meant that new opportunities were appearing, and it was vital to rekindle the development group's enthusiasm:

> The new director travelled to the plant with the local manager, so that the new strategies could be sold to the local engineers. Obviously there was initially a feeling of 'here we go again, another change'. However, as the meeting progressed with the group as a candid two-way discussion, attitudes changed. It was obvious that the new director was willing to accept inputs from the staff, and he was displaying a lot of trust in them by agreeing to give his most important development project to the UK group. Team work was the new message.
>
> New tasks have been agreed for the engineers, and these have now been initiated. Both engineers have eagerly produced plans and schedules for completion of their responsibilities on this task. The fact that both are now working long hours at their own instigation suggests that the corner has been turned, and that we are now getting 100 per cent commitment.

The same idea can be applied to smaller projects – some activity, presentation, brainstorming session, to mark the start of work, and to raise the profile of the project with team members and their departments.

Publicise success

Remind the team of their successes, and make sure they are widely publicised. Problems and difficulties always attract attention, and are quickly talked about around the organisation. Balance that by ensuring people know about the successes, the work done, the progress made – and about the team responsible. Boddy *et al.* (2002) reported how The Royal Bank of Scotland used the idea of 'Quick Wins'.

> People respond to . . . 'Quick Wins', (which) can take many forms – such as something which generate new income, cuts a cost, or improves conditions for a visible unit. This has a number of benefits:
>
> - Staff gain a sense of achievement.
> - Management can claim a success for the programme.
> - Board members see a return on their investment.
>
> If they can build enough Quick Wins of real value into the (project), management can claim that the (change) is self-funding. This sends a powerful message to the stakeholders about the overall value of the (change), and severely weakens objectors. In the early days of Project Columbus, the team identified a number of Quick Wins including:
>
> - reducing the cost of cash stocks in branches through more frequent movements;
> - removing charges which cost more to administer than they earned;
> - adding charges for services whose costs were not covered;
> - identifying and stopping inefficient work processes.

A Director gave the following responses to questions about Quick Wins:

> *'Like every other area of the Bank, the project has been set tough commercial targets. It must deliver radical improvements in the performance of Branch Banking Division (BBD) while effectively being self-financing. This means that the ongoing cost of the project has to be met from measurable improvements in BBD's bottom line. Quick Wins are initiatives which can be introduced rapidly and require limited investment in technology, people or buildings. Next year the Quick Wins programme is intended not just to meet the cost of Columbus but to deliver benefits worth over £30 million' (p. 246).*

Effective working methods

Groups and teams need to decide a common approach to how they will work together to accomplish their common purpose. This includes some mechanical but vital aspects of planning meetings, communication patterns, dealing with disagreements.

Common approach

A primary outcome of an effective 'norming' stage is that team members agree both the administrative and social aspects of working together. This includes deciding who does which jobs, what skills members need to develop, and how the group should make and modify decisions. In other words, the group needs to agree the work required and how it will fit together. It needs to decide how to integrate the skills of the group and use them cooperatively to advance performance.

The common approach includes supporting and integrating new or reticent members into the team. It also includes practices of remembering and summarising group agreements and discussions. Working together on these tasks helps to promote the mutual trust and constructive conflict necessary to team success. Groups need to spend as much time on developing a common approach as they do on developing a shared purpose.

Group problem-solving processes

Mike Robson (1993) offers more detail on the skills which group members need to develop as a common approach to getting things done. His model combines both analytical and creative methods, and team members often need both. The elements he suggests are:

- **Brainstorming** – a well known but often badly used technique to generate many ideas in a short time, and to ensure that everyone contributes.
- **Define the problem clearly** – people often pay too little attention to defining the real problem. Problem statements may be thinly disguised solutions; or may tackle the wrong issue because of the assumptions made. He recommends spending time to get at the root cause, by rigorously asking exactly what issue would be solved by dealing with the stated problem.

- **Multiple causes and solutions** – analyse the problem by methods that help to identify a wide range of possible causes and solutions. Successful groups do not accept the obvious causes, but think their way around the problem thoroughly. One technique here is to have six headings – people, environment, methods, plant, equipment and materials – and assess how each of these (or other items) can be possible causes of the difficulty.
- **Collect data** – facts not opinion, and gather in a single document.
- **Interpret the data** – use some organised tools for looking at the data and exploring what it means, e.g. Pareto charts, histograms. These allow data to be organised in descending order of priority, so indicating where to concentrate effort.
- **Find or generate possible solutions** – using a fishbone diagram to generate ideas via brainstorming or techniques like force field analysis.
- **Agree the best solutions** – ensuring that the criteria for selection are specified.
- **Cost-benefit analysis** – to establish what costs will be incurred, and what benefits obtained.
- **Implement solutions** – often the most difficult part of the whole exercise.
- **Monitor and evaluate** – to check on progress and to learn lessons for the future.

Source: Robson (1993)

Plan meetings

Hold regular meetings, say weekly, at which all interested parties are present. These can be used for strategy and planning, but also to keep everyone up-to-date with the progress of each other's work. One company has daily meetings on some fast-moving projects, limited to 15 minutes. Experience has shown them that if they are kept short, people do not see them as a chore, turn up, stay on the subject and enhance productivity.

Team members need to control their meetings effectively. That involves ensuring it is conducted in way that suits the purpose of the task, without participants feeling they are being manipulated. Here are some observations that may help achieve this:

- People are easier to persuade when they are feeling good about being in a meeting.
- Ask members at the beginning if there are items they would like you to add to the agenda.
- Fast and regular communications are vital to commitment, especially in projects linking several parts of the organisation.
- Keep sub-groups informed of each others' progress.
- Ensure minutes of meetings are prepared quickly – preferably the same day – and circulated immediately.
- Minutes should clearly show what action steps were agreed, and who was to be responsible.

Table 9.2 contains some points about effective and ineffective meetings.

Table 9.2 Five factors affecting the success of meetings

Meetings are more likely to succeed if:	*Meetings are more likely to fail if:*
• they are scheduled well in advance	• are fixed at short notice (absentees)
• have an agenda, with relevant papers distributed in advance	• have no agenda or papers (no preparation, lack of focus, discussion longer)
• have a starting and finishing time	• are of indefinite length (discussion drifts as people raise irrelevant issues or repeat themselves)
• follow prearranged time limits on each item	• time is lost, and important items not dealt with (delay, and require a further meeting)
• decisions recorded and circulated within 24 hours	• decisions lack clarity (misunderstanding what was agreed, delay, reopening issues)

Pattern and content of communication

Group members depend on information and ideas from others to help them perform the group task. Figure 9.6 shows five distinct patterns of communication.

In the chain pattern, each person only passes information to the next member, while in the circle or star patterns information flows much more freely amongst the

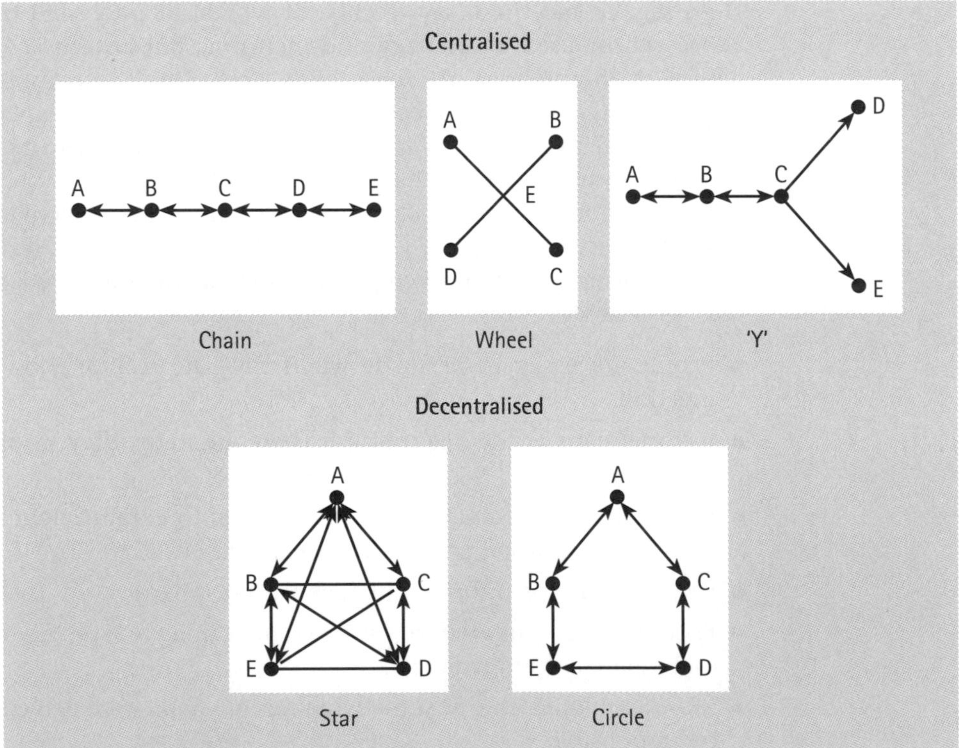

Figure 9.6 Alternative patterns of communication

members. Different patterns are better suited to certain types of task. Centralised networks seem to work best if the tasks are simple and routine. Decentralised patterns are more effective in complex and uncertain tasks. Allowing information and ideas to flow freely around the group produces better results in that kind of task.

Another step in observation is to identify the communication processes. This provides information about communication events (who speaks to whom), and allows the observer to draw some inferences about the structure of the group. It shows if the group has a centralised communication structure, or a decentralised one.

Communication also concerns the kind of contribution which people make, and whether this helps the group to manage the task. To study and learn how people behave in groups, we need a precise and reliable way to describe events. There are many such models and you can develop one depending on the particular focus of interest. Table 9.3 illustrates one list of behaviours. The point is that if, for example, a group spends a lot of time proposing ideas and disagreeing with them, it will not progress far. A more effective group will spend more time proposing and building, which of course implies developing better listening skills.

Face up to disagreements

It is dangerous to ignore disagreements. One man was developing a performance reporting system, assisted by a steering group of three senior managers. They all had their own idea of what the report should be like:

> *'In order to overcome this I took the initiative and, working to the brief, designed a set of reports and a system specification that I put forward at the next Steering Group meeting. The three managers pushed for their own measures, but the positional and personal power of the Development Director overcame their resistance and brought agreement.*

Table 9.3 Categories of communication within a group

Category	*Explanation*
Proposing	Behaviour which puts forwards a new suggestion, idea or course of action
Supporting	Behaviour which declares agreement or support for an individual or their idea
Building	Behaviour which develops or extends an idea or suggestion from someone else
Disagreeing	Behaviour which states a criticism of another person's statement
Giving information	Behaviour that gives or clarifies facts, ideas or opinions
Seeking information	Behaviour which asks for facts, ideas or opinions from others

'On subsequent meetings, when challenged about the approach, I continually referred back to this meeting, at which they had agreed to the Development Director's proposals. In other words, I used the combination of prior agreement and proxy positional power to overcome the positional power base of the senior managers.'

Provide physical support

Make sure the team's physical working environment supports them. Provide an office where they can meet easily, in good working surroundings. This also gives a tangible signal that the project is being taken seriously by management, as well as providing a convenient place to leave messages or collect information. Modern communication methods help overcome the problems of dispersed project teams, but do not replace the benefits of personal contact. If the team is able to use groupware or video-conferencing systems, so much the better. But they will have more value if they are additional to at least some face-to-face meetings, rather than in place of them.

Monitoring progress – observing the team

The project manager needs to assess how well a team is performing during a project, so that they can take corrective action. There are many guides to help them do this. The following notepad uses a model from the previous chapter to give the project manager an interim assessment of how well the team is working. Anyone can develop their ability to observe groups by concentrating on this aspect rather than on the content of the immediate task. They work slightly apart from the team for a short time and keep a careful record of what members say or do. They also note how other members react, and how that affects the performance of the team.

With practice, and of course in the reality of the workplace, skilled members of a team are able to observe what is happening at the same time as they work on the task itself. They can do this more easily and powerfully if they focus their observations on certain behaviour categories. These vary with the purpose of the observation.

There are many other diagnostic instruments that can help those observing a group to understand what is happening. At the very least, members can reflect on these questions at the end of a task:

- What did people do or say which helped or hindered the group's performance?
- What went well during that task that we should try to repeat?
- What did not go well, which we could improve?

Figure 9.7 represents a simple group rating scale that team members can use to assess how well the team is performing, based on the ideas about team development presented earlier. It is a way of summarising both individual and collective views about the team's current position. They can then see where it needs to focus effort to improve its own working methods.

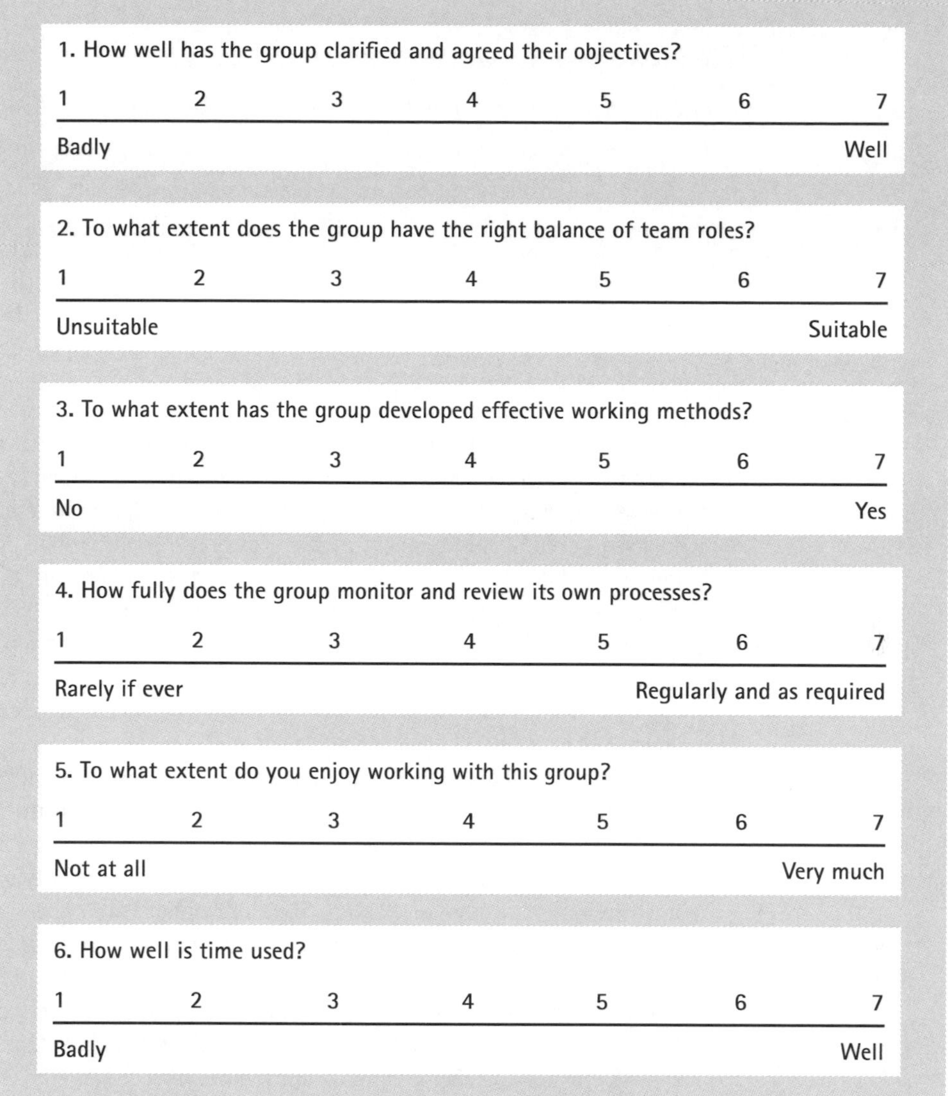

1. How well has the group clarified and agreed their objectives?

1	2	3	4	5	6	7
Badly						Well

2. To what extent does the group have the right balance of team roles?

1	2	3	4	5	6	7
Unsuitable						Suitable

3. To what extent has the group developed effective working methods?

1	2	3	4	5	6	7
No						Yes

4. How fully does the group monitor and review its own processes?

1	2	3	4	5	6	7
Rarely if ever						Regularly and as required

5. To what extent do you enjoy working with this group?

1	2	3	4	5	6	7
Not at all						Very much

6. How well is time used?

1	2	3	4	5	6	7
Badly						Well

Figure 9.7 Rating scales for reviewing group performance

Manage external relations

This section has concentrated on things which project managers can do within the team to enhance performance. Team performance is also affected by conditions surrounding the team, and these also need attention. This includes ensuring that wider factors support the commitment of the team, and that there are good reporting links to senior management. These and related issues are dealt with in Chapters 10 and 12, respectively.

NOTEPAD 9.3

Reviewing a group's progress

- Use the questions in Figure 9.7 to assess the way a project group is working.
- Circle the number which best reflects your opinion of the position.
- If possible, ask other members to do the same, and compare your results.
- You should then have a better common understanding of where to focus effort.

CASE STUDY

The evolution of a project team

A local authority created a project team to select and implement a computer-based Housing Management System for a local authority. The Chief Executive appointed the Assistant Head of the Information Technology (IT) Department as project leader, who then asked some members of the Housing Department to join the team. The Director of the Housing Department allocated some project duties to his staff without reference to the project leader. The Housing Department believed the IT Department was invading their territory. Both incidents caused relationship problems until managers clarified roles and expectations. To help get the group's commitment the project leader explained the plan to the team. They discussed and agreed it in principle.

The group members pointed out that they could not work on the project as well as on their normal duties. They believed that they would be distracted if they worked in their normal open-plan offices alongside other Housing Department staff. The Chief Executive agreed to a limited amount of time off for the project, and allocated a separate room for those working on it. One member still refused to commit to time-scales. The other members told him forcefully that they were equally busy but able to comply, implying his behaviour was affecting team performance. This was enough to persuade him to participate more fully. There was another early conflict when members of two functional groups put forward opposing system requirements and were reluctant to specify in writing what their joint requirements would be. The team, with the encouragement of the project leader, established some guidelines on the working practices they would use.

Members contacted suppliers and other sites that had installed similar systems, to gather information about potential systems. The project leader noted that team members enjoyed these visits, and used them as a motivator to encourage the completion of more boring but essential tasks like systems documentation. Performance improved as the project continued. Each member had prepared a checklist for meetings with suppliers and users. As they learned how each other worked, this process improved, with each evaluation increasing their effectiveness as a team. They completed document preparation, evaluation and recommendation on time and to the level of performance required. The group would adjourn once they implemented the project.

Case study questions

1 Use the Tuckman and Jensen model to note behaviours that indicate the stages the group had reached, such as establishing norms.

2 Note any actions that helped the group move to the next stage.

3 Was the Housing Director right in the way he made appointments?

4 Is the team leader using intrinsic or extrinsic factors to motivate staff?

5 What have (a) the project leader and (b) the team members done to make the team work effectively?

6 Was the Chief Executive wise to appoint the Head of IT to lead the team? What are the consequences of that likely to be?

Summary

This chapter has introduced some theories about the development of teams, and the factors that help them to succeed or to fail. Effective teams depend on having clear objectives, and the chapter has suggested a technique for developing these. Effective teams also depend on securing and motivating the right members, which the project manager can facilitate by using established ideas on motivation – especially by ensuring that team members see work on the project as being in their interests. Tactics of generating excitement and publicising success also help. Teams also benefit from having developed a set of common working methods through which to conduct their work, and the chapter included some practical suggestions on these. The foundation of any team's development rests, however, on members developing the skill of observing the group's processes, so that they can improve and correct these as required. The chapter concluded with some examples of the instruments that members can use.

The key points from this chapter are:

- Creating a team does not in itself ensure that projects receive the benefits of team-working.
- Project managers need to understand team development theories.
- The stages of team development model were outlined.
- Five steps in setting objectives were presented.
- Project managers can use established theories of motivation to support team commitment.
- Several techniques for observing group processes were introduced.
- Teams are not only affected by internal team factors but also by wider organisational factors, which are examined in Chapters 10 and 12.

Chapter questions

1 Why are teams likely to go through the stages of development many times during their life?

2 Would such recycling be a sign of weakness?

3 What ideas from motivation theory would support the method for setting objectives presented in this chapter?

4 What is the primary influence affecting the motivation of team members?

5 Give examples, with illustrations if possible, of working practices that help team performance. How does this part of the chapter relate to the theory of the stages of team development?

6 Why does process observation help people work better in teams?

7 Give at least one example from your experience of teams which supports, and one which contradicts, a theory presented here.

Further reading

Belbin, R.M. (1993) *Team Roles at Work*. Oxford: Butterworth-Heinemann. Reports the original research on which the now widely used model of team roles is based.

Hayes, N. (1997) *Successful Team Development*. London: International Thompson Business Press. A lively and well-referenced account of many team development issues.

References

Boddy, D. and Buchanan, D.A. (1992) *Take the Lead: Interpersonal Skills for Project Managers*. Hemel Hempstead: Prentice Hall.

Boddy, D., Boonstra, A. and Kennedy, G. (2002) *Managing Information Systems: An Organisational Perspective*. Harlow: Financial Times Prentice Hall.

Robson, M. (1993) *Problem Solving in Groups*, 2nd edn. Aldershot: Gower.

Tuckman, B. and Jensen N. (1977) 'Stages of small group development revisited', *Group and Organizational Studies*, 2, 419–27.

Part 4

Managing beyond the team

10 Managing across

Introduction

Project managers usually depend on the support of people in other departments, functions or organisations. They need them to support the objectives of the project, to supply resources for the project team, and perhaps to change the way they work. One difficulty for the project manager is that others may see disadvantages in the proposal and oppose it – especially if it conflicts with personal ambitions. They probably report to a different senior manager and have their own priorities and interests. They may also be under pressure from other changes taking place in the business, and so ignore the project manager. The second difficulty for the project manager is that they will usually lack any formal authority over the other managers they are trying to influence.

Project managers therefore need to spend time and effort anticipating what they need from other areas, and use a variety of methods, other than formal authority, to secure their support. They need to influence these other managers to accept the legitimacy of the project, in competition with other claims. They do this in many ways, but especially through negotiation – a common practice in managing projects. It occurs wherever two or more parties depend on each other, and have conflicting interests.

This chapter begins by describing the range of issues on which project managers need the support of others. These centre on the areas identified earlier as being critical for project success – agreeing goals, securing resources and monitoring progress. A short section discusses the danger signals to look out for, as early signs of difficulty. The next section presents a model describing seven influencing strategies – these form the basis of this chapter and the following two. This chapter focuses on one of those methods – negotiating, which is developed in the final two sections, dealing with individual skills and formal structures, respectively.

Objectives

After reading this chapter you should be able to:

- describe the areas in which a project manager depends on the support of others;
- recognise the signs that such support is lacking;
- outline a model of influencing tactics which managers can use to secure support;
- explain why negotiating is a major project management skill, and outline the main steps in successful negotiation;
- use these principles during individual negotiation and in more formal settings.

The project manager depends on others

Almost by definition, a change project will involve several departments, which the project manager needs to move forward in a coherent way. This is not always possible, and they need to adapt the pace of implementation. Boddy and Buchanan (1992) reported an example from a local authority, where some departments displayed resistance and uncertainty to a project:

> There were, however, some cases of resistance to change and instances of protectionism. This had an effect on how, when and where the project should progress. We implemented in the areas where we had total support so that when we reached the areas where we were expecting opposition, we had proved our point and we were able to display examples of our success.

The project manager will be balancing the needs of different departments. Those that are keen to press ahead may need to be slowed down, while those that need to move more slowly are given more time. But the interests of the latter cannot be protected so well that the enthusiasm of the former is lost.

Projects often involve other organisations, including customers. Technology allows people to move information electronically between organisations – and many projects are created to turn that vision into reality. Another common business trend is to work in partnership with other organisations, to improve performance or service to clients – such as between housing, social work and health services.

The more outside links there are in a project, the more 'managing across' the project manager will need to do. Small projects present few problems, as most of what is needed lies within the control of the manager responsible. The larger the task, the more likely it is that success will depend on integrating the work of those in other departments or organisations. Busy managers often forget these external stakeholders or make incorrect assumptions about how they will react. Yet they are often highly influential in the success of a project, and those managing a change need to influence their behaviour towards it.

The focus of the project manager's attempts to influence the activities of other units is to ensure, as far as possible, that they act in ways that support the project. Recall that Chapter 5 identified the factors in successful projects – goals, resources and control. It follows that these should be the strategic focus in dealing with other units, as shown in Figure 10.1.

Support for project objectives

Other departments or organisations need to express some degree of support for a project's goals before they will invest time and effort in making it work. Some functions or departments that need to be involved in the work will have no difficulties in demonstrating this, but others will feel the project is distracting them from their more urgent priorities. The project manager needs to build some sense of ownership and support amongst other managers towards the project, so that it is not seen as someone else's problem.

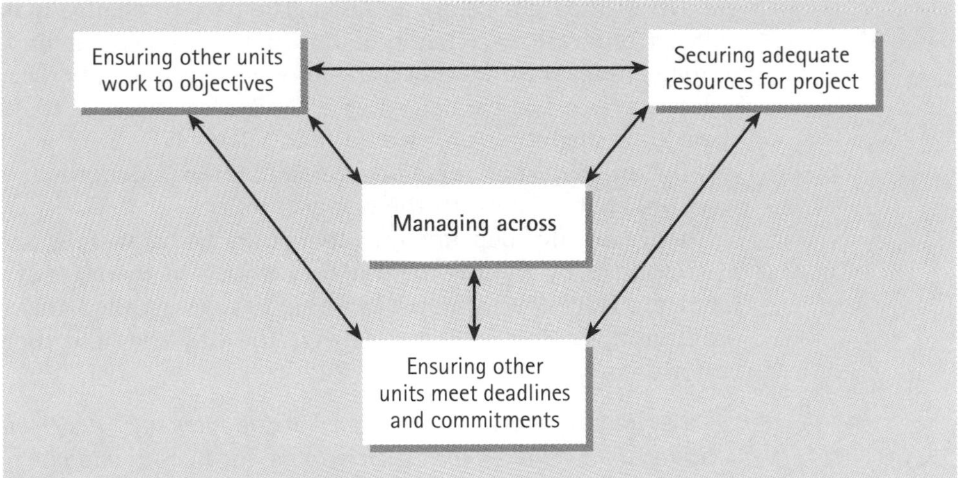

Figure 10.1 How managing across can support effective project management

For example, a manager in the UK plant of a US-based company (with four US plants) was leading the local effort to implement an Enterprise Resource Planning System by the end of 1999. He saw the huge potential of the system radically to change the way the business worked. He was keen to put time, energy and enthusiasm into the project. Managers at the US sites were much less committed to these objectives, and were satisfied when the financial modules of the system had been implemented. They were less committed to the more radical changes the system made possible, and did not support the UK manager's bolder objectives.

The box shows how the manager of a Europe-wide project succeeded in securing the support of other units to bold objectives in his project.

Brainstorming for objectives

'Very soon after the project was established, the manager called for a one-week brainstorming team-building session. All managers of the various [world-wide] groups reporting to the Vice-President participated, including representatives from the European Business group. As a result of this meeting, relationships were established and objectives agreed. The meeting developed overall objectives for the project, which translated into specific tasks for our group. I saw it as a major benefit for the participants, and helped gain the commitment of the functional areas to become involved in these state-of-the-art developments.'

Source: Boddy and Buchanan (1992)

Securing and using resources

Project managers usually depend on other units to release resources, or to support the case for more senior management. This especially includes providing staff for a project – and the project manager will usually experience difficulty getting enough of the right people released. The pace of change makes this more difficult. In one case of a European integration project, senior management had fundamentally misunderstood the resource requirements. They had assumed the separate systems to be merged were similar, so expected the task of transferring them to a single location would be a relatively routine technical and administrative matter. They therefore appointed inexperienced staff to the work who were unable to cope with the complex tasks.

Change usually depends on other units being willing to change how they use resources, by altering the way they work. The manager of a product development group designing new electronic devices recalled that this depended on other groups being willing to change the way they did their part of the task. Unfortunately:

> *'Other product groups were not prepared to alter their design methods at that particular time, to allow their devices to be fitted easily into our system. This made it impossible for us to offer the full range of possibilities to the customer.'*

Monitoring and control

The project manager also depends on separate functions providing accurate information about current operations and likely future needs – otherwise the most basic aspects of the project can be incorrectly designed. This takes time, and commitment. Without that, other departments will not respond, or will do so in an unhelpful way.

The project manager also expects other departments to meet deadlines set, and come up with ideas to overcome difficulties. This will only happen if the staff in the respective functions feel a sense of ownership and responsibility towards the change. Monitoring and controlling events is additionally difficult when a project involves physically separate operations. It is more difficult to know what is happening, and easier for things to go badly wrong before they come to the manager's attention. The more a project depends on consistent action by separately managed functions, and the more distant these are, the more effort the project manager needs to put into getting their informed cooperation.

What are the danger signals?

When a change involves extensive work with other departments, danger signals such as those set out below warn the manager of impending problems, and other managers having different priorities:

- giving low priority to requests for help;
- persistently over-running of deadlines;
- staff not attending meetings;
- sending relatively junior or low-status staff to meetings;
- questioning whether the project is really necessary;

- making promises but doing little;
- recalling previous failures.

Peter Keen (1981) developed the idea of counter-implementation tactics. He pointed out that it is not necessary for those who oppose a project to express their resistance openly – that carries too many risks. A more subtle move is to use one or more tactics which appear to demonstrate support, but which in practice are likely to obstruct the project. These moves will tend to dissipate the team's energies and slow the progress of the project. Observing such symptoms may forewarn the project manager of impending difficulties with other departments. He went on to suggest that overt resistance to change is often risky, and may not in practice be necessary. There are several ways in which those wanting to block a change can do so – even while appearing to support it. The box indicates some possible tactics.

Peter Keen on the tactics of counter-implementation

- *Divert resources.* Split the budget across other projects; have key staff given other priorities and allocate them to other assignments; arrange for equipment to be moved or shared.
- *Exploit inertia.* Suggest that everyone wait until a key player has taken action, or read the report, or made an appropriate response; suggest that the results from some other project should be monitored and assessed first.
- *Keep goals vague and complex.* It is harder to initiate appropriate action in pursuit of aims that are multi-dimensional and that are specified in generalised, grandiose or abstract terms.
- *Encourage and exploit lack of organisational awareness.* Insist that 'we can deal with the people issues later', knowing that these will delay or kill the project.
- *'Great idea – let's do it properly.'* And let's bring in representatives from this function and that section, until we have so many different views and conflicting interests that it will take forever to sort them out.
- *Dissipate energies.* Have people conduct surveys, collect data, prepare analyses, write reports, make overseas trips, hold special meetings . . .
- *Reduce the champion's influence and credibility.* Spread damaging rumours, particularly among the champion's friends and supporters.
- *Keep a low profile.* It is not effective openly to declare resistance to change because that gives those driving change a clear target to aim for.

These inertial forces may make the implementation of the structural and organisational issues identified earlier that much more difficult.

Source: Based on Keen (1981)

The support of other managers can only be secured through the efforts of the project manager to influence them. The next section introduces an empirically-based theory on which to build an influencing strategy.

Influencing strategies

Kipnis *et al.* (1980) conducted extensive research on how managers influenced others. They analysed over 700 incidents in which managers had influenced other managers, their subordinates, and those above them in the hierarchy. From this they identified a set of influencing tactics which managers used in dealing with subordinates, bosses and coworkers. Yukl and Falbe (1990) replicated this work in a wider empirical study, and refined the categories. Table 10.1 defines the Yukl and Falbe influence categories.

The nine tactics cover a variety of behaviours that project managers are likely to use as they try to influence others – whether subordinates, bosses or colleagues. Yukl and Tracey (1992) extended the work by examining which tactics managers used most frequently with different target groups. Most relevant to practitioners, they tried to establish the relative effectiveness of the different methods. They used questionnaire data provided by 128 managers, who also secured matching questionnaires from 128 superiors, 526 subordinates and 543 peers with whom

Table 10.1 Influence tactics and definitions

Tactic	*Definition*
Rational persuasion	The person uses logical arguments and factual evidence to persuade you that a proposal or request is viable and likely to result in the attainment of task objectives
Inspirational appeal	The person makes a request or proposal that arouses enthusiasm by appealing to your values, ideals and aspirations or by increasing your confidence that you can do it
Consultation	The person seeks your participation in planning a strategy, activity or change for which your support and assistance are desired, or the person is willing to modify a proposal to deal with your concerns and suggestions
Ingratiation	The person seeks to get you in a good mood or to think favourably of him or her before asking you to do something
Exchange	The person offers an exchange of favours, indicates a willingness to reciprocate at a later time, or promises you a share of the benefits if you help accomplish the task
Personal appeal	The person appeals to your feelings of loyalty and friendship towards him or her before asking you to do something
Coalition	The person seeks the aid of others to persuade you to do something, or uses the support of others as a reason for you to agree also
Legitimating	The person seeks to establish the legitimacy of a request by claiming the authority or right to make it or by verifying that it is consistent with organisational policies, rules, practices or traditions
Pressure	The person uses demands, threats or persistent reminders to influence you to do what he or she wants

Source: Based on Yukl and Falbe (1990)

the manager interacted frequently. The questionnaires covered the extent to which the manager used the nine tactics, how many of the attempts resulted in complete commitment by the target, and the overall effectiveness of the influence agent (the manager). The main conclusions were that:

- Rational persuasion was used most in an upward direction.
- Inspirational appeal and pressure were used most in a downward direction.
- Exchange, personal appeal and legitimating tactics were used most in managing across.

The study also sought to establish the effects of different approaches by the 'agent' on the targets' commitment to the task. They concluded that:

- Rational persuasion, inspirational appeal and consultation by the agent had a positive effect on task commitment – in whatever direction the target was exercising influence.
- Pressure, coalition and legitimating were usually ineffective.
- Ingratiation and exchange had a positive effect on the task commitment of subordinates and peers, but were ineffective when the agent was trying to influence superiors.

All of these approaches have a place in the project manager's toolkit. They will do their job more effectively if they are able to draw on these approaches as necessary, and use them effectively. This chapter focuses on the tactic of exchange – otherwise known as bargaining or negotiation – as this is an effective influence tactic for managing across. Chapter 11 (on managing staff and users) concentrates on motivation and consultation, while in Chapter 12, on managing up, the emphasis is on rational persuasion. Remember this is only for presentational clarity – in reality managers will often want to use the tactics in combination.

The background to negotiating

The key strategy in managing across is to negotiate with a range of outside interests, so as to integrate their interests with those of the project. The project manager has to ensure that these other interests give what is needed to the project, mainly by negotiating with them about the benefits that can be offered in return. Some tactics and practices which will help are set out below.

Find out whose commitment you need

Work out, by using the stakeholder analysis in Chapter 6, who will have an interest in the project, and whose support will be needed for a successful conclusion. Then set out exactly what it is that you want from them, during and after the project. Until it is clear what they are expected to provide – staff, premises, changes in the way they work, political support, and so on – little will happen. Establishing such targets – how much? when? for how long? – is the first step in the process of influence. Particular attention should be paid to what is expected of customers at this stage.

Ignoring the customer

'Communications with the small customer was a big problem. We were under pressure to save costs but we've realised that we made a mistake in not going to the customer base and selling the idea to them properly. We didn't sell or explain the idea to customers. So when the customer rang the Call Centre and got a poor response he didn't bother to call again but went to one of the independent service engineers. We could have sold the benefits better. We didn't take our branch managers or our customers along with us.'

Source: Quoted in Boddy (2000), p. 34

Some essential preliminary activities to conducting negotiations are to anticipate the invisible committee, distinguish between interests and position, understand the major elements in their interests, and consider your sources of power.

The 'invisible committee'

How people respond to a proposal reflects the forces acting upon them. These can be:

- *internal*:
  - personality
  - motivation and objectives
  - experience
- *external*:
  - personal life (e.g. family)
  - past commitment
  - organisational forces.

These forces play a critical role in influencing what people think and say. In preparing for a negotiation, the manager needs to consider how these forces will be affecting each member of the other side. The manager will of course also be influenced by their own invisible committee.

One way to think about such forces is to imagine an 'invisible committee' standing behind each negotiator. This 'committee' is composed of the forces that influence his/her behaviour. When people make a decision or state a position, it reflects the influence of these forces, and how they interpret them. Often people are well aware of the forces that influence them, but some may be unconscious.

Recognising that everyone in a negotiation is influenced by an invisible committee permits you to look beyond surface expressions and actions, and to attempt to determine the motivations underlying them. When X makes a comment at a meeting, you have to decide if it is X speaking for himself, or if X is representing a member of his invisible committee. The key point is to recognise that each individual has an invisible committee that may be exerting very strong pressures.

NOTEPAD 10.1

Drawing the invisible committee

- Draw your invisible committee in your role as a project manager (which is different from the stakeholder map of your project, though the idea is similar).
- Which of these influences are the most powerful?
- How do you think this may have affected your attitudes to issues raised?
- Do the same for the invisible committee of one or more of the stakeholders with whom you are negotiating.
- How may the invisible committee affect the way the stakeholders have reacted?

Interests and positions

Fisher and Ury (1991) recommend that negotiators distinguish between interests and positions. A position is what the other side demands or requests. It is a public expression of what each party to a negotiation hopes to achieve. An interest is what lies behind the position, and represents what a particular position is meant to achieve. They recommend that negotiators who have trouble getting the other party to move from a **position** they have taken should turn their attention to the **interests** that lie behind the position. The approach is useful because any interest or long-term goal can probably be equally well satisfied by any of several positions. While one of these positions may be unacceptable to the project manager, others may pose less of a problem. If the project manager can find a way of showing the other side that their interests can be just as well served by position B as by position A, an agreement acceptable to both sides may be in sight. Problems arise when people get locked into defending one particular position. Understanding the interests behind the position can point the way to a solution that meets both sets of interests. Table 10.2 obtains some ideas on how to put this into practice.

Understanding what the target values are

In a sense this is trying to understand some of the elements in a person's invisible committee. In trying to reach agreement through negotiating, it can greatly help if we present ideas or proposals in a way that acknowledges (directly or indirectly) the interests that are important to the other side. Cohen and Bradford (1989) see negotiation as a process of give and take, in which people agree to certain things, in the expectation that they will receive something valuable to them in return.

Table 10.2 Ideas on how to identify interests

Tactic	*Possible questions*
Try to identify their interests – what lies behind their stated position?	'Why are they taking that line?' 'What makes that position important to you?' 'I'm trying to see why you're sticking on that' 'Is there an aspect of this I've not understood?'
Try to identify the source – what expectations are they having to meet?	Basic psychological influences – Economic well-being – Acceptance by their group – Recognition
Ways of discussing interests – acknowledge that their interests are part of the situation	'As I understand it, your basic interests are . . .' 'Have I understood you correctly to be meaning that . . . ?'
Look forward (purposes), not back (causes)	Speak in terms of purpose, of where you want to end up, not in terms of causes and past events. Interests will be satisfied better by working on suitable future arrangements than by arguing about why things have got into the state they are

They classified such transactions in terms of five currencies which the parties can use to conduct the deal. Table 10.3 illustrates a selection of the currencies. The central point is that understanding the other person's needs is at the heart of a successful influence attempt. This enables the negotiator to present ideas and requests in a way that helps the influencee see that they will benefit from agreeing to the request – the payoff to them matches their interests. They will do things for the project, if they believe that in doing so they are acting in their best interests.

The interests of the stakeholders themselves also need to be understood and taken into account as far as is practicable. The change needs to be viewed from their point of view. While to the project manager the changes proposed will look positive and exciting, others may see them as threatening, time-consuming and foolish.

Priorities and expectations should be presented in a way that seems reasonable to them. Make your approaches in a way that is sensitive to this, and which recognises the need to earn their willing cooperation. People may follow instructions, but this may not be the most productive approach in the long run.

Prepare to discuss not only the preferred solution, but also what would be acceptable as a fall-back position. Decide the arguments you will use, and try to anticipate their likely reaction. One way of anticipating the reactions of interested parties is to ask persistently, before making a move, 'who will that affect, and who am I likely to upset next?'

There are clear parallels between the Cohen and Bradford currencies and theories of human needs. The benefit of their approach is that it gives a greater level of operational precision to broader categories of human needs.

Table 10.3 Cohen and Bradford classification of exchange currencies

Currency	*Type*	*Description*
Inspirational	Vision	The chance to become involved in a significant or exciting task
	Excellence	The chance to do something well, to the highest standards
	Moral/ethical	The chance to do something for moral or ethical reasons
Task	Resources	Offering new resources (budget, staff, etc.)
	Challenge	Tasks that increase learning or experience
	Assistance	Help with existing projects or unwanted tasks
	Task	Giving support to promote a project
	Rapid response	The promise to deal with requests quickly
	Information	Offering access to organisational or technical knowledge
Position	Recognition	Acknowledging a contribution, especially publicly
	Visibility	Especially to those higher in the organisation
	Reputation	Offering to promote a positive reputation in the eyes of others
	Insiderness	Access to places of power where important decisions are made
	Contacts	Opening up access to networks with whom relationships can be established
Relationship	Acceptance and inclusion	Friendship and inclusion in a working group
	Understanding	Readiness to acknowledge and listen to concerns
	Personal support	Providing emotional support to the influencee
Personal	Gratitude	Thanks, showing appreciation
	Ownership and involvement	The chance to influence important tasks, and so feel part of the work
	Self-concept	Confirms value and self-worth, by the tasks undertaken
	Comfort	Avoiding public fuss or confrontation

NOTEPAD 10.2

Using the Cohen and Bradford currencies

- Which of the Cohen and Bradford currencies have you offered to one of the groups you want to influence?
- Are there others on the list which you may be able to use, such as:
  - promotion or better career prospects;
  - career visibility;
  - networking in high status groups or places.
- Have you tried taking such an approach?
- How well did it work, and why?

In return for the commitments sought from other departments, project managers need to consider what rewards and incentives they can offer in return. What benefits will value? Giving a group a particular task may help their promotion chances, give them visibility amongst senior managers, or provide them with opportunities to build a network of contacts.

Offering support to secure commitment

The project manager may win support by providing a department with resources or assistance that they need for other aspects of their work. Boddy and Buchanan (1992) reported the example of a project manager who persuaded a unit to give him systems support, by arranging for the unit to be given extra staff in another area. They also quoted another who wanted a department to change priorities in favour of his project:

> The tactic used was to offer task-related help, in this case with problems they were experiencing with other MIS systems. In return the project team received the desired commitment to the project. This task was made easier by the existing good working relationships already built up.

Conducting negotiations

A key point for project managers negotiating with another department or unit to remember is that they will probably need to work with them again. So it is important to conduct the negotiations in a way that helps to build and maintain good long-term relationships. The following tactics, based on studies of effective negotiators, will help project managers develop their skills in this area.

Preparation

As in all attempts to influence the behaviour of other people, preparation pays off in negotiating. Refer back to the section in Chapter 6 on 'Planning the approach', and use that as a guideline in your preparations. Specifically, you will need to identify the objectives you are hoping to achieve by the end of the negotiation, what standards or targets you are hoping to achieve, and what you will do in order to reach those targets. Write down your objectives, targets and behaviour plans, try them out with your colleagues, perhaps rehearse some of the more important arguments you want to use. Then read the rest of this section, which gives some ideas on negotiating practice.

Label your behaviour

Skilled negotiators are clear communicators, and one technique they use is to signal that they are about to suggest a solution, or to ask a question. It has the effect of capturing the attention of the whole group, and putting pressure on the person to whom the signal has been directed. Without the clear labelling, the target may be able to avoid responding – but the label makes their position more visible to everyone present.

Test and summarise

A very useful technique, especially in a long negotiation, is to test that both sides fully understand what is being proposed, and have a common understanding of the stage the negotiations have reached. This helps to clarify key points, and also helps to create mutual trust. It shows that although you may not accept the other side's point, you have listened to it sufficiently well to be able to summarise the argument. Above all, the practice of testing and summarising helps to ensure that when an agreement is reached, it is not undermined by misunderstandings amongst the parties about what was being agreed.

Do not dilute a good argument

It may seem that the more individual arguments you can bring out in support of a case, the more persuasive the case becomes. This is not the case – skilled negotiators tend to use fewer, but stronger arguments, rather than a lot of weak ones, to support a position.

A weak argument does not add to a strong one – it dilutes and weakens it. The reason is that a skilled opponent will spot the weakest in a series of points being made and attack it hard. This tends to put the other side on the defensive very quickly, and to undermine the credibility of their case as a whole.

Use questions to persuade

The negotiator is obviously keen to get his or her point of view over to the other side, and a common fault is to stress, repeat or emphasise an argument that is not being accepted. Repeatedly telling a person something that they are clearly unwilling to accept is unlikely to change their view – if anything, it will reinforce their opposition.

A better approach is to ask the other side questions – carefully designed to let them realise the strength of your case. Good negotiators ask a lot of questions, which gradually reveal the legitimacy of their point. Allowing the other side to think about the issue in a particular way is more likely to reduce their opposition, and thus secure their agreement. Trying to force acceptance on them is unlikely to work.

Use questions to control

Asking questions gives the questioner more control over the conversation. The other side is forced to respond to what is being asked, rather than leading with points which they wanted to make. It also gives the questioner more thinking time – while the other is responding to the question, the questioner can be planning his or her next move.

Skilled use of a question also allows the negotiator to avoid disagreeing directly with the other side's proposal. So instead of saying 'that wouldn't work here', the skilled negotiator would say something like: 'Could you please tell me how that might work here?' If the question allows the other side to see the weakness of their idea, the point is won: if they can respond convincingly, the questioner is no worse off, as their disagreement would have been countered anyway.

Plan your questions

Because questions play such an important part in negotiations, prepare, and write down before the negotiations, a list of questions you are likely to want to use. They will not only help you to persuade and control, they will also come in useful if you get into difficulty, and want to take the pressure off. Asking a question, to which they have to think up a reply, gives you time to think.

CASE STUDY

Digital Europe, Part B

This case continues the account begun at the end of Chapter 2.

'It's now 6th November and a number of interesting things have happened. I personally have now been legitimised by my own plant management team and have also been legitimised as the European Programme Manager for order scheduling. Of the 17 part-timers that started the white paper, we now have at least 10 of them committed full-time to the programme and another five individuals across the sites committed full-time to the programme. The process of engagement has begun. The full team is coming together again in mid-November to compile a European paper supported by plant experts. Another major milestone.

In many ways system and process design is going through the very same as happens to some product design in its early days. An individual or a group of individuals need to go out on a limb with an idea and be able to articulate that idea to a wider audience before they can get any interest and therefore any support and investment to go forward. In our company, where the products and the business plan change very quickly, it is enormously difficult to get people to focus on what is important rather than on what is urgent.

There are some interesting organisational discussions going on in each of these plants which have a direct bearing on this programme. We have seven sites, all at different stages of development. We have in some way to make sure that each of them is positioned both in terms of resources, energy and commitment to support an integrated European programme. It is because we have a business which is fairly complex and so diverse that we have adopted the approach that basically says – generate a common level of understanding of what needs to be done, then allow each area to specify their unique requirements within this overall framework. It also allows each individual location to move at their own pace as long as they don't get too far out of line.

The team member from Valbonne wrote to me two weeks ago indicating that he's now been asked to do another European programme. Therefore because his particular group in Valbonne are very short of resources he will not be able to support this team. From my point of view as a programme manager that is totally unacceptable as his plant is a very big part of the order-fulfilment process. So without a representative from there any solution that we devise will only be partially successful.

I have had to speak to the individual himself who I know well from the past is making a very clear statement around availability. I understand the circumstances in Valbonne, having worked there for some time. I have therefore agreed that we will put together a plan to augment the materials and planning resource in Valbonne. I will take that plan to the manager in Valbonne and also to the European management team to try to provide the support required so that he can support both programmes. I will also personally join the team for a week to help them with some of the technical aspects of the specification.

Christmas holidays are looming but prior to that next week in London I have to do an up-date on this programme to all my peers and my functional boss. They are obviously getting anxious about just exactly where we are. They are aware of some of the road-blocks that are causing me and the rest of the team pain. So I am putting together a presentation that tries to be constructive about what is required to get the road-blocks out of the way and get us moving.

The European management team, from the conversations that I have had with them, are talking about some fairly unusual methods to drive this. For example the concept of 'gold cards' which means that I can have the power to get whoever I want from wherever I want in Europe to drive the design for this system. Looks like we are in for a very interesting time within the first two to three weeks of January.'

Source: Information provided by the manager

Case study questions

1 In what ways does the project manager depend on people in other departments?

2 What forms of power has he used, or acquired?

3 What has he done to try to increase his power?

4 What forms of influence has he used to try to secure their support?

5 Which of the Cohen and Bradford 'currencies' has he used?

6 Are there any other currencies in the Cohen and Bradford list which he could use? Explain how these might be expressed in this case.

Summary

This chapter has examined how project managers can influence those in other departments or organisations whose support they need. It has drawn on other research on influencing to outline a range of influencing tactics, and has examined one of the tactics, negotiating.

The key points from this chapter are:

- Project managers need the support of those in other departments and organisations to help clarify objectives, secure and use resources, and in monitoring and control.
- The danger signals include a variety of delaying tactics, reverting to past difficulties, and a variety of other less apparent tactics to indicate lack of support.
- Managers exercise influence through one or more tactics of rational persuasion, inspiration, consultation, ingratiation, negotiation, personal appeal, coalition, legitimating and pressure.
- In preparing to negotiate managers can identify the invisible committee behind those they are negotiating with, distinguish interests from positions, and identify likely substantive interests of the target group.
- In conducting negotiation, theory suggests paying attention to factors such as preparation, labelling, summarising, not diluting good arguments with weak ones, and the effective use of questions.

Chapter questions

1. Do you agree with the reasons given for project managers depending on others? Can you add other reasons?
2. What examples can you give of the danger signals identified, including those associated with Keen's counter-implementation tactics?
3. Which of the influencing strategies would you expect to be used most often in seeking to 'manage across', and why?
4. What is meant by 'the invisible committee', and why is the idea important to negotiators?
5. Explain in your own words the difference between an interest and a position. Give an example from an actual negotiation if you can.

Further reading

Bragg, M. (1996) *Reinventing Influence*. London: Pitman. Excellent account of how those without formal authority can develop their powers of influence.

Fisher, R. and Ury, W.L. (1991) *Getting to Yes: Negotiating Agreements Without Giving In*. Boston, MA: Houghton Mifflin. The second edition of a well-regarded book, containing a convincing account of the theory and tactics of negotiating.

Gillen, T. (1995) *Positive Influencing Skills*. London: Institute of Personnel Development. Clearly presented account of the author's views on the fundamental principles of influencing, and the core skills required to put them into practice.

References

Boddy, D. and Buchanan, D.A. (1992) *Take the Lead: Interpersonal Skills for Project Managers*. Hemel Hempstead: Prentice Hall.

Boddy, D. (2000) 'Implementing inter-organisational IT systems: lessons from a call centre project', *Journal of Information Technology*, 15, 29–37.

Cohen, A.R. and Bradford, D.L. (1989) 'Influence without authority: the use of alliances and reciprocity to accomplish work', *Organizational Dynamics*, Winter, 4–17.

Fisher, R. and Ury, W.L. (1991) *Getting to Yes: Negotiating Agreements Without Giving In*. Boston, MA: Houghton Mifflin.

Keen, P. (1981) 'Information systems and organization change', in Rhodes, E. and Weild, D. (eds) *Implementing New Technologies*. Oxford: Blackwell/Open University Press.

Kipnis, D., Schmidt, S.M. and Wilkinson, I. (1980) 'Intra-organizational influence tactics: explorations in getting one's way', *Journal of Applied Psychology*, 65, 440–52.

Yukl, G. and Falbe, C.M. (1990) 'Influence tactics in upward, downward and lateral influence attempts', *Journal of Applied Psychology*, 75, 132–40.

Yukl, G. and Tracey, J.B. (1992) 'Consequences of influence tactics used with subordinates, peers and the boss', *Journal of Applied Psychology*, 77, 525–35.

11 Managing staff and users

Introduction

Project managers have to influence staff and users to give an adequate degree of commitment and effort to the change they are implementing. They need to generate this during the project itself, but also in a way that will continue to energise those who will be working or using the new systems and procedures long after the project team has moved on.

The most visible group are the people whose work is directly altered by the change, and who will be living with the results in their daily work. They have to set up the system, and run it thereafter. They have a direct interest in the change, and detailed operating knowledge of the situation. These are assets which the project manager would be foolish to ignore. It would be equally unwise to ignore those who receive the results of the work done in the area – members of the public, customers, suppliers or people in other departments.

A stakeholder analysis will probably have identified the staff and users most likely to experience the change. This chapter shows how project managers can attempt to influence them so that they react positively towards the change, rather than with grudging compliance. The chapter begins by showing how the project manager depends on staff and users, and the symptoms which can warn of difficulties. The next section shows how they can use theories of human motivation to plan their influence attempt, because understanding the needs of the person being influenced leads to practical suggestions. The final section considers the process of change, focusing on how to ensure staff are consulted in planning the change. This in itself is a form of influence.

Objectives

After reading this chapter you should be able to:

- describe why a manager needs to influence staff and users during a project;
- identify the danger signals that indicate falling commitment or possible opposition;
- summarise the implications of motivation theories for the project manager;
- describe practices which can be used to meet different motivational needs;
- explain when and why consultation may help the influence process, and outline how this can be achieved.

The project manager depends on staff and users

Conducting a stakeholder analysis will identify those affected by the change, including operational staff or users of new systems. Project managers will depend on them during and after the project, in the areas of objectives, resources and control. Figure 11.1 summarises the potential benefits of managing this possibly very diverse group of people effectively.

Support for project goals

Broad objectives for a project are likely to be set by senior management. Yet those who are closest to the work are most aware of the detail of how the work is done now, and what the possibilities are of significant change. The job of the project manager is made a great deal easier if he or she is able to draw on the skills and experience of the staff in the area. They know what the equipment needs to be able to do, how new systems would need to fit in with old, how the transitional problems could be handled. Boddy and Gunson (1996) quote the example of the project manager who recalled that a successful feature of his project had been the decision:

> To involve local supervising management in route planning, which introduced and involved them at an early and critical stage in the project, and we were able to benefit from their local knowledge and experience.

Important aspects of an operation are easily missed – especially the new, unusual, uncertain or occasional elements. These can only be captured if staff and designers work closely together. Expectations will also be more realistic: consulting staff

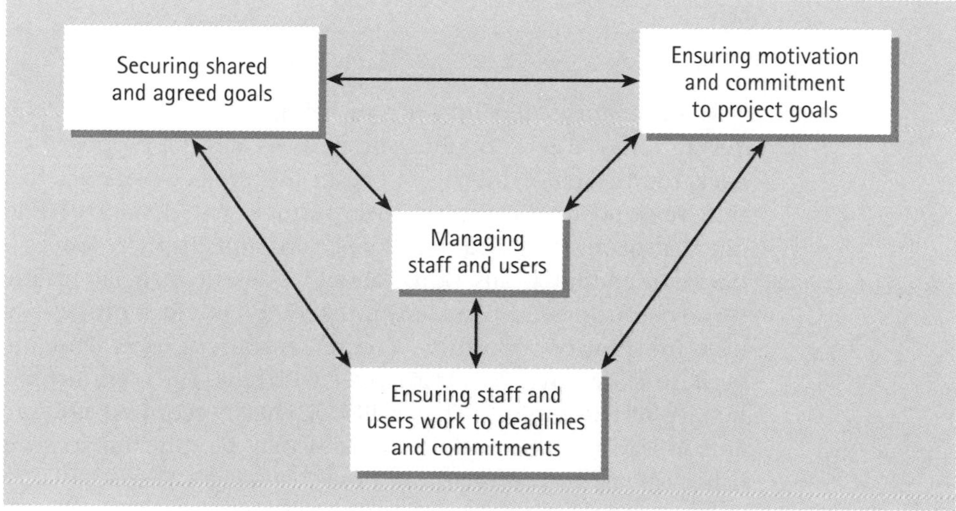

Figure 11.1 How managing staff and users can support effective project management

allows them to form a balanced view between what they would ideally like from the change, and what they are likely to get.

Securing high commitment from staff and users

Change will place new demands on staff – to contribute ideas to the project, to manage the transition and to use the system productively after implementation. The scale of the physical work of the transition should never be underestimated. As new systems take shape countless problems occur. The manager can gain credibility with staff by ensuring that adequate resources are available to help them through this transitional stage. Small problems will be kept small, not allowed to grow out of proportion. Enabling staff or users to be part of the design process is likely to ensure that better decisions are taken about the design of the new system – but will take time, and often be competing with current work. The box contains an example.

Managing 'the day job'

A senior nurse who was managing a project to develop new 'care pathways' through a hospital for patients with dementia commented in early 2001:

> *'Another difficult aspect of this project is freeing up time for the team to be involved. Everyone on the team is a skilled and valuable member of staff (that's why they were selected) and they already have very heavy workloads. A healthy budget has been allocated to recruit locums or replacements for intensive periods of the project but this is currently hugely underspent as it has proved difficult or impractical to secure these staff. We have therefore had to be flexible in how we have allocated and carried out the various tasks.'*

Source: Communication from the senior nurse

Major changes depend on staff being able and willing to put in extra work. Yet staff may also be anxious and nervous about a proposed system. Against that background, senior managers expect the project manager to influence the way staff respond to the project in a positive way. Charles Handy (1993) pointed out that people respond to influence attempts in three ways – compliance, identification and internalisation. Table 11.1 describes the alternatives. He argues that merely securing compliance is unlikely to benefit a project – even if there is no outward show of opposition. Compliant staff (or users who put up with a change because they have no alternative) will have no commitment to the ultimate quality of the project. They will do what is required grudgingly, and without enthusiasm or imagination. While it may be quickest to secure compliance by using threats or coercion, the project manager needs to consider whether that will be the most useful reaction in the longer term. Identification too has limitations, if long-term success depends on further innovation.

Table 11.1 Three responses to influence attempts

Responses to influence	*Description*	*Commentary*
Compliance	Target accepts proposal because manager has power – but does so grudgingly	Produces the desired outcome, but not voluntarily. Can deny responsibility for results
Identification	Target accepts proposal as they identify emotionally with source of influence	Difficult to maintain, and uncritical acceptance leads to dependence, not initiative
Internalisation	Target accepts proposal as their own	Most likely to develop and improve the idea, after voluntary acceptance. Influence attempt may be invisible to the target

Only when staff are fully committed because they have internalised the goals of the project and see themselves as part of the project's creative process will the full benefits be realised. Only then is there likely to be an environment of creativity and innovation.

Monitoring and control

As a change is introduced and implemented, the staff closest to it are most aware of its strengths and limitations. Project managers depend on accurate monitoring of progress by those working with a new system, both to publicise success and to deal with problems rapidly. Blocking or ignoring such data represents a lost opportunity. The managers at Pensco missed this – to quote from the case study at the end of Chapter 4:

> The company maintained the public position that despite the many difficulties the project was successful. The authors of the case study reported different views from the clerical staff who were processing new proposals (without adequate IS support). As a team leader commented:
>
> > They [the managers] don't have a grasp of what's going on. They just want the figures. They don't appreciate our problems. I wish they'd acknowledge there is one (Knights and Murray, 1994, p. 162).

More positively, momentum and interest has to be maintained in the aftermath of the change. Staff need to learn how to use the new system to full advantage, further organisational changes may be needed if the full benefits are to be realised, and the change will be refined in the light of experience. These opportunities to learn open up new possibilities for developing the project, and for refining the objectives of the project. These are more likely to be experienced if staff have internalised the change, and are highly committed to making it work. They will not arise when the manner of the influence attempt has led to compliance.

What are the danger signals?

The project manager can be alert to signals that staff lack enthusiasm for the change. Overt and prolonged resistance is rare, but indifference and reluctance can be just as damaging to a project. It takes many forms, disguised or overt, including:

- refusing to use the equipment or system;
- deliberate misuse of the system;
- using the system as rarely as possible;
- maintaining old procedures;
- delaying other changes necessary for a system to work;
- missing meetings about the change;
- making no effort to learn how to use it;
- not attending training sessions;
- excessive fault finding and criticism;
- endless discussion and requests for more information;
- suggesting new features, which make the change more complex;
- bringing other interest groups into the discussion, delaying agreement.

Any of these symptoms, if present, will result in the new system performing below expectation.

NOTEPAD 11.1

Assessing staff commitment to the project

If you are involved in a project, consider these questions:

- Which groups of staff or users will the project affect?
- What is their current attitude – compliance, identification or internalisation?
- Are any of these danger signals evident?
- What plans have you at this stage about how to get staff commitment?

Strategies for influencing staff and users

Understanding the needs of the target is the basis of every successful attempt at influence. People will be willing to do things for the project manager if they feel they are acting in their best interests, and that they are achieving their personal goals. Project managers need to establish what these interests are, and present their proposal in a way that staff or users believe will meet them. If they do so,

Table 11.2 Applying Maslow's hierarchy to project activities

Level	*Need*	*Project example*
Self-actualisation	Developing full potential	Additional responsibilities, more challenging work
Esteem	Recognition, attention, respect of others	Invitations to join senior teams, present at conferences, networking
Social	Relationship, affection, belonging	Membership of team, retaining close working relationships after change
Safety	Security, order, predictability	Leaving some aspects of work unchanged, providing regular information on what is happening
Physiological	Survival	Reassurance about job security, compensation for loss

people will respond positively, as they see that in doing so they will meet their needs. To do so is to do themselves a favour.

Motivation is a decision process through which an individual chooses desired outcomes, and sets in motion behaviours that will help achieve those outcomes. As discussed in Chapter 8, project managers need a practical guide to understanding the needs of the target – in this case the staff and users affected by the change. One such usable theory is, of course, that put forward by Abraham Maslow (1943). Despite its age, the theory is still useful for those trying to influence others in the workplace. The five needs represent points which influencers can touch in their efforts to gain support of staff and users for their proposals. Table 11.2 illustrates this.

One difficulty for project managers is to identify the needs of those they are trying to influence. People have hidden needs which, though unstated, may be their fundamental driving forces. To identify these can be problematic, especially when so much else is going on in the project. The project manager can recall that people are usually trying to satisfy their current primary need. Observing how they behave, what they put their energies to, what they complain about, the manager will soon get a sense of what is important to them. Getting to know the staff and users affected by a change is a worthwhile experience for any project manager.

In addition, the manager can use the Cohen and Bradford (1989) approach outlined in Chapter 10. Table 11.3 contains some links between that model and the world of projects.

Table 11.3 Applying the Cohen and Bradford model to staff and user interests

Currency	*Description*	*Project example*
Inspiration	Vision, excellence, ethics	Taking part in high-tech, state-of-the-art work
Task	Resources, challenge, assistance, response, information	New responsibilities, learning opportunities, access to scientific developments
Position	Recognition, visibility, reputation, insiderness, contact	Praise, visits, presentations, meeting customers or other professionals
Relationship	Acceptance and inclusion, understanding, personal support	Project team, maintaining established relationships, valuing past work
Personal	Gratitude, ownership and involvement, comfort	Thanks for work well done, allowing staff to develop sense of ownership of tasks

Satisfying the needs of staff and users

The project manager needs to recognise that staff have diverse attitudes, preferences, skills and interests. They will value different things at work; whatever these are, the project manager will have an easier time if he or she identifies benefits that staff value. These will be more persuasive than an approach which only stresses the features and broad objectives. The change has to be promoted to staff, in ways that will meet their needs. Some examples of actions during projects that meet one or more of Maslow's categories follow.

Physiological

Projects can meet these needs if they help ensure that basic needs for income and survival are being met. Some staff will fear losing their job, status or career prospects. These fears may be well founded – in which case they are probably best dealt with openly and early. Those who are secure can then concentrate on the job, rather than have it undermined by needless anxieties. Boddy and Buchanan (1992) quote these examples:

> The other major factor used in persuading staff the system was worth using was the knowledge of another system, which calculated a bonus for branch staff if they reached certain profit targets. The system we were proposing would help them improve their sales and thus their profit by focusing their attention on particular areas on a weekly basis. This would help improve their chances of meeting targets, and earning a bonus.

Another project manager recalled some decisions which helped the project:

> To increase bonus performance levels where possible, which acted as a carrot to the manual workers, as it provided the opportunity to earn more money. The staff were given four to six weeks to settle into the new method of operation, and to familiarise with their new routes. During this period their bonus levels were guaranteed; to protect the loss of earnings for a period of nine months for the manual workers who became surplus to requirements.

Ezzamell and Wilmott (1998) studied a project at 'Stitchco', whereby management intended to introduce self-managing teams into a clothing factory. Staff had previously worked on an individual incentive scheme, in which a person's income depended on what they produced. The new system grouped staff into teams which deliberately combined experienced, high-earning staff and younger, less productive staff. The former were expected to help the latter to increase their earnings through training and advice. Earnings now depended on group output. The experienced staff became highly dissatisfied, as, amongst other complaints, their earnings were reduced by the lower productivity of the younger staff.

Safety

Some people will be enthusiasts, others will feel unable to cope, uncertain and lacking in confidence. They may become stressed and defensive. They need time to adjust, and time to absorb training. Boddy and Gunson (1996) quote the example of an ambulance service that was introducing computer-aided systems to support staff in its control rooms. To ensure that all staff, especially those unfamiliar with modern technology of any sort, became familiar, terminals were placed in the control rooms several weeks before training was due to start. Staff were able to experiment at their own pace and overcome any anxieties, well before the extended training began. Management stressed throughout that the system would only go live once staff were completely comfortable with their skills, and confident that they could manage the change. This reassurance contributed to the smooth introduction of a highly successful system.

Staff will feel more secure with the system if they are confident it will work, with minimum disruption. This implies taking care over the design and planning of the technical aspects of the change – whether of equipment, procedures, or systems:

> Members of the project team, from past experience, suggested that although staff in the branch network were very enthusiastic about the new system, they would probably lose interest and not use it. The problem was to get them to accept ownership of the system.

This was tackled by ensuring that the system was as simple as possible to use, and by providing full help facilities. In addition each region was asked to nominate a representative who would act as coordinator for their region. This person would receive advance training, and would be responsible for allowing access to the system in their region.

Social

Change often means new patterns of working which take away valued parts of the role, or which threaten to disrupt established working relationships, alter the status or prospects of people and interests. The Stitchco case illustrates this too. As well as complaining about loss of earnings, experienced staff also underwent a change of role within the new groups. Management expected them to encourage and if necessary discipline the less productive staff, to help the latter meet team targets. They were in effect being asked to take on some aspects of the supervisory role. This conflicted with their sense of how they should relate to fellow workers, and was a further source of dissatisfaction.

More positively, projects can be a way of rearranging work so that people work more as teams rather than individuals. Most people welcome the chance to have good social relations with colleagues at work, and well-designed teams can support this need. Simple adjustments to the layout of a working area can improve the chances of this happening.

Esteem

Lloyd and Newell (1998) reported on a study of a project which appears to have lowered the self-esteem of staff, with negative effects on performance. Representatives visited doctors, nurses and pharmacists to promote 'Pharma' products. They were well-educated, and 40% had been with the company for more than seven years. They covered a defined territory and had developed their own target lists, based on their knowledge of doctors and their prescribing practices.

In 1996 management installed a marketing database of the most fruitful sales prospects in their area on the reps' lap-top computers. They were expected to call on these prospects at a specified frequency and to ignore contacts not on the list.

Staff were keen to use new technology but complained about the poor quality of the database. It had been compiled by a market research company and was widely perceived to be inaccurate. They were not permitted to change more than 10% of the entries in any year. Moreover: 'The computer system linked to the database meant that the reps' performance was being assessed on the basis of calls which could not be made because the targets were no longer in the territory, were not interested in (the product) or never saw reps. The system would only accept data about recognised target customers' (p. 112).

The reps claimed the database information did not reflect their knowledge and experience. Staff turnover rose sharply, sales targets were not met, and the number of calls declined. Boddy and Gunson (1996) reported how the ambulance service quoted earlier (see p. 183) made radical changes to its command and control system. The service continued to develop the system in ways that added to the responsibility and self-esteem of the staff, as described in the box.

Enhancing self-esteem

'The basic system has not changed but we have made some changes in how we use it. We used to tell the crew how to action the run: what we do now is put all the patients in a geographic area onto a log sheet, with their appointment times. We have devolved responsibility to the crew members to decide how best they should schedule that journey to meet the appointments of the patients.

'How they pick them up is up to them – they also take breaks to suit the overall schedule: we don't schedule them. Initially we told them in much more detail, manually intervening with the computer data. But it was very labour-intensive, and we didn't see the traffic jams. We hand out the work in the morning, and we only want to hear if they have operational problems.

'The planning officer's role has developed into a liaison role with the hospitals. Building up a relationship with them, because there has to be some come and go. The person in the planning department becomes a crucial personality, not just a worker. Someone coming into the job now could take two years to build up those working relationships. The routine bits are done by the machine and by the control assistants. At first the planning officer did that: now it's been pushed down.

'The Command and Control system identifies the patient by urgency, and instantly recommends the most suitable resource. I stress "recommends" – the essential point is that the controller makes the decision as to who goes. It only recommends the deployment – we don't want the computer deciding. We will keep the human element in. The decision of the control officer will be transmitted via a screen. It is user-friendly because we insisted that the software writers made it so. It mirrored very closely the old paper system, and it has been a great success. It is now extremely quick to deploy ambulances.'

Source: A control manager, quoted in Boddy and Gunson (1996)

Self-actualisation

The final element in Maslow's hierarchy can be used to describe the extent to which work helps people realise their full potential, by learning new skills and taking on new tasks. Most people welcome the opportunity to extend their role in this way, provided other more tangible rewards are also received. The manager of a plant had used the introduction of an Enterprise Resource Planning system as an opportunity to change the work of his staff. As the box describes, he gave them much greater responsibility and opportunity to learn new skills and work in a wider range of tasks – with positive effects on their motivation.

Using ERP to increase responsibility

'A culture change has happened, that says the power and the information are no longer in the management team. The people who are driving the business process, and producing the management reports, are the people at other levels in the organisation who have not generally been looked on as the people who have that knowledge. The whole ERP process is pushing that. They can see the information directly on the screen. The system generates information for each process rather than in a global form. That means the people down there doing the work have more information than management has got. If we then bolster that by them going to other plants to see how they use the next generation of software you are driving a whole improvement process on the spine of ERP.

'They see the things that are possible. The (next project) team has four members, of which three are manufacturing operatives. They will be going to Company X to see their system: they would never have had that opportunity before. Probably no one else other than myself will go and see it. They'll come back, and probably be spending 100k on software for the system. A whole change of management style. The structure I've got now is taking the pressure off me – and I'm happy. The people are making decisions, whereas before they looked to me – they wanted me to do it. But I don't have the up-to-date operating information. They had knowledge of the operations, but not the information. Now they have access to the management information.

'As a process finishes they key in what's happened – and they realise that is going to inform the management. They understand the significance of what they are doing. I've asked them to structure the reports and explain to me what's happening. It's a very closed job if you're just keying in information. We've opened the job up, by asking them to produce the report, investigate what you think are problems are come and talk to me about them. They can raise purchase orders based on the information, which is another change. We never had a mechanism for that before. It was left to me to check how much raw material we had, and decide we need to order some. Now they know what they've used, and they decide if they need to order some. I'm not part of the process.'

Source: Manufacturing manager, speaking in February 2001

Projects offer many opportunities to enhance the work of staff in this way – provided managers see the potential, and have the incentive to make it happen. Understanding individual motivation is the essential starting point.

Consulting staff and users

The Yukl and Tracey (1992) research cited in the previous chapter showed that consultation was an effective means of influencing subordinates. It helps to maintain users' sense of control over their work. In the normal course of events staff and users come to exercise some degree of control and influence over the task. The work itself becomes familiar, expectations are established, rewards are predictable, status is established, social relationships are worked out.

A restructuring project at a Government agency

In July 2000 the Board of a Government agency decided to create a new structure, to clarify the roles and direction of staff effort. The Director of HRM commented on how the change was initially handled:

> *'The Board had very clear ideas on the new structure, and in effect imposed it on the senior management team. They in turn all had different views on how the new structure should look, but weren't allowed to express those views properly and argue them through. That left a certain disaffection with the process. It wasn't a structure they created, even though they are directors. It was created by the Board.'*

Source: Interview with the Director of HRM

A change threatens all of this. Fearing a loss of control, staff become apprehensive or antagonistic towards the project. Elements of the situation which bring this about include:

- Change – differences in the objective features of the old and new situations.
- Contrast – differences that are personally significant to those affected (some staff may welcome a feature, others dislike it).
- Surprise – significant differences between what was expected to happen, and what does happen.

This analysis leads to the proposition that acceptance of change will be helped by implementation activities that enable users to cope with change, contrast and surprise. The case in the box about a restructuring project is an example where this was not done. It appears to have created a sense among senior managers that they were unable to maintain an acceptable degree of control. Practical possibilities include activities to deal with each of the elements, shown in Table 11.4.

A regular theme in discussions with project managers has been that consulting staff about the project is a worthwhile activity. It helps to meet the higher level needs for esteem and self-actualisation, because being asked for

Table 11.4 Ways of preventing a loss of control

Element	*Activity*
Change	Staff briefed in a discussion format Staff actively take part in system demonstration Demonstration designed to highlight not features, but what users would see
Contrast	Staff able to discuss in small groups what the change might mean Staff able to express personal anxieties about the change Staff given degree of choice over when or whether they personally had to be part of the change (e.g. by making transfers available)
Surprise	Implementation staff present at meetings, to ensure accurate information is passed out Staff told in advance about surveys, visits from consultants, deliveries of equipment, etc. Staff given significant influence over working methods

opinions and experience implies that skills are recognised and valued. It also helps people gain the satisfaction of making a greater contribution than is normally the case.

Effective consultation

The practices below all offer ways of using the experience of staff to gain their commitment, and to benefit the project.

Ask staff for ideas

People become anxious when they do not know what is going on, or when they feel that their views are ignored. Encourage people to raise doubts and objections. If these are unfounded, they can be reassured; if they have substance, dealing with them will gain support. Questionnaires are an effective way of gathering views from a large number of staff about a proposed change programme, especially in the early stages. They give an overview of what staff want and expect from a change. Individual discussions allow the project manager to check their understanding of what users anticipate from the system. But it is time-consuming and open to misinterpretation.

Secondment to the project team

This is a common way of ensuring that staff are represented – not just at the planning stage, but throughout the project. Remember that having staff representatives on the project team does not guarantee they will be effective. Do they transmit all requests from their colleagues, and do they take back all the relevant information? If in doubt, create other channels so that information reaches the staff directly.

Seminars and newsletters

Seminars and newsletters can be used to keep groups of staff informed about project progress, and to cut down on any secrecy about the change which might be developing. Staff will be able to ask questions directly, and the discussion itself will probably generate new ideas, and increase willingness to use the system.

On large-scale projects, it will be difficult to arrange progress seminars for all users. To make sure that all staff are up-to-date, produce a project progress newsletter. In this way you ensure that the information you want to transmit goes directly to the users. Consider using videos or Intranet web sites to convey information consistently and widely.

Avoiding communication distortions

The manager of a management information project in a local authority realised that ambiguities were arising between what staff and potential users were being told by working party representatives and how the project was progressing in reality. The project managers decided that the best solution was to hold user seminars backed up by information sheets. The information sheets were sent directly to the staff, by name, a few days before the seminar.

Deal with snags and publicise success

If difficulties with the new system arise, do not ignore them. A utility company which experienced a lot of problems in adapting existing software to a new situation found this was beginning to undermine staff commitment. They adopted a deliberate policy of concentrating effort on to problem areas as soon as they arose, and told everyone what the problems were. They believed that this helped to reassure staff that their difficulties were being taken seriously and helped to maintain morale.

Bad news travels fast, whereas good news is taken for granted. Aim for some early victories, however small, and then make sure that everyone, including management, knows what has been achieved. Continue to report the benefits being experienced, and how reluctant people would be to go back to the old system.

Moving a factory

The project manager of a move which had become controversial reported on how he had gained staff support:

> *'The apparent changes in strategy had created a feeling of disbelief in some of the staff who will be obstacles to the move unless their opinions can be altered. The project manager must publicise the positive steps being taken towards the achievement of the move. Something we did was to use the informal network to put out the message that the furniture has been ordered, the new equipment is being installed, the desk layout is being drawn up, etc. This encouraged people by showing that finance was available, and that the change was happening.*
>
> *'Another means to help the reality to become clearer was to allow some of the staff to visit the new premises, and let them see the partitions being erected, and the phone lines put in.'*

Manage the timing of consultation

The timing of consultation raises a dilemma. 'As early as possible' sounds sensible, but this needs careful thought. Advantages of early participation include:

- replacing rumour with fact;
- people have time to accept that the changes are going to happen;
- people are more enthusiastic at the start of a new project.

To have extensive discussions with staff is, however, very time-consuming. Early involvement can also raise people's expectations and lead to disillusion if the project is delayed or postponed. So it is worth stressing that:

- these are initial investigations;
- the projects may not happen;
- the change may not do all they want.

CASE STUDY

Finco

Finco was established in 1998 as a joint venture between a major oil company and a consulting business. The purpose was to centralise and harmonise the oil company's transaction processing activities in a single location. This would lead to cost savings and encourage sharing of knowledge across the European operations. Historically, the separate European companies had operated independently and the company embodied many different national cultures. Finco would be established in the UK, and would draw work from the 18 existing national operating companies.

The concept of centralising back-office accounting and administration activities into Finco was based on the assumption that the tasks were standard, the computer systems consistent and the procedures harmonised. This would allow Finco to organise its workload by procedure to secure the benefits of common processes. This assumption was unfounded. The oil company's processes and systems were discrete, haphazard and customised in each national company. There were no standard processes – for example, no consistency in the way supplier invoices were processed in Denmark as compared to Belgium or Greece.

The company established a separate migration team for each location. A work transfer leader was appointed to coordinate each migration and report to the Operations Director in the UK. The work transfer leaders were mainly seconded consultants. They were technically competent, and focused on software design issues. When each team returned to Finco the consultant was typically moved to another project by the consultancy. The migration teams had about 20 employees and their task was to work in the respective local offices for about 12 weeks and learn the tasks. They would then return to the UK and perform the tasks in the Finco centre. Employees were recruited to join Finco on the basis of their technical competencies, and were well trained in that aspect of the work.

The national offices continued to work and react autonomously to the work transfer project. The project was sensitive as local employees were being asked to hand over their jobs and train the Finco employees to perform them.

The project met significant resistance in many of the local business units. Under pressure to meet revenue targets, Finco speeded up the migration process. They also tried to reduce costs by hiring less well-qualified staff and spending less on training. This affected quality and customer satisfaction fell. This in turn frustrated experienced employees, who left the company.

These difficulties led the oil company Board to terminate future migrations until stability was achieved. By this time Finco employed 400 staff. There was significant conflict between the joint venture partners, which resulted in the oil company buying out the consultancy and changing senior management. In early 2001 Finco was working to stabilise its current processes.

There was no high-level central sponsorship for the project. The support may have been implied but was not real and available when required. The support from the parent company was neutral – resulting in limited ownership and responsibility providing an atmosphere of resistance and politics.

Source: Documents and interviews with a senior Finco manager

Case questions

1 What decisions has management made about the staff to employ at Finco, both initially, and when the first migrations ran into difficulty?

2 What assumptions lay behind these decisions?

3 What different assumptions could they have made, and how would they have led to different decisions?

4 How will these decisions have affected the users of the service?

5 How could the company have handled the process when the teams returned to Finco better?

Summary

This chapter has examined how project managers can influence staff and users to support the project, in the areas of objectives, resources and control.

The key points from this chapter are:

- In exercising influence, it is easy to ensure compliance; however, internalisation of project needs is more useful.
- Motivation theories provide guidance on how the manager can secure commitment.
- The project manager should look for opportunities to design work that satisfies needs for esteem and self-actualisation.
- Acceptance can be fostered by encouraging consultation in the project design and implementation.
- Several practical techniques for encouraging consultation were introduced.

Chapter questions

1 Because projects are essentially about creating something new, how can they also be a way of satisfying basic physiological and safety needs?

2 Why are projects especially suited as a way to increase the satisfaction of the need for self-actualisation?

3 If time is short to implement a project, how can a manager justify consulting staff?

4 In what circumstances may consultation be a waste of time?

Further reading

Wickens, P.D. (1995) *The Ascendant Organisation*. Basingstoke: Macmillan. This account of the author's experience of running Nissan's UK manufacturing site includes many insights into ways of managing staff during a time of rapid change.

References

Boddy, D. and Buchanan, D.A. (1992) *Take the Lead: Interpersonal Skills for Project Managers*. Hemel Hempstead: Prentice Hall.

Boddy, D. and Gunson, N. (1996) *Organizations in the Network Age*. London: Routledge.

Cohen, A.R. and Bradford, D.L. (1989) 'Influence without authority: the use of alliances and reciprocity to accomplish work', *Organizational Dynamics*, Winter, 4–17.

Ezzamel, M. and Wilmott, H. (1998) 'Accounting for teamwork: a critical study of group-based systems of organizational control', *Administrative Science Quarterly*, 43, 358–96.

Handy, C. (1993) *Understanding Organisations*. Harmondsworth: Penguin Books.

Huczynski, A.A. (1996) *Influencing Within Organizations*. Hemel Hempstead: Prentice Hall.

Knights, D. and Murray, F. (1994) *Managers Divided: Organisation Politics and Information Technology Management*. Chichester: Wiley.

Lloyd, C. and Newell, H. (1998) 'Computerising the sales force: the introduction of technical change in a non-union workforce', *New Technology, Work and Employment*, 13, 104–15.

Maslow, A.H. (1943) 'A theory of human motivation', *Psychological Review*, 50, 370–96.

Yukl, G. and Tracey, J.B. (1992) 'Consequences of influence tactics used with subordinates, peers and the boss', *Journal of Applied Psychology*, 77, 525–35.

12 Managing up

Introduction

Project managers need to influence senior management to act in ways that support the project. That support has to be earned, and argued for, in the face of competing claims. In some cases, the competition is for resources or other forms of backing that the job requires, or to demonstrate a sense of ownership towards the project. In other cases ensuring clarity of objectives is critical, because members of senior management are likely to have different priorities. It is also valuable to ensure that others in the organisation recognise that the senior team supports the project. Finally, there may be issues to do with monitoring and control – as problems arise the project manager will, in severe cases, need senior support to help resolve them. Given the political nature of organisations, a project will suffer if others can challenge or undermine the status or legitimacy of the change. The sponsors of the project may need to 'manage up' to ensure they have a defence against that argument.

This chapter shows how the project manager can take a positive, active role in managing their relationship with senior management. The chapter begins by outlining more fully why project managers need support from those above them in the hierarchy, and then indicates some danger signals. The second section introduces relevant research on effective tactics for managing up, especially the use of rational persuasion. The final sections offer suggestions on how to ensure that appropriate structures are in place to support individual efforts to influence senior management.

Objectives

After reading this chapter you should be able to:

- describe why project managers need to influence upwards during a project;
- identify the danger signals that indicate a lack of senior management support or commitment;
- summarise research on effective upward influence tactics;
- outline practices for influencing upwards effectively;
- evaluate the structures and formal mechanisms that support individual efforts.

The project manager depends on senior managers

Projects begin in a loose and unstructured way. Someone has an idea, sees a possibility, observes an opportunity for improvement. Through a process of trying out the idea on colleagues, discussing how it might work, and lobbying for support, an identifiable project comes into being. Its ultimate fate will depend on how well or otherwise those responsible for the project manage their relationship with senior management. They need their support in the areas of objectives, resources and control, as summarised in Figure 12.1.

Clarifying goals

A project manager who is active at this stage can ensure that the project emerges with a clear vision of what the change is for, and has a clear set of objectives. Unless this is done, the later stages of the change will be difficult to handle:

> *'The size and specification of the project – the tonnages of oils to be made, and the specifications of the products – was not handled well by the commercial functions within the company. It affected results in that when the products eventually emerged from the refinery, we did not have ready customer outlets. Another problem was the decision to develop all our own technology . . . this was a mammoth task and would never have been entertained by a major company.'*

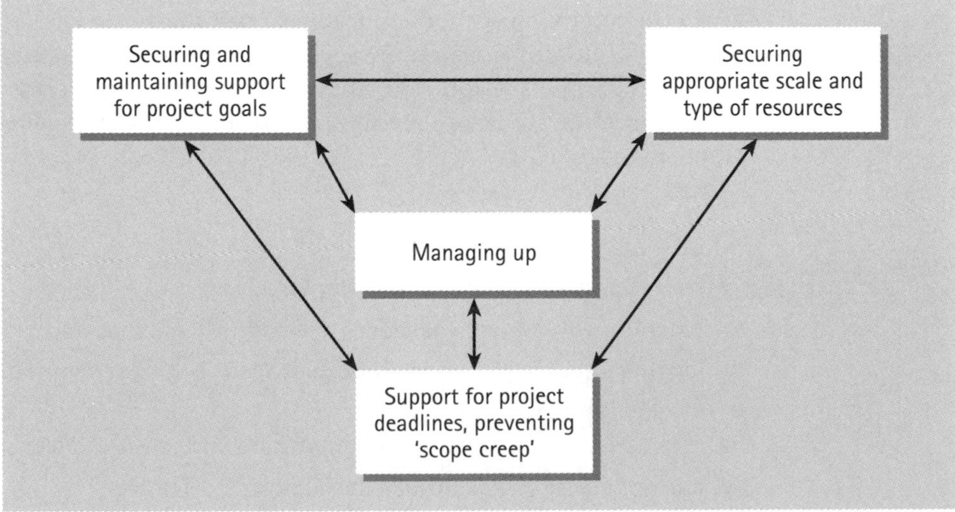

Figure 12.1 How managing up can support effective project management

Senior management has other preoccupations, and knows little of the project. They will be unclear about the detailed implications of moving from the broad idea to a realistic plan, and of the problems that will need to be solved on the way through. The project manager will try to engage the attention of senior management in this process.

Visions can easily turn into fantasies – so the project leader needs to ensure that senior managers' expectations are visionary, but also achievable and realistic. The danger of unrealistic expectations seems to be particularly strong in projects involving new technology, where it is easy to underestimate the problems, and to overestimate the benefits:

'A major drawback was that, for a small family company with no experience of implementing a complex project, there was an inadequate allowance for the teething problems to be overcome. They did not appreciate that large, modern process plants are complex in design and layout and need many weeks of familiarisation, by skilled operators, before they can be operated efficiently. There seemed to be the idea that once the plant was mechanically complete, then it was simply a case of pushing a button and product would flow. Of course, in the real world, nothing could be further from the truth.'

The case study at the end of Chapter 11 (Finco) revealed a similar misconception by senior management about the nature of the task they were initiating. Their underestimation of its complexity severely hindered the success of the project, from which it is only now recovering.

Securing resources

Big projects need big resources – and the project manager has to secure these from senior management or functional heads. In the latter case, they may then need the support of senior managers to secure them (as the case study at the end of Chapter 10 showed):

'The product engineering manager has been championing the project, but no resources have yet been allocated, despite several presentations to senior management. This has resulted in virtually no progress.'

Money and facilities are often less of a problem than staff of the right quality:

'We need people who are good at the travel business, and who can help develop and implement the new systems. Getting people who are good at one of these aspects is OK – but those who are good at both are like gold-dust. And of course the operations side don't want to lose them to the project.'

Staff who are put on the project may lack commitment. If they are still attached to a line department, working for the project part-time, they are always likely to be pulled back by their line manager to meet a greater departmental priority:

> *'The situation in X is no better. In fact it's probably degraded a little bit in the sense that resource in that area has become even tighter, as one of the key individuals is about to transfer inside the company. The Y situation has gone from bad to worse. One of my key team players there has decided – or his organisation has decided – that they have other priorities and he needs to do other work.'*

And a few months later:

> *'This is the second time we have been to that management team, to pose how we wish to move forward, and to try and get the resources that are required. It is, however, worth taking the time up front to get all members fully supportive of what we are trying to do. Although it takes a bit longer we should, by pressure and by other individuals demonstrating the benefits of the system we are proposing, eventually move them forward.'*

Misunderstanding the task at Finco

As the case study at the end of Chapter 11 showed, senior management's misunderstanding of the task led them to employ the wrong type of people in the new centre. Believing it was a routine administrative task, they recruited mainly young, inexperienced staff. These proved unable to deal with both the technical complexities and the interpersonal issues that arose in transferring the work from the separate national companies.

Securing adequate resources from the top helps the project manager in other ways. It shows in a tangible way that senior management takes the project seriously, and so increases the prestige and authority of those working on it. A well-supported project will be more attractive to people who are asked to work on it. Slack will be available to cope with unexpected difficulties and to use unexpected opportunities.

Monitoring and control

In a dynamic environment all projects are likely to change as circumstances change, and as people learn during design and implementation. Project managers need the support of senior managers to protect against 'scope creep' – the tendency for new things to be added to a project after people have agreed the specification. Inadequate monitoring is also at the root of the problem of project escalation, where projects appear to consume ever more resources, with less and less sign of producing the expected results (Drummond, 1996).

Project managers can also use milestones and targets set by senior management as a tool for influencing other senior managers, as the box illustrates.

Using a deadline to drive a project

The HR manager of a public agency who was leading a project to implement a new management structure commented in early 2001:

> *'I basically ignored blockages from senior managers and just carried on. If people were being difficult by not settling issues or not setting budgets, I would just go ahead. I would tell people in meetings that if they had problems, then come and see me. I really drove it forward: instead of talking about things we showed that we were doing it.*
>
> *'The driver was that we had to meet the April 1 2001 target. That meant that I knew that we had to do a, b and c before Christmas, we had to do the interviews about now, etc. Just no time for chat or worries. The Board had set the time – the restructuring had to be in to fit the financial year. It had to be April. I could use that to keep the thing moving. My remit came from the Chief Executive – she said it must be April 1.'*

Source: Discussions with the HR manager

NOTEPAD 12.1

Assessing the role of senior managers in the project

- In what ways are senior managers involved in your project?
- How have you worked with them to create a clear vision of the change?
- How realistic have they been in their expectations, and what have you tried to do to manage these?
- What changes are taking place elsewhere that could affect your project in the next 3–6 months?
- Are senior managers aware of the costs of changing targets?

What are the danger signals?

There are visible danger signals that give early warning to the project team of possible trouble with senior management. These include:

- interfering without consulting the project manager;
- not providing support when needed;
- appointing junior staff to the project (and requiring to be consulted on most decisions);
- not giving public support;
- not including the project manager on relevant decision-making bodies;
- making unfounded promises or commitments;
- ignoring, or discounting, unfavourable information;
- paying too much attention to unfounded criticism;
- delaying decisions and approvals;
- allocating resources to other projects.

A technical or a business problem?

Boddy and Buchanan (1992) reported the difficulties which the project manager of a new refinery faced with his senior management:

> During the very difficult commissioning period it was apparent that the Managing Director, himself having a technical bias, had formed the view that most of the problems were technical, and that it was necessary to bring in certain consultants to help us. He also allowed another director to recruit a new senior manager from the oil industry. At this time the project was actually technically in good shape, although there were still things to finish off . . . it was becoming apparent that the major problems were now almost entirely commercial, in that markets could not be found for the product.

Source: Boddy and Buchanan (1992, p. 79)

Strategies for managing up

The starting point is for the project manager to recognise that he or she needs to be active rather than passive in dealing with those above them in the hierarchy. Gabarro and Kotter pointed out many years ago that 'effective managers take time and effort to manage not only relationships with their subordinates but also with their bosses, (yet) some . . . nevertheless assume an almost passively reactive stance *vis-à-vis* their bosses. Such a stance almost always hurts these managers and their companies' (1980, p. 1). They point out that the relationship is essentially one of mutual dependence between fallible human beings. The boss needs the manager – and equally the manager needs the boss – especially in providing a link to other parts of the organisation, in providing resources and in ensuring priorities match those of the organisation. Gabarro and Kotter advise that both need to understand each other's world, and to develop a healthy working relationship – summed up in Table 12.1.

Table 12.1 Managing the relationship with your boss

- **Make sure you understand your boss and his/her context**, including:
  - their goals and objectives
  - the pressures on them
  - their strengths, weaknesses, blind spots
  - their preferred working style
- **Assess yourself and your needs**, including:
  - your own strengths and weaknesses
  - your personal style
  - your predisposition towards dependence on an authority figure
- **Develop and maintain a relationship** that:
  - fits both your needs and styles
  - keeps your boss informed
  - is based on dependability and honesty
  - selectively uses your boss's time and resources.

Source: Based on Gabarro and Kotter (1980)

A general approach such as that advocated in Table 12.1 will help project managers to build their credibility as they compete for the time and attention of senior management.

The work of Yukl and Tracey (1992) described in Chapter 10 provides a theoretical basis for managing up effectively. Their research showed that rational persuasion was used most often by those trying to exercise influence in an upward direction (and hence the focus on that approach in this chapter). This is consistent with the work of Case *et al.* (1988), who conducted an empirical study into how managers influenced those above them in the hierarchy. They analysed self-reports of 271 influence attempts (145 successful, 126 unsuccessful) by managers. The research team asked managers to specify which methods of influence they had used, and whether the attempt had been successful. They concluded that the most commonly used methods in successful influence attempts were:

- presenting facts, data and documentation in support;
- presenting a complete plan;
- using persistence and repetition;
- developing and showing support of others.

In summary, they concluded that 'those who are effective at influencing superiors appear to be those who prepare well, touch many bases for support, use a combination of approaches and persist until they win their case' (p. 30).

Effective upward influence

The background to upward influence

Before outlining useful tactics, it is worth recalling some essential steps in any influence attempt. These were set out in Chapter 10 (pp. 165–70) and include such fundamental preparatory tasks as:

- find out whose support you need (i.e. select the target carefully);
- be clear about your own objectives, and express them in terms of specific results, such as, 'by the end of the meeting, the manager of European distribution will have agreed to release one member of staff to the project for two weeks';
- try to identify their 'invisible committee' which will be influencing their attitude;
- distinguish between their interests and their positions;
- understand the target of influence values.

Spending time on these preliminary tasks is likely to mean that the more detailed tactics can be designed and targeted more accurately.

Presenting facts, data and documentation in support

The conclusion by Case *et al.* (1988) on the effectiveness of this approach is in line with case study evidence from Boddy and Buchanan (1992). Changing the views of sceptical senior managers needed significant planning and preparation:

> A great deal of time was wasted earlier, when the choice of the project team was vetoed by the Board, who imposed their own solution. So (this time) a more rigorous approach to report-writing must be adopted, to ensure that ideas are communicated with maximum clarity. Although these reports may not necessarily be read by the Group Board, it is more likely that a well-written and well-presented document will be noticed, and less likely that it will be rejected without recourse to the author (p. 85).

Another project manager drew on past experience to reach a similar conclusion, in preparing a verbal presentation:

> Previous presentations had been rejected, because of poor planning, and weak proposals for achieving objectives. The manager was in favour of the concepts, but would not give his support until a detailed plan was presented. To manage upwards in this company, the presenter must anticipate all questions, and present the data in a logical and concise manner. So the new presentation contained both Gantt and Pert charts for the first time. It was accepted (p. 85).

In taking this approach, the following practices will increase the chance of success:

- **Manner of presentation.** Think out who will receive the proposal, or be at the meeting to discuss it. Consider what their interests are, and how they are likely to view the proposal. What might allay their fears, enhance their commitment? Use the right language; think of the perspective from which the audience will view it. This will probably mean phrasing recommendations in the language of finance or business, rather than of technology or human relations.
- **Facts and data in support.** Find out how others have dealt with similar changes and give examples of how what is proposed has worked elsewhere. Find out who you know there, and arrange to learn from their experiences. Decide on the best arguments, evidence, examples that senior managers will be able to identify with.
- **Supporting documentation.** Decide what material to send out before a meeting, and how it should be prepared. It has a better chance of success if it shows knowledge of current policy relevant to the matter, and is presented concisely and reasonably, in clear terms, without technical jargon.

Presenting a complete plan

A project leader for a radical information system in a bank depended on top management support against attacks from another service department. He and his team made presentations about the intended system to senior managers, which appeared to work:

'Each demonstration was carefully planned and rehearsed. Credibility was also gained by using the external consultant's experience, where he had introduced similar projects in major high street banks.

'The system was demonstrated to a key manager, who was also the Deputy Chairman of one of the businesses. He was impressed by what he saw, the ease of use, and immediately ordered a personal computer for his own use. This information was made known to all concerned, and soon even those who had sworn never to have a personal computer were ordering one too.'

Three specific practices which are likely to help approval include:

1 **Work it through.** If possible, present a worked-through solution, not one that evidently needs further work. This will help convince people that you are committed to the idea, and have anticipated the possible snags.

2 **Timing.** There are always competing pressures on senior management time. Think carefully about when to push a thing, and when to hold back. What events or changes are imminent that will make senior people more receptive to a proposal?

3 **Make their decision easy.** Another useful aim is to try to make their decision easy. Make it appear uncontroversial, neat, no further angles to worry about or that need further consideration and another meeting. The more the influencer can do this, the more likely it is that senior managers will approve.

Persistence and repetition

Senior management may not pay attention straight away, and the project manager needs to be prepared to persist with their argument. This can be highly discouraging, and adds to the vulnerability of the role. A project manager wanting senior management attention needs to remain visible and prominent:

'It's the same as happens to some product design in its early days. An individual or a group of individuals need to go out on a limb with an idea, and be able to articulate that idea to a wider audience before they can get any interest and therefore any support and investment to go forward.'

Persistence can also involve being proactive, and creating opportunities. The effective project manager does not always wait to be asked to present ideas to senior managers. They can take the initiative by looking for opportunities to get their views across – forthcoming meetings, presentations, seminars. They take or create opportunities to meet as many as possible informally before a meeting, to sense their reaction, and to get clues about areas of concern or opposition.

Developing and showing support of others

Finally, the research showed that attempts to influence senior managers were more likely to succeed if the proposal was backed by other groups. Surprisingly, managers rarely used this tactic, despite its evident effectiveness. It involves more preparation, as those whose support the manager wants need to be briefed and persuaded. Doing so pays off, however – not least by reassuring senior managers that others have considered and been convinced by the case. It reduces the risk to them of agreeing what is being asked.

The project manager therefore needs to prime key people to write or speak in support of the project. They could be other line departments, or staff groups such as personnel or finance. Persuading them to act on behalf of the project will in itself be an exercise in influence.

Building support by showing progress

In early 2001 the manager driving a Social Work Information System in a local authority commented:

> *'The project will have big effects on staff and departments right across the authority. Securing the funding itself was no mean achievement. Having done that I still had to keep my end up, and protect the work we had done. I have to be there to protect it from other claims on the budget.*
>
> *'I think the leadership in my case has been more in the background, getting the funding, getting the infrastructure in place. If people see that on the ground they are more likely to work with you: they say "well, she's moving it, let's get in on this". Doing various committee things in the background. Because the project is something people never thought they would see in a lifetime in the council – technically a very advanced system for a social work department.*
>
> *'Even if the timetable slips they can see that things are happening – and they are then willing to put their time into it. It's very easy to put off work on a project like this, with so many other things going on with reorganisations, etc. I keep the thing focused, ensure that we take a few steps forward, remind them of it – and they work with you.'*

Source: Discussions with the manager

Support needs long-term planning, as relationships and credibility have to be built before support can be called upon. Look for opportunities to build credit, by helping other managers, or building resources which you can offer in return for their support.

A caution

In deciding how best to put these ideas into practice, the manager should recall that while necessary, they are not necessarily sufficient. For while the Case *et al.* (1988) study showed that 'Presenting facts and data as support' was used in 76 successful influence attempts, it was also used in 48 unsuccessful attempts. So the tactic is more likely to succeed than fail, but is not guaranteed. Failure could arise from the quality of the data presented, competition from yet more convincing proposals, or other factors in the situation. More fundamentally, it perhaps draws attention to the ritualistic aspects of the rational approach. Those who emphasise the political aspects of influence stress that an appearance of rationality is deeply entrenched in the culture of most Western organisations. Senior managers expect proposals to be presented in this way – but their choice may be influenced by factors other than the apparent rationality of the proposal.

Building mechanisms for upward influence

The earlier comments have centred on a range of interpersonal skills which can help project managers influence senior managers. The ability to manage up can also be supported by appropriate formal mechanisms. These include building communication links and documentary methods for keeping top management informed and supportive.

Create the communication links

Project managers need to review the links they have with the sponsor of the project, the Board, or other senior management. Boddy and Buchanan (1992) reported the difficulty one manager had faced:

> My role as adviser to the senior management group means that I am not actually part of that group, and therefore not involved in all issues. It is therefore difficult with something like this to get a hearing for it in that group. Perhaps I need to identify someone within that group to talk the issues through with, and who may then take them forward or help me to take them forward.

The HR manager in the case on page 197 faced a similar problem, in that she was not part of the main Board which made many decisions about the new structure during 2000.

The general danger is that the Board will be getting information about the project, even if only in the form of rumours and innuendo. And bad news travels faster than good. So it is in the project manager's interest to ensure that they have accurate, factual information about progress – good and bad. It will be easier to win if the sponsor is managed, so that the project has a respected backer, rather than one who is low in status. If necessary, those promoting the change may need to use some initiative to seek out a favourably inclined, *and* respected, member of senior management to provide the link. They must then make doubly sure that that person is attracted by the project, and kept up-to-date with developments, positive or negative, so that they are always at least as well informed as any other senior manager. Practices have included:

- A project manager made a point of briefing his director fully before each Board meeting during a project, just in case questions arose. Subsequently he persuaded his sponsor to secure a one-hour spot at every second Board meeting, at which the Board were brought up-to-date with current technology issues in the business, and possible future moves.

- A project manager in a local authority identified an elected member who showed an interest in new technology, and invited her to a full briefing on current and proposed systems. This again helped ensure that there was at least one informed opinion being expressed at policy meetings.
- Another recalled that he deliberately solicited the support from a Development Director, in order to influence the rest of senior management.

These examples show project managers actively managing their sponsors. They did not play a passive role, but actively sought out opportunities to build links to the higher levels. In another case, a manager used success in one task to gain power with her boss's boss. Her immediate superior was lukewarm towards the task, but by completing it successfully the project manager showed it could be done. This allowed her to gain visibility and credibility; it also improved her access to the political levels of the organisation, to the benefit of later projects. Delivering successfully on something which is valued by senior management is a major tactic in managing up.

Create regular reports

Senior managers will also expect the project managers to provide a written report on progress. A common method is to establish a weekly reporting mechanism whereby project managers feed details on their progress to senior managers. This used to be a paper exercise, but is now likely to use shared files on a computer network, or an Intranet site.

Web-based reporting at a semiconductor company

A multinational firm in the electronics industry reorganised its worldwide facilities during 1999 and 2000. This involved rearranging capacity between the sites, and implementing various information systems to support manufacturing. The IS department designed a web-based reporting system, in which each sub-project manager completed a standard report showing progress against actions. The site also contained standard programme documents which would previously have been on paper files.

The information entered by each project manager was visible to everyone with access to the site (most staff). In addition the programme manager called a weekly meeting of all project managers. Each brought up their report on a large screen in the conference room, and talked the programme manager through the report, and any issues on which they needed support.

The system worked so well that it has now been adopted as standard programme management practice throughout the company.

Source: Personal communication from a project manager

Figure 12.2 shows an example Weekly Project Report that was used during the Columbus Project at The Royal Bank of Scotland. This very radical change meant that the Board required constant reassurance about progress, and staff

Programme Office
Composite Progress Report

Week Ending: – 7 April 2000

Programme Status (Red / Amber / Green): Green

Summary:
Product tables for database delayed six weeks due to marketing re-planning. Communications plan re-scheduled. Systems Development Phase 2 at Amber due to resourcing problems, but no major impact expected.

Major Activities Carried Out This Week
- Consolidated May results produced and completed monthly report
- Risks Workshop held, and Risk Log distributed for comment
- Most Union submissions are now complete
- Finance re-forecasts completed
- High-level plan for property agreed

Major Activities Planned for Next Week
- Issue Board papers for May
- Complete population of database with YTD May information, actual and budget
- Input to systems work on tactical solutions – consolidation
- Union consultations
- Follow-up Risk Log to confirm gaps and establish action plans to close gaps

Missed / Slipped Milestones Reported This Week

	Completion Date:		
	Baseline	**Estimated**	**Actual**
Database Build			
Create entities on system for customer data and populate YTD April actuals	1 April		6 April
Create integrated product tables	20 March	30 April	
System Development Phase 2			
Preliminary coding modules completed	4 April	7 April	7 April
Decide on processes for maintenance of account figures	20 April	25 April	

Issues / Actions Required
1. Fast-track internal recruitment processes to allow earliest possible start dates for systems development team members.
   Project Director to discuss with HR Director.
2. The uncertainty of external reporting requirements impacts a number of areas.
   Conclude discussions as fast as possible.

Figure 12.2 Example Weekly Progress Report

Programme Office
Composite Progress Report

Week Ending: – 7 April 2000

Programme Status (Red / Amber / Green): Green

Summary:
Product tables for database delayed six weeks due to marketing re-planning. Communications plan re-scheduled. Systems Development Phase 2 at Amber due to resourcing problems, but no major impact expected.

Major Activities Carried Out This Week
- Consolidated May results produced and completed monthly report
- Risks Workshop held, and Risk Log distributed for comment
- Most Union submissions are now complete
- Finance re-forecasts completed
- High-level plan for property agreed

Major Activities Planned for Next Week
- Issue Board papers for May
- Complete population of database with YTD May information, actual and budget
- Input to systems work on tactical solutions – consolidation
- Union consultations
- Follow-up Risk Log to confirm gaps and establish action plans to close gaps

Missed / Slipped Milestones Reported This Week

	Completion Date:		
	Baseline	**Estimated**	**Actual**
Database Build			
Create entities on system for customer data and populate YTD April actuals	1 April		6 April
Create integrated product tables	20 March	30 April	
System Development Phase 2			
Preliminary coding modules completed	4 April	7 April	7 April
Decide on processes for maintenance of account figures	20 April	25 April	

Issues / Actions Required
1. Fast-track internal recruitment processes to allow earliest possible start dates for systems development team members.
   Project Director to discuss with HR Director.
2. The uncertainty of external reporting requirements impacts a number of areas.
   Conclude discussions as fast as possible.

Figure 12.3 Example Composite Progress Report

designed these forms to provide that. The project reports fed into the Composite Plan Report, shown in Figure 12.3.

The Composite Plan Report can then provide the programme owners (the budget holders and executive decision-makers) with a quick and accurate update on the overall programme situation. The box below describes another device used in the Columbus project.

Project Columbus: 'The Black Box'

As a high-profile project, the Bank's Board were demanding constant reassurance of progress and control. Realising the need for rapid, accurate updates on the various projects, the Columbus Programme Office team devised a method of gathering regular information from each project area against an agreed set of measures. They developed a system – nicknamed the 'Black Box' – for collating these reports and producing an overview of the current situation.

Providing information on project performance to the Black Box took time – which stressed project managers often felt they did not have. Where projects were behind plan or above budget, project managers were reluctant to provide accurate information. Staff operating the Black Box had to be skilled relationship-managers. They had to encourage project managers to support the process, while at the same time challenging and probing for the most accurate information.

Source: Boddy *et al.* (2002)

The Black Box and other reports were in a simple, easy to understand format that focused on exceptions. They kept people adequately informed and 'surprises' were kept to a minimum. Above all, they helped the project to retain the support of the Board and other senior managers during a long and complex series of projects.

CASE STUDY

Chem Tec

Chem Tec is the holding company for a group of companies in the USA (Chem Inc.), and one in the UK (Chem Ltd) which manufacture chemicals for the semiconductor industry. Chem Tec senior management decided to implement an Enterprise Resource Planning system across the group, which could electronically link the Finance, Purchasing, Sales & Marketing, Manufacturing and Quality Control departments.

The project was led corporately by an implementation team from Chem Tec. The project also included the UK plant, Chem Ltd. Their Manufacturing Manager reflected:

'My role meant that I was heavily involved in designing the systems with the consultants. As the project progressed my role grew and I became the manufacturing lead in implementing the project not just at Chem Ltd but also at Chem Inc.

'The original goal of the project was to improve financial control through increased visibility of daily accounting information – for example to allow better cash management through centralised control. They also intended only to implement the software

at Chem Inc., with Chem Ltd being completed later. We felt that little additional resource would be required to include Chem Ltd. We also had to point out to senior management that as we work in several European currencies our reporting requirements are complex. Unless we were included in the project from the start, all of these would still have to be done in the old way and then fed into the Chem Tec system. So there would be few benefits without simultaneous implementation at Chem Ltd. Together with Chem Inc. we persuaded top management to implement simultaneously.

'Chem Inc. wanted the new system to match as closely as possible their current practices to avoid confusion on system launch and minimise the training effort. This group felt that current business systems were "efficient enough". At Chem Ltd we intended to challenge all our current systems during implementation and, where agreed, change them. We are a vibrant, dynamic plant which welcomes change.

'The atmosphere at Chem Inc. is very different and less dynamic. Chem Inc. also has the corporate head office and the Vice-Presidents play a significant role in day-to-day operations. Change is not really welcomed. The presence of the VPs at Chem Inc. slows decisions as even small ones need their approval. They are more used to debating issues as a group, gaining consensus and then implementing slowly.

'April 1999 saw the first Chem Inc./Chem Ltd implementation team meeting and discussion was commenced about whether Chem Ltd were included. This was the key decision at this point. Inc. were keen for us to be involved, as we had shown great enthusiasm and built a clear understanding of the system and how it could support our business. The same enthusiasm was not present at Inc. I believe that this was a major driving force in the decision to include Ltd in a parallel implementation as without us Inc. would not have implemented. At this point the decision-making power was fully in the hands of the few individuals from Ltd and the project started really gathering speed.

'Around this time, in late May/early June the scope of the project changed. Firstly the group wanted to reduce the scope to a basic financial reporting system. I felt this blow the hardest as this was where I realised that the system would only allow financial tracking of manufacturing operations. It did not provide any new data in the production process. About this time I proposed a different architecture, which would support the long-term vision I had. Corporate management disapproved, and we had lengthy debates with them. They demanded that the architecture was changed to use different functions. This was their first involvement in the process and came as a bombshell to us as we had already proved that the system they were proposing was not suitable for our operation. This became a big issue but I persisted in my point of view. Eventually they agreed that we would move forward with the approach we had proposed, though it was made clear in a number of conference calls that this was against the project manager's wishes.

'Two key learning points for both organisations centre around top level management involvement or at least understanding of the key benefits to be gained from such a system, and also of what the implementation involved, what the end product was likely to look like. This problem still exists and is now critical for the future development of any IT strategy within Chem Tec. The main reason for this is ignorance of the system and what is possible.

'We at Ltd were the first to grasp the opportunity that was presented, and quickly gained an understanding of how this would change the business in a positive manner. After this realisation it was then left to us to convince the Inc. team that the same was true in their organisation.'

Source: Discussion with the Manufacturing Manager

Case questions

1. What problems is the manager at Chem Ltd having in dealing with his senior management at Chem Tec?
2. What differences are there over the objectives and potential of the project?
3. Are there any issues regarding resources?
4. What evidence is there in the case about how the manager at Ltd has influenced senior management to agree with his position?
5. Has he solved the long-term problem?
6. What are the risks in taking the line he has? How can he minimise those risks?

Summary

This chapter has examined how project managers can influence those above them in the hierarchy, with whom they have a mutually dependent relationship. It has used research on upward influencing to outline a range of practical tactics.

The key points from this chapter are:

- Project managers need the support of senior managers, and vice versa, to help clarify objectives, secure resources, and ensure flexible control. They should manage this relationship actively.
- The danger signals include interfering without consultation, not providing support when needed, not providing adequate links, and making unreasonable commitments.
- Managers are more likely to be successful in their upward influence attempts when they use reason, persistence and build coalitions that show their idea has the support of others.
- In preparing to use these tactics the manager should be aware that they are necessary rather than sufficient, and that non-rational factors will also be significant.
- Managing up can also be supported by creating good communication links through influential people, and through regular formal reporting systems.

Chapter questions

1 Do you agree that the project manager and senior managers are mutually dependent? Can you add other reasons to those given in the chapter?

2 What are the dangers of taking an active role towards senior management?

3 Which of the strategies identified by Yukl and his colleagues would you expect managers to use in support of rational methods?

4 How can a manager increase their power to influence senior managers (see Chapter 6)?

5 Why do interpersonal skills benefit from appropriate institutions?

Further reading

Bragg, M. (1996) *Reinventing Influence*. London: Pitman. Excellent account of how those without formal authority can develop their powers of influence.

Gillen, T. (1995) *Positive Influencing Skills*. London: Institute of Personnel Development. Clearly presented account of the author's views on the fundamental principles of influencing, and the core skills required to put them into practice.

References

Boddy, D. and Buchanan, D.A. (1992) *Take the Lead: Interpersonal Skills for Project Managers*. Hemel Hempstead: Prentice Hall.

Boddy, D., Boonstra, A. and Kennedy, G. (2001) *Managing Information Systems: An Organisational Perspective*. Harlow: Pearson Education.

Case, T., Dosier, L., Murkison, G. and Keys, B. (1988) 'How managers influence superiors: a study of upward influence tactic', *Leadership and Organizational Development Journal*, 9, 25–31.

Drummond, H. (1996) *Escalation in Decision-making: The Tragedy of Taurus*. Oxford: Oxford University Press.

Gabarro, J.J. and Kotter, J.P. (1980) 'Managing your boss', *Harvard Business Review*, 58:1, 92–100.

Yukl, G. and Tracey, J.B. (1992) 'Consequences of influence tactics used with subordinates, peers and the boss', *Journal of Applied Psychology*, 77, 525–35.

13 Conclusions and questions

Introduction

This short concluding chapter is intended to bring together the main points developed earlier in the book, and to suggest some remaining questions of interest to practitioners and academics. The central argument is that our knowledge of the unique issues faced by those managing organisational projects is tentative and provisional. Our knowledge of project management is essentially 'work in progress'. Projects offer considerable opportunities for learning by those who work on them as part of their careers. They offer equally good opportunities for learning more about many of the processes of project management examined in this book. A synopsis of the main themes leads to some suggestions of areas of research that would meet the requirements of both academic rigour and practical usefulness.

Perspective

The central theme of this book has been that people managing large projects depend on other people, and that they need to influence these other people to act in a particular way. These people are not subordinates – they are in a variety of positions in and around the organisation, and the manager typically lacks any formal or positional authority over them. This is a risky position, but if a project has a high profile in the organisation, the rewards of success are probably greater than the same effort put into managing a routine, background operation. Projects can help the manager's career – not least because they can use the skills required to manage projects in other high-profile management roles.

This book has been designed to help those wanting to develop their understanding of the project management role, and so begin to enhance further the skills which it seems to require. Drawing on extensive research with active project managers, it has presented a distinctive view of the project manager's role. This is no longer about drawing up schedules, Gantt charts and critical paths. These are useful techniques, but modern project managers need above all to understand human motivation, team development, and how to influence people with different interests in volatile environments. They need to be able to influence a wide range of interested parties, using both personal skills and institutional support. They need to deal with both the processes and politics of projects.

The book is possible because although the specific nature of every project is unique, they have features in common:

- the requirement to meet some performance targets – however ambiguous and fluid these may be in practice;
- they depend on people, not techniques – project managers need to influence other people;
- projects take place within a context – the project is intended to partially change this context, and at the same time the context will affect the success or otherwise of the project.

These common features of apparently unique projects provide opportunities for learning, as managers can learn from others' experience in dealing with the common themes of influencing people to meet fluid performance criteria in a volatile context. The book has tried to support that learning by offering a framework within which to consider the issues, drawing on the author's research and that of other writers.

It deals with major organisational and other changes which are novel, and where there are usually different interests. Not only is the outside world likely to change during these projects; so too will the actions of the interested parties. This implies that political and interpersonal aspects of projects will matter. The book gives most attention to these. It also acknowledges that models and frameworks inevitably appear much tidier than the reality they try to represent. They are tools to help reflection and understanding – which only project managers themselves can gain by reflecting on the messy and turbulent state that is the nature of most organisational projects of any significance.

Overview

Part 1 introduced some ideas about the nature of projects in contemporary organisations. While these were once seen as relatively discrete, physical, construction-type projects, they are now usually deeply embedded in the way organisations work. This has implications for the skills required to manage them. One of the distinctive themes of the book is the emphasis on the uniqueness of projects, and Part 1 also outlined the features of particular projects that make them unique. Awareness of the features in Chapter 2 allows the project manager to diagnose significant project features, and anticipate areas likely to cause most difficulty. Chapter 3 introduced the theoretical basis of the book, namely the idea that projects interact with their context. It is the project manager's central role to ensure that the project changes elements of the context – such as technology, processes or structures. The aim is that those changes encourage behaviour which supports project objectives.

How people approach the project management task depends on their implicit theory of projects or of organisational change. Chapter 4 outlined four contrasting theories, each of which can be an accurate description of a project or an aspect of a project. Each theory implies a different approach to managing projects, so the manager needs diagnostic skills to decide which approach to use in which circumstances.

The central chapter in Part 2 used a variety of empirical sources to outline the nature of the project management role. It showed that, in addition to the traditional aspects of the work, many project managers now work in relatively political settings, and need to exercise a variety of influencing skills. Managers use their influencing skills to promote the interests of the project in three areas which research suggests make a difference to project performance:

- Goals and objectives – around which there is often conflict and uncertainty.
- Resources – for which there is competition with other managers.
- Monitoring and control – to ensure relevant players understand the position and can act on it.

Chapter 6 began the process of applying these ideas by offering a technique for identifying those with a stake in the project – who may be above the project manager in the hierarchy, in other departments or, increasingly often, in other organisations. Managing stakeholders is essentially a matter of developing and using power to influence behaviour that supports the project in the critical areas of goals, resources and control. The chapter identified the forms of power and methods of influence that a manager can use to influence any of the target groups. All these activities depend on the project manager influencing others – sometimes using their individual bases of power, at other times drawing support from positional or formal sources.

A major source of formal support takes the form of various management structures created by organisations within which to conduct project activities. While small projects can be handled informally, projects soon require some visible structure. Part 3 was devoted to this topic, especially the idea of the project team. Chapter 7 outlined the various forms of project structure and project teams that organisations use. It also made the point that project teams have both advantages and disadvantages, and project managers need to be aware of the potential costs of team-working – and to question whether it is always worth the time and effort. The other two chapters in Part 3 presented ideas from the organisational behaviour literature on the development and composition of teams. Management practices that can help improve their performance – in the areas of motivation, composition and working methods – were discussed, drawing on Hackman's (1990) research on team performance.

Part 4 moved beyond the team to consider the other sets of players that the project manager is likely to need to influence – to ensure support in the areas of goals, resources and support. The empirical work presented in Chapter 10 provided a structure for Part 4 as a whole, because each of the several methods of influence appear to work best with different target groups. Chapter 10 (Managing across) therefore focused on negotiating, Chapter 11 (Managing staff and users) on motivation and consultation, and Chapter 12 (Managing up) on rational presentation of arguments. In doing so, it was stressed that this was for presentational clarity only, and that effective project managers probably use the methods in combination.

Remaining questions

In an area as volatile as organisational change and project management there are very few certainties. The book has tried to present the available evidence on the relevant topic, but quite often this is based on limited sources of data. Elsewhere theories have been introduced to the field of project management which seem plausible – but which cannot avoid the fact that they were developed in quite different areas of management or organisational study. So the evidence throughout must be tentative, and is likely to be revised as research on the topic is extended.

There are several areas in which research could be of interest to both academics and practitioners. Just a few of the topics are mentioned, to indicate the kind of issues that could be fruitful topics of study:

1 Are the project features and contextual elements outlined in Chapters 2 and 3 the most useful categories for distinguishing projects and contexts? Such schemes are only of practical value if their use as a diagnostic tool allows the user (the project manager) to make some significant and deliberate adjustment to the way they approach the project. The schemes in Chapters 2 and 3 are based on the evidence available – but should be regarded as work in progress, awaiting refinement.

2 Are the four theories (or perspectives) on organisational change a valid description of the alternative ways in which people see the topic? Academics may then be interested in why people come to hold one view rather than another. Practitioners may find greater value in considering the implications for the skills of project management of each alternative. In particular there could be considerable value in working out in some depth the skills required to manage projects which fit the 'emergent' and 'political' perspectives.

3 There is considerable scope for research directly on project teams. The evidence on teamwork, and so the theory developed from that, comes from a largely accidental set of team types and circumstances. Very little appears to originate in direct empirical work on project teams, and the particular circumstances in which they operate. For example, a replication of Hackman's approach, focused on project teams (which accounted for only three of the 27 teams in that study) would be of great interest to academics and practitioners alike.

4 A similar suggestion can be made about the topics covered in Part 4. This is based on research and theory on how managers exercise influence, and the bases of the power sources that they use. Given the peculiar and essentially transient nature of project relationships, there must be considerable scope for examining the way project managers develop their power bases, how they use this in relation to different targets, and how those targets react.

As already mentioned, the research offered in support of the arguments throughout this book has (like so much management knowledge) come from a wide variety of disciplines, having been generated by an equally wide variety of research methods. The topics outlined above are clearly concerned not only with knowing more about the topics, but also with knowing how managers could put such knowledge to practical use. As such it would be ideally suited to be undertaken within what is now referred to as a 'Mode 2' system of knowledge production, in the sense that the 'research problems are framed in the context of application, and research activity is driven by trans-disciplinary concerns at the levels of both theory and practice' (Tranfield and Starkey, 1998). If that were to become the case, then the scope for projects to be vehicles for learning would be more widely realised amongst both academics and practitioners.

References

Hackman, J.R. (1990) *Groups that Work (and Those That Don't)*. San Francisco: Jossey-Bass.

Tranfield, D. and Starkey, K. (1998) 'The nature, social organization and promotion of management research: towards policy', *British Journal of Management*, 9, 341–53.

Index